Equal

Educational

Opportunity

This volume, prepared by the Editorial Board of the *Harvard Educational Review,* is an expansion of its Winter 1968 Special Issue.

HARVARD
EDUCATIONAL
REVIEW

Equal

Educational

Opportunity

HARVARD UNIVERSITY PRESS
Cambridge, Massachusetts

Contents

Introduction

The complacent belief that our public schools provide their students with "equal educational opportunity" has been shattered in the last fifteen years by a combination of social action and social science research. This book examines the American commitment to "equal educational opportunity" in light of the record of massive educational failure that these activities have brought into sharp focus.

Black Americans and their allies have repeatedly underlined the destructive effects of the present school system on black children, both in the South and the North. Since before the 1954 Supreme Court decision and continuing through the current demands for black control of black schools, civil rights leaders and black militants have consistently argued that the expression "equal educational opportunity" is meaningless for a large number of American school children.

Recent social science research supports this contention, revealing huge gaps in educational achievement between racial groups and social classes. The most dramatic evidence concerning the limited effectiveness of our schools is contained in *Equality of Educational Opportunity*, which is generally called the Coleman Report.[1] The Report finds, for example, that the average Negro in the urban Northeast still in school at the twelfth grade achieves at a ninth-grade level in reading and a seventh-grade level in mathematics. Further, after analyzing the effect of schools in closing this racial achievement gap, the Report concludes:

Schools bring little influence to bear on a child's achievement that is independent

[1] James S. Coleman, *et al., Equality of Educational Opportunity* (Washington: U.S. Government Printing Office, 1966).

1

of his background and general social context; this very lack of independent effect means that the inequalities imposed on children by their home, neighborhood, and peer environment are carried along to become the inequalities with which they confront adult life at the end of school. For equality of educational opportunity through the schools must imply a strong effect of the schools that is independent of the child's immediate social environment, and that strong independent effect is not present in American schools.[2]

Buried in the Report's 737 pages of text, graphs, and tables are additional conclusions that undercut popular beliefs about what contributes to effective education. The Report finds, for example, that the quality of a school's physical facilities has almost no relation to the achievement levels of its typical student, while the social class of the student's peers has a dramatic effect on his reading and math scores.[3]

The essays in this book probe the meaning of the American belief in equal educational opportunity in the context of the present social crisis and the findings of the Coleman Report and other research studies. Contributors to this volume attempt to answer the following closely related questions:

What has equal educational opportunity meant in the past and what should it mean in the future?

What do empirical studies of the schools have to say about our effectiveness in achieving equal educational opportunity?

What public policies will be most effective in implementing equal educational opportunity?

In the first article in this volume, James Coleman attacks the basic problems of defining equal educational opportunity. He traces its past meanings and argues that recent social science findings require a new definition of this concept. For a school system to have provided equal educational opportunity, Coleman argues, the *results* of its educational program in terms of achievement must be equal for all racial and social groups; the average black child must be equipped with the same skills as the average white child.

Naturally, neither the findings of the Coleman Report nor the implications drawn from it by its principal author have gone unchallenged by those with an

---

[2] *Ibid.*, p. 325.
[3] A summary of the Report, written by James Coleman, will be found on pp. 253 to 261.

interest in the public schools. These empirical conclusions and policy implications have become the focus for an intense debate on the concept of equal educational opportunity. In "Sources of Resistance to the Coleman Report," Daniel P. Moynihan provides one analysis of the general form that this debate has taken, as educators, social activists, and social scientists have reacted to the Report. The reader may wish to evaluate the adequacy of Moynihan's analysis as he reads the work of the educators, social activists, and social scientists that comprises the remainder of this book. Their contributions discuss both research issues and public policy issues related to equal educational opportunity.

American educators have historically exhibited little interest in comprehensive evaluation of the quality of their efforts. The Coleman Report, commissioned by the Civil Rights Act of 1964, was not clearly aimed at rectifying this situation. The charge given by Congress was fairly narrow and specific:

The Commissioner shall conduct a survey and make a report to the President and the Congress, within two years of the enactment of this title, concerning the lack of availability of equal educational opportunities for individuals by reason of race, color, religion, or national origin in public educational institutions at all levels in the United States. . . .[4]

The language of the section hints that the legislators were looking for documentation of what they felt to be obvious: that is, that minority groups had poorer schools and poorer teachers, were generally segregated by race, and reflected these disadvantages in poor achievement.

It is only because Coleman and his fellow investigators interpreted their mandate quite broadly, seeking to maximize the amount of information that could be gained within the bounds of the Congressional charge, that the Coleman Report is a seminal study of the factors which influence educational achievement.

Since Coleman's findings challenge much of the conventional wisdom of the educational establishment and seem to lend support to certain social policies about which there is strong public disagreement (for example, integration), the validity of this research deserves the most careful scrutiny. Thus, the Report has preoccupied many social scientists interested in education for several years, and this interest is likely to continue for some time.

[4] Section 402, Civil Rights Act of 1964.

The quality of the Report has been debated in a series of reviews, articles, and symposia throughout the country. Such discussions have concentrated on several types of methodological issues:

(1) Alleged flaws in the design of the study (for example, a weak set of attitude questions).

(2) Difficulties in the execution of the survey which may have affected the results (for example, the refusal of a substantial number of school systems to cooperate).

(3) Alleged shortcomings in the analysis of the data (for example, the decision to control for the child's social class before examining the influence of the school on his achievement).

(4) Limitations of a survey taken at one point in time as a basis for forecasting the effects of changes in the educational system (for example, the effect of school integration).

The reader will encounter these issues many times in the following articles. However, a systematic consideration of all the specific methodological disputes surrounding the Report is beyond the scope of this book.[5] The section on "Research Issues and Equal Educational Opportunity" in this volume has a much narrower purpose. Much published criticism of the Coleman Report has treated its findings in isolation from related research. The usual approach has been to detail under each of the Report's major findings a series of alleged methodological shortcomings which cast doubt on the validity of the Report's conclusions.

Although such criticism is useful, it gives the unfortunate impression that conclusions about equal educational opportunity are dependent on how well the Report, by itself, withstands methodological analysis. The Report, however, is not an isolated study. In each of the major subject areas it touches, the

---

[5] The interested reader is referred to the following reviews of the Coleman Report, which provide further information on the specifics of some of these methodological issues: William H. Sewall, Leonard A. Marascuilo, and Harold W. Pfautz, "Review Symposium," *American Sociological Review*, XXXII (1967), 475-483. Samuel Bowles and Henry M. Levin, "The Determinants of Scholastic Achievement—An Appraisal of Some Recent Evidence," *The Journal of Human Resources*, III (1968), 475-483. Responses to Bowles and Levin appear in the correspondence sections of the Spring, Summer, and Fall 1968 issues of the *Journal of Human Resources*. Robert C. Nichols, "Schools and the Disadvantaged," *Science*, CLIV (1966), 1312-1314. Responses to Nichols appear in *Science*, CLVI (1967), 731-734.

Coleman Report is merely one piece of research (albeit the largest piece) among many. Its findings on the effect of social class on school achievement, for example, can be compared with earlier small-scale studies, several of which are not subject to the methodological limitations of the Coleman survey data.

In this volume four noted scholars—specialists in the relationships of race, social class, motivation, and school characteristics related to achievement—analyze the findings of the Report in the light of other research in these fields. These reviews, and everything else that has been written about the findings of the Report up to this time, must be viewed as part of a long-range process of evaluating the basic data collected in the survey.

The analyses published in the original Report were completed under great time pressure to meet a Congressional deadline. A major re-analysis of the data was later conducted by the Civil Rights Commission and included in *Racial Isolation in the Public Schools*.[6] A group of Harvard social scientists have just completed a second major re-analysis of the Coleman data which is being prepared for publication in 1969.[7] Preliminary results from the Harvard re-analysis indicate that the Report's major conclusions (that is, the racial achievement gap, the influence of a child's social class background and the social class of his peers on his achievement, and the relatively small effect of education in overcoming social differences) are holding up under closer scrutiny.

Whatever the specific conclusions reached in this continuing re-analysis, however, the conclusions of the social scientist have emerged as an important force in the formulation of educational policy. In the policy section of this book, contributors were asked to analyze what public policies would be most effective in implementing equal educational opportunity. In addressing this question, they discuss not only the Coleman Report and other empirical data, but also a variety of political, legal, and moral issues. Despite the diversity of their viewpoints and proposals, they face a common frustration: the social and political forces that bind together the present public school system are highly resistant

U.S. Commission on Civil Rights, *Racial Isolation in the Public Schools* (Washington: U.S. Government Printing Office, 1967). This report is a readable summary of many of the major findings of the Coleman Report and clear analysis of factors leading to racial isolation.

[7] A Harvard Faculty Seminar, chaired by Professors Daniel P. Moynihan and Thomas Pettigrew, was established in 1966 with the support of a grant from the Carnegie Corporation to re-analyze and discuss the policy implications of the data from the Coleman Report. The findings of the Seminar will be published in a book in 1969 which is being edited by Harvard Professors Charles F. Mosteller and Daniel P. Moynihan.

to change. New educational programs must contend with the strong social class influence of the child and his peer group, the rigid bureaucracy that governs most school systems, and the status quo political forces that want to preserve the schools the way they are.

This frustrating resistance to change is reflected clearly in the fight over integration. For at least a decade, there was a general consensus among those seeking educational change that the schools should be integrated by race. The Coleman Report and the Civil Rights Commission Report give evidence that minority group students in racially integrated schools achieve somewhat better than students with similar backgrounds in segregated schools. They also show that white students do not suffer academically from moderate integration.

Yet Southern school integration has not even kept up with population increases; as a result, more students attend totally segregated schools in the South today than were attending them in 1954. In the North, local efforts to force integration have met with very limited success, and the Federal Government has failed to use its power to cut off funds to promote integration in the North. In the North's largest cities, prospects for substantial integration are particularly remote. New York, Washington, Baltimore, Chicago, Detroit, Philadelphia, and St. Louis all have majority non-white populations in their public elementary schools. In view of the difficulty of achieving metropolitan cooperation on such noncontroversial problems as waste disposal, the likelihood of attaining large-scale metropolitan integration is at best problematical.

Nor have other alternative policies met with greater success. At the same time demands for school integration were being pressed most strongly, Federal, state, and local governments began to pour large amounts of money into various types of compensatory education aimed at improving existing segregated schools. So far, there is no research evidence that any such compensatory programs have produced lasting gains in achievement. The proponents of compensatory education counter that such programs as More Effective Schools have not been given sufficient time to succeed. They argue further that the compensatory programs tried to date have not departed radically enough from traditional practice. The fact remains that they have yet to prove their effectiveness.

With integration facing formidable social and political barriers and little discernible pay-off from compensatory education, many critics of the schools have advocated various schemes for transferring control of the schools to individuals more responsive to the needs of minority group children. One solution along these

6

lines asks that community residents control the education of their children directly by electing their own school governing boards. Another solution calls for the development of competing alternatives to the public schools. Under one such scheme, families from poverty backgrounds would be given $1200 a year per child with which to buy the best available education for their children. Both of these plans attempt to give the parent increased control over his child's education. Neither has been tried out yet in any extensive fashion.

All of these ideas and related political, legal, and moral problems are discussed at length in this book. Moreover, many ideas are advanced that do not fit into any of the pigeon-holes constructed for the purposes of this brief introduction. Perhaps the best way to provide the reader with a preliminary feeling for the breadth of the policy suggestions presented and the problems considered is to present a series of questions about which the contributors are often in basic disagreement:

Is integration still a desirable public policy? Is it still acceptable to the majority of the black community? Are there schemes for promoting large-scale integration that have some chance of success?

How important is it that current social science research indicates that minority group students achieve better in integrated schools? Are there other results of schooling besides achievement that should be considered more important in the formulation of public policy?

Does equal educational opportunity imply that students emerge from the educational process with equal skills?

What role should various branches of the Federal government (the Congress, the Courts, the Office of Education) play in the implementation of equal educational opportunity? Will meaningful change come through the initiative of any governmental division or must it come through social action?

Will community control in ghetto areas lead to desirable educational outcomes? Will it further racial separatism? Can the effects of increased parental involvement overcome the negative effects on achievement of attending a predominantly lower-class school?

Are schemes for dismantling the present school bureaucracy or for providing massive amounts of compensatory education any more feasible politically than integration?

Will broad policy changes produce any results at the classroom level without new mechanisms for retraining teachers and for implementing new curriculum ideas?

Can equal opportunity be promoted in a meaningful way by any reform of the educational system or must educational change follow from broader social change?

This book represents the first comprehensive assault on the tangle of research and policy issues related to equal educational opportunity. Though no resolution of these issues is achieved in this book, it is our belief that the outlines of this continuing debate have been sharpened in the following essays.

The Editors

September 1968
Cambridge, Massachusetts

The Concept of Equality of Educational Opportunity *

JAMES S. COLEMAN

Johns Hopkins University

Although there is wide agreement in the United States that our society accepts and supports the fundamental value of equal opportunity, when it comes to areas of specific application there is considerable disagreement over its meaning. In this article, the author traces the evolutionary shifts in interpretation of the concept of equality of educational opportunity, not only putting into perspective the different views which form the basis for disagreement today but also indicating how the current direction of change may influence the interpretation of this concept in the future.

The concept of "equality of educational opportunity" as held by members of society has had a varied past. It has changed radically in recent years, and is likely to undergo further change in the future. This lack of stability in the concept leads to several questions. What has it meant in the past, what does it mean now, and what will it mean in the future? Whose obligation is it to provide such equality? Is the concept a fundamentally sound one, or does it have inherent contradictions

* This article appeared originally in the Winter 1968 issue of the *Harvard Educational Review*. It was based on a paper delivered at the Conference on the *Equality of Educational Opportunity* Report sponsored by the Colloquium Board of the Harvard School of Education, October 21, 1967.

or conflicts with social organization? But first of all, and above all, what is and has been meant in society by the idea of equality of educational opportunity?

To answer this question, it is necessary to consider how the child's position in society has been conceived in different historical periods. In pre-industrial Europe, the child's horizons were largely limited by his family. His station in life was likely to be the same as his father's. If his father was a serf, he would likely live his own life as a serf; if his father was a shoemaker, he would likely become a shoemaker. But even this immobility was not the crux of the matter; he was a part of the family production enterprise and would likely remain within this enterprise throughout his life. The extended family, as the basic unit of social organization, had complete authority over the child, and complete responsibility for him. This responsibility ordinarily did not end when the child became an adult because he remained a part of the same economic unit and carried on this tradition of responsibility into the next generation. Despite some mobility out of the family, the general pattern was family continuity through a patriarchal kinship system.

There are two elements of critical importance here. First, the family carried responsibility for its members' welfare from cradle to grave. It was a "welfare society," with each extended family serving as a welfare organization for its own members. Thus it was to the family's interest to see that its members became productive. Conversely, a family took relatively small interest in whether someone in *another* family became productive or not—merely because the mobility of productive labor between family economic units was relatively low. If the son of a neighbor was allowed to become a ne'er-do-well, it had little real effect on families other than his own.

The second important element is that the family, as a unit of economic production, provided an appropriate context in which the child could learn the things he needed to know. The craftsman's shop or the farmer's fields were appropriate training grounds for sons, and the household was an appropriate training ground for daughters.

In this kind of society, the concept of equality of educational opportunity had no relevance at all. The child and adult were embedded within the extended family, and the child's education or training was merely whatever seemed necessary to maintain the family's productivity. The fixed stations in life which most families occupied precluded any idea of "opportunity" and, even less, equality of opportunity.

With the industrial revolution, changes occurred in both the family's function as a self-perpetuating economic unit and as a training ground. As economic organizations developed outside the household, children began to be occupationally mobile outside their families. As families lost their economic production activities, they also began to lose their welfare functions, and the poor or ill or incapacitated became more nearly a community responsibility. Thus the training which a child received came to be of interest to all in the community, either as his potential employers or as his potential economic supports if he became dependent. During this stage of development in eighteenth-century England, for instance, communities had laws preventing immigration from another community because of the potential economic burden of immigrants.

Further, as men came to employ their own labor outside the family in the new factories, their families became less useful as economic training grounds for their children. These changes paved the way for public education. Families needed a context within which their children could learn some general skills which would be useful for gaining work outside the family; and men of influence in the community began to be interested in the potential productivity of other men's children.

It was in the early nineteenth century that public education began to appear in Europe and America. Before that time, private education had grown with the expansion of the mercantile class. This class had both the need and resources to have its children educated outside the home, either for professional occupations or for occupations in the developing world of commerce. But the idea of general educational opportunity for all children arose only in the nineteenth century.

The emergence of public, tax-supported education was not solely a function of the stage of industrial development. It was also a function of the class structure in the society. In the United States, without a strong traditional class structure, universal education in publicly-supported free schools became widespread in the early nineteenth century; in England, the "voluntary schools," run and organized by churches with some instances of state support, were not supplemented by a state-supported system until the Education Act of 1870. Even more, the character of educational opportunity reflected the class structure. In the United States, the public schools quickly became the common school, attended by representatives of all classes; these schools provided a common educational experience for most American children—excluding only those upper-class children in private schools, those poor who went to no schools, and Indians and Southern Negroes who were without schools. In England, however, the class system directly manifested itself through the schools. The state-supported, or "board schools" as they were called, became the schools of the laboring lower classes with a sharply different curriculum from those voluntary schools which served the middle and upper classes. The division was so sharp that two government departments, the Education Department and the Science and Art Department, administered external examinations, the first for the products of the board schools, and the second for the products of the voluntary schools as they progressed into secondary education. It was only the latter curricula and examinations that provided admission to higher education.

What is most striking is the duration of influence of such a dual structure. Even today in England, a century later (and in different forms in most European countries), there exists a dual structure of public secondary education with only one of the branches providing the curriculum for college admission. In England, this branch includes the remaining voluntary schools which, though retaining their individual identities, have become part of the state-supported system.

This comparison of England and the United States shows clearly the impact of the class structure in society upon the concept of educational opportunity in that society. In nineteenth-century England, the idea of *equality* of educational opportunity was hardly considered; the system was designed to provide *differentiated* educational opportunity appropriate to one's station in life. In the United States as well, the absence of educational opportunity for Negroes in the South arose from the caste and feudal structure of the largely rural society. The idea of differentiated educational opportunity, implicit in the Education Act of 1870 in England, seems to derive from dual needs: the needs arising from industrialization for a basic education for the labor force, and the interests of parents in having one's own child receive a good education. The middle classes could meet both these needs by providing a free system for the children of laboring classes, and a tuition system (which soon came to be supplemented by state grants) for their own. The long survival of this differentiated system depended not only on the historical fact that the voluntary schools existed before a public system came into existence but on the fact that it allows both of these needs to be met: the community's collective need for a trained labor force, and the middle-class individual's interest in a better education for his own child. It served a third need as well: that of maintaining the existing social order—a system of stratification that was a step removed from a feudal system of fixed estates, but designed to prevent a wholesale challenge by the children of the working class to the positions held for children of the middle classes.

The similarity of this system to that which existed in the South to provide differential opportunity to Negroes and whites is striking, just as is the similarity of class structures in the second half of nineteenth-century England to the white-

Negro caste structure of the southern United States in the first half of the twentieth century.

In the United States, nearly from the beginning, the concept of educational opportunity had a special meaning which focused on equality. This meaning included the following elements:

(1) Providing a *free* education up to a given level which constituted the principal entry point to the labor force.

(2) Providing a *common curriculum* for all children, regardless of background.

(3) Partly by design and partly because of low population density, providing that children from diverse backgrounds attend the *same school.*

(4) Providing equality within a given *locality,* since local taxes provided the source of support for schools.

This conception of equality of opportunity is still held by many persons; but there are some assumptions in it which are not obvious. First, it implicitly assumes that the existence of free schools eliminates economic sources of inequality of opportunity. Free schools, however, do not mean that the costs of a child's education become reduced to zero for families at all economic levels. When free education was introduced, many families could not afford to allow the child to attend school beyond an early age. His labor was necessary to the family—whether in rural or urban areas. Even after the passage of child labor laws, this remained true on the farm. These economic sources of inequality of opportunity have become small indeed (up through secondary education); but at one time they were a major source of inequality. In some countries they remain so; and certainly for higher education they remain so.

Apart from the economic needs of the family, problems inherent in the social structure raised even more fundamental questions about equality of educational opportunity. Continued school attendance prevented a boy from being trained in his father's trade. Thus, in taking advantage of "equal educational opportunity," the son of a craftsman or small tradesman would lose the opportunity to enter those occupations he would most likely fill. The family inheritance of occupation at all social levels was still strong enough, and the age of entry into the labor force was still early enough, that secondary education interfered with opportunity for working-class children; while it opened up opportunities at higher social levels, it closed them at lower ones.

Since residue of this social structure remains in present American society, the dilemma cannot be totally ignored. The idea of a common educational experience implies that this experience has only the effect of widening the range of opportunity, never the effect of excluding opportunities. But clearly this is never precisely true so long as this experience prevents a child from pursuing certain occupational paths. This question still arises with the differentiated secondary curriculum: an academic program in high school has the effect not only of keeping open the opportunities which arise through continued education, but also of closing off opportunities which a vocational program keeps open.

A second assumption implied by this concept of equality of opportunity is that opportunity lies in *exposure* to a given curriculum. The amount of opportunity is then measured in terms of the level of curriculum to which the child is exposed. The higher the curriculum made available to a given set of children, the greater their opportunity.

The most interesting point about this assumption is the relatively passive role of the school and community, relative to the child's role. The school's obligation is to "provide an opportunity" by being available, within easy geographic access of the child, free of cost (beyond the value of the child's time), and with a curriculum that would not exclude him from higher education. The obligation to "use the opportunity" is on the child or the family, so that his role is defined as the active one: the responsibility for achievement rests with him. Despite the fact that the school's role was the relatively passive one and the child's or family's role the active one, the use of this social service soon came to be no longer a choice of the parent or child, but that of the state. Since compulsory attendance laws appeared in the nineteenth century, the age of required attendance has been periodically moved upward.

This concept of equality of educational opportunity is one that has been implicit in most educational practice throughout most of the period of public education in the nineteenth and twentieth centuries. However, there have been several challenges to it; serious questions have been raised by new conditions in public education. The first of these in the United States was a challenge to assumption two, the common curriculum. This challenge first occurred in the early years of the twentieth century with the expansion of secondary education. Until the report of the committee of the National Education Association, issued in 1918, the standard curriculum in secondary schools was primarily a classical one appropriate for college entrance. The greater influx of noncollege-bound adolescents into the high school made it necessary that this curriculum be changed into one more appropriate to the new majority. This is not to say that the curriculum changed immediately in the schools, nor that all schools changed equally, but rather that the seven "cardinal principles" of the N.E.A. report became a powerful influence in the movement toward a less academically rigid curriculum. The introduction of the new nonclassical curriculum was seldom if ever couched in terms of a conflict between those for whom high school was college preparation, and those for whom it was terminal education; nevertheless, that was the case. The "inequality" was seen as the use of a curriculum that served a minority and was not designed to fit the needs of the majority; and the shift of curriculum was intended to fit the curriculum to the needs of the new majority in the schools.

In many schools, this shift took the form of *diversifying* the curriculum, rather than supplanting one by another; the college-preparatory curriculum remained though watered down. Thus the kind of equality of opportunity that emerged from the newly-designed secondary school curriculum was radically different from the elementary-school concept that had emerged earlier. The idea inherent in the new secondary school curriculum appears to have been to take as given the diverse occupational paths into which adolescents will go after secondary school, and to say (implicitly): there is greater equality of educational opportunity for a boy who is not going to attend college if he has a specially-designed curriculum than if he must take a curriculum designed for college entrance.

There is only one difficulty with this definition: it takes as *given* what should be problematic—that a given boy is going into a given post-secondary occupational or educational path. It is one thing to take as given that approximately 70 per cent of an entering high school freshman class will not attend college; but to assign a *particular child* to a curriculum designed for that 70 per cent closes off for that child the opportunity to attend college. Yet to assign all children to a curriculum designed for the 30 per cent who will attend college creates inequality for those who, at the end of high school, fall among the 70 per cent who do not attend college. This is a true dilemma, and one which no educational system has fully solved. It is more general than the college/noncollege dichotomy, for there is a wide variety of different paths that adolescents take on the completion of secondary school. In England, for example, a student planning to attend a university must specialize in the arts or the sciences in the later years of secondary school. Similar specialization occurs in the German gymnasium; and this is wholly within the group planning to attend university. Even greater specialization can be found among noncollege curricula, especially in the vocational, technical, and commercial high schools.

The distinguishing characteristic of this concept of equality of educational opportunity is that it accepts as given the child's expected future. While the concept discussed earlier left the child's future wholly open, this concept of differentiated curricula uses the expected future to match child and curriculum. It should be noted that the first and simpler concept is easier to apply in elementary schools where fundamental tools of reading and arithmetic are being learned by all children; it is only in secondary school that the problem of diverse futures arises. It should also be noted that the dilemma is directly due to the social structure itself: if there were a virtual absence of social mobility with everyone occupying a fixed estate in life, then such curricula that take the future as given would provide equality of opportunity relative to that structure. It is only because of the high degree of occupational mobility between generations—that is, the greater degree of equality of *occupational* opportunity—that the dilemma arises.

The first stage in the evolution of the concept of equality of educational opportunity was the notion that all children must be exposed to the same curriculum in the same school. A second stage in the evolution of the concept assumed that different children would have different occupational futures and that equality of opportunity required providing different curricula for each type of student. The third and fourth stages in this evolution came as a result of challenges to the basic idea of equality of educational opportunity from opposing directions. The third stage can be seen at least as far back as 1896 when the Supreme Court upheld the southern states' notion of "separate but equal" facilities. This stage ended in 1954 when the Supreme Court ruled that legal separation by race inherently constitutes inequality of opportunity. By adopting the "separate but equal" doctrine, the southern states rejected assumption three of the original concept, the assumption that equality depended on the opportunity to attend the same school. This rejection was, however, consistent with the overall logic of the original concept since attendance at the same school was not an inherent part of that logic. The underlying idea was that opportunity resided in exposure to a curriculum; the community's responsibility was to provide that exposure, the child's to take advantage of it.

It was the pervasiveness of this underlying idea which created the difficulty for the Supreme Court. For it was evident that even when identical facilities and identical teacher salaries existed for racially separate schools, "equality of educational opportunity" in some sense did not exist. This had also long been evident to Englishmen as well, in a different context, for with the simultaneous existence of the "common school" and the "voluntary school," no one was under the illusion that full equality of educational opportunity existed. But the source of this inequality remained an unarticulated feeling. In the decision of the Supreme Court, this unarticulated feeling began to take more precise form. The essence of it was that the *effects* of such separate schools were, or were likely to be, different. Thus a concept of equality of opportunity which focused on *effects* of schooling began to take form. The actual decision of the Court was in fact a confusion of two unrelated premises: this new concept, which looked at results of schooling, and the legal premise that the use of race as a basis for school assignment violates fundamental freedoms. But what is important for the evolution of the concept of equality of opportunity is that a new and different assumption was introduced, the assumption that equality of opportunity depends in some fashion upon effects of schooling. I believe the decision would have been more soundly based had it not depended on the effects of schooling, but only on the violation of freedom; but by introducing the question of effects of schooling, the Court brought into the open the implicit goals of equality of educational opportunity—that is, goals having to do with the *results* of school—to which the original concept was somewhat awkwardly directed.

That these goals were in fact behind the concept can be verified by a simple mental experiment. Suppose the early schools had operated for only one hour a week and had been attended by children of all social classes. This would have met the explicit assumptions of the early concept of equality of opportunity since the school is free, with a common curriculum, and attended by all children in the locality. But it obviously would not have been accepted, even at that time, as providing equality of opportunity, because its effects would have been so minimal. The additional educational resources provided by middle- and upper-class families, whether in the home, by tutoring, or in private supplementary schools, would have created severe inequalities in results.

Thus the dependence of the concept upon results or effects of schooling, which had remained hidden until 1954, came partially into the open with the Supreme Court decision. Yet this was not the end, for it created more problems than it solved. It might allow one to assess gross inequalities, such as that created by dual school systems in the South, or by a system like that in the mental experiment I just described. But it allows nothing beyond that. Even more confounding, because the decision did not use effects of schooling as a criterion of inequality but only as justification for a criterion of racial integration, integration itself emerged as the basis for still a new concept of equality of educational opportunity. Thus the idea of effects of schooling as an element in the concept was introduced but immediately overshadowed by another, the criterion of racial integration.

The next stage in the evolution of this concept was, in my judgment, the Office of Education Survey of Equality of Educational Opportunity. This survey was carried out under a mandate in the Civil Rights Act of 1964 to the Commissioner of Education to assess the "lack of equality of educational opportunity" among racial and other groups in the United States. The evolution of this concept, and the conceptual disarray which this evolution had created, made the very definition of the task exceedingly difficult. The original concept could be examined by determining the degree to which all children in a locality had access to the same schools and the same curriculum, free of charge. The existence of diverse secondary curricula appropriate to different futures could be assessed relatively easily. But the very assignment of a child to a specific curriculum implies acceptance of the concept of equality which takes futures as given. And the introduction of the new interpretations, equality as measured by results of schooling and equality defined by racial integration, confounded the issue even further.

As a consequence, in planning the survey it was obvious that no single concept of equality of educational opportunity existed and that the survey must give information relevant to a variety of concepts. The basis on which this was done can be seen by reproducing a portion of an internal memorandum that determined the design of the survey:

The point of second importance in design [second to the point of discovering the intent of Congress, which was taken to be that the survey was not for the purpose of locating willful discrimination, but to determine educational inequality without regard to intention of those in authority] follows from the first and concerns the definition of inequality. One type of inequality may be defined in terms of differences of the community's input to the school, such as per-pupil expenditure, school plants, libraries, quality of teachers, and other similar quantities.

A second type of inequality may be defined in terms of the racial composition of the school, following the Supreme Court's decision that segregated schooling is inherently unequal. By the former definition, the question of inequality through segregation is excluded, while by the latter, there is inequality of education within a school system so long as the schools within the system have different racial composition.

A third type of inequality would include various intangible characteristics of the school as well as the factors directly traceable to the community inputs to the school. These intangibles are such things as teacher morale, teachers' expectations of students, level of interest of the student body in learning, or others. Any of these factors may affect the impact of the school upon a given student within it. Yet such a definition gives no suggestion of where to stop, or just how relevant these factors might be for school quality.

Consequently, a fourth type of inequality may be defined in terms of consequences of the school for individuals with equal backgrounds and abilities. In this definition, equality of educational opportunity is equality of results, given the same individual input. With such a definition, inequality might come about from differences in the school inputs and/or racial composition and/or from more intangible things as described above.

Such a definition obviously would require that two steps be taken in the determination of inequality. First, it is necessary to determine the effect of these various factors upon educational results (conceiving of results quite broadly, including not only achievement but attitudes toward learning, self-image, and perhaps other variables). This provides various measures of the school's quality in terms of its effect upon its students. Second, it is necessary to take these measures of quality, once determined, and determine the differential exposure of Negroes (or other groups) and whites to schools of high and low quality.

A fifth type of inequality may be defined in terms of consequences of the school for individuals of unequal backgrounds and abilities. In this definition, equality of educational opportunity is equality of results given *different* individual inputs. The most striking examples of inequality here would be children from households in which a language other than English, such as Spanish or Navaho, is spoken. Other examples would be low-achieving children from homes in which there is a poverty of verbal expression or an absence of experiences which lead to conceptual facility.

Such a definition taken in the extreme would imply that educational equality is reached only when the results of schooling (achievement and attitudes) are the same for racial and religious minorities as for the dominant group.

The basis for the design of the survey is indicated by another segment of this memorandum:

Thus, the study will focus its principal effort on the fourth definition, but will also provide information relevant to all five possible definitions. This insures the pluralism which is obviously necessary with respect to a definition of inequality. The major justification for this focus is that the results of this approach can best be translated into policy which will improve education's effects. The results of the first two approaches (tangible inputs to the school, and segregation) can certainly be translated into policy, but there is no good evidence that these policies will improve education's effects; and while policies to implement the fifth would certainly improve education's effects, it seems hardly possible that the study could provide information that would direct such policies.

Altogether, it has become evident that it is not our role to define what constitutes equality for policy-making purposes. Such a definition will be an outcome of the interplay of a variety of interests, and will certainly differ from time to time as these interests differ. It should be our role to cast light on the state of inequality defined in the variety of ways which appear reasonable at this time.

The survey, then, was conceived as a pluralistic instrument, given the variety of concepts of equality of opportunity in education. Yet I suggest that despite the avowed intention of not adjudicating between these different ideas, the survey has brought a new stage in the evolution of the concept. For the definitions of equality which the survey was designed to serve split sharply into two groups. The first three definitions concerned input resources: first, those brought to the school by the actions of the school administration (facilities, curriculum, teachers); second, those brought to the school by the other students, in the educational backgrounds which their presence contributed to the school; and third, the intangible characteristics such as "morale" that result from the interaction of all these factors. The fourth and fifth definitions were concerned with the effects of schooling. Thus the five definitions were divided into three concerned with inputs to school and two concerned with effects of schooling. When the Report emerged, it did not give five different measures of equality, one for each of these definitions; but it did focus sharply on this dichotomy, giving in Chapter Two information on inequalities of input relevant to definitions one and two, and in Chapter Three information on inequalities of results relevant to definitions four and five, and also in Chapter Three information on the relation of input to results again relevant to definitions four and five.

Although not central to our discussion here, it is interesting to note that this examination of the relation of school inputs to effects on achievement showed that those input characteristics of schools that are most alike for Negroes and whites have least effect on their achievement. The magnitudes of differences between schools attended by Negroes and those attended by whites were as follows: least, facilities and curriculum; next, teacher quality; and greatest, educational backgrounds of fellow students. The order of importance of these inputs on the achievement of Negro students is precisely the same: facilities and curriculum least, teacher quality next, and backgrounds of fellow students, most.

By making the dichotomy between inputs and results explicit, and by focusing attention not only on inputs but on results, the Report brought into the open what had been underlying all the concepts of equality of educational opportunity but had remained largely hidden: that the concept implied *effective* equality of opportunity, that is, equality in those elements that are effective for learning. The reason this had remained half-hidden, obscured by definitions that involve inputs is, I suspect, because educational research has been until recently unprepared to demonstrate what elements are effective. The controversy that has surrounded the Report indicates that measurement of effects is still subject to sharp disagreement; but the crucial point is that *effects* of inputs have come to constitute the basis for assessment of school quality (and thus equality of opportunity) in place of using certain inputs by definition as measures of quality (e.g., small classes are better than large, higher-paid teachers are better than lower-paid ones, by definition).

It would be fortunate indeed if the matter could be left to rest there--if merely by using effects of school rather than inputs as the basis for the concept, the problem were solved. But that is not the case at all. The conflict between definitions four and five given above shows this. The conflict can be illustrated by resorting again to the mental experiment discussed earlier—providing a standard education of one hour per week, under identical conditions, for all children. By definition four, controlling all background differences of the children, results for Negroes and whites would be equal, and thus by this definition equality of opportunity would exist. But because such minimal schooling would have minimal effect, those children from educationally strong families would enjoy educational opportunity far surpassing that of others. And because such educationally strong backgrounds are found more often among whites than among Negroes, there would be very large overall Negro-white achievement differences—and thus inequality of opportunity by definition five.

It is clear from this hypothetical experiment that the problem of what constitutes equality of opportunity is not solved. The problem will become even clearer by showing graphs with some of the results of the Office of Education Survey. The highest line in Figure 1 shows the achievement in verbal skills by whites in the urban Northeast at grades 1, 3, 6, 9, and 12. The second line shows the achievement at each of these grades by whites in the rural Southeast. The third shows the achievement of Negroes in the urban Northeast. The fourth shows the achievement of Negroes in the rural Southeast.

When compared to the whites in the urban Northeast, each of the other three groups shows a different pattern. The comparison with whites in the rural South shows the two groups beginning near the same point in the first grade, and diverging over the years of school. The comparison with Negroes in the urban Northeast shows the two groups beginning farther apart at the first grade and remaining about the same distance apart. The comparison with Negroes in the rural South shows the two groups beginning far apart and moving much farther apart over the years of school.

Which of these, if any, shows equality of educational opportunity between regional and racial groups? Which shows greatest inequality of opportunity? I think the second question is easier to answer than the first. The last comparison showing both initial difference and the greatest increase in difference

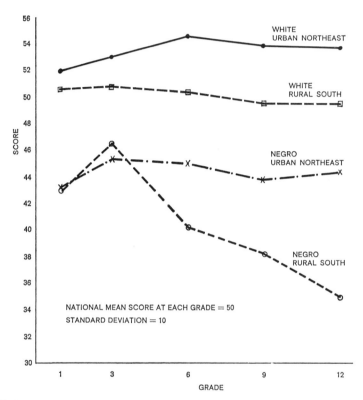

FIGURE 1

Patterns of Achievement in Verbal Skills at Various Grade Levels by Race and Region

over grades 1 through 12 appears to be the best candidate for the greatest inequality. The first comparison, with whites in the rural South, also seems to show inequality of opportunity, because of the increasing difference over the twelve years. But what about the second comparison, with an approximately constant difference between Negroes and whites in the urban Northeast? Is this equality of opportunity? I suggest not. It means, in effect, only that the period of school has left the average Negro at about the same level of achievement relative to whites as he began—in this case, achieving higher than about 15 per cent of the whites, lower than about 85 per cent of the whites. It may well be that in the absence of school those lines of achievement would have diverged due to differences in home environments; or perhaps they would have remained an equal distance apart, as they are in this graph (though at lower levels of achievement for both groups, in the absence of school). If it were the former, we could say that school, by keeping the lines parallel, has been a force toward the equalization of opportunity. But in the absence of such knowledge, we cannot say even that.

What would full equality of educational opportunity look like in such graphs? One might persuasively argue that it should show a convergence, so that even though two population groups begin school with different levels of skills on the average, the average of the group that begins lower moves up to coincide with that of the group that begins higher. Parenthetically, I should note that this does *not* imply that all students' achievement comes to be identical, but only that the *averages* for two population groups that begin at different levels come to be identical. The diversity of individual scores could be as great as, or greater than, the diversity at grade 1.

Yet there are serious questions about this definition of equality of opportunity. It implies that over the period of school there are no other influences, such as the family environment, which affect achievement over the twelve years of school, even though these influences may differ greatly for the two population groups. Concretely, it implies that white family environments, predominantly middle class, and Negro family environments, predominantly lower class, will produce no effects on achievement that would keep these averages apart. Such an assumption seems highly unrealistic, especially in view of the general importance of family background for achievement.

However, if such possibilities are acknowledged, then how far can they go before there is inequality of educational opportunity? Constant difference over school? Increasing differences? The unanswerability of such questions begins to give a sense of a new stage in the evolution of the concept of equality of educational opportunity. These questions concern the *relative intensity* of two sets of influences: those which are alike for the two groups, principally in school, and those which are different, principally in the home or neighborhood. If the school's influences are not only alike for the two groups, but very strong relative to the divergent influences, then the two groups will move together. If school influences are very weak, then the two groups will move apart. Or more generally, the relative intensity of the convergent school influences and the divergent out-of-school influences determines the effectiveness of the educational system in providing equality of educational opportunity. In this perspective, complete equality of opportunity can be reached only if all the divergent out-of-school influences vanish, a condition that would arise only in the advent of boarding schools; given the existing divergent influences, equality of opportunity can only be approached and never fully reached. The concept becomes one of degree of proximity to equality of opportunity. This proximity is determined, then, not merely by the *equality* of educational inputs, but by the *intensity* of the school's influences relative to the external divergent influences. That is, equality of output is not so much determined by equality of the resource inputs, but by the power of these resources in bringing about achievement.

Here, then, is where the concept of equality of educational opportunity presently stands. We have observed an evolution which might have been anticipated a century and a half ago when the first such concepts arose, yet one which is very different from the concept as it first developed. This difference is sharpened if we examine a further implication of the current concept as I have described it. In describing the original concept, I indicated that the role of the community and the educational institution was relatively passive; they were expected to provide a set of free public resources. The responsibility for profitable use of those resources lay with the child and his family. But the evolution of the concept has reversed these roles. The implication of the most recent concept, as I have described it, is that the responsibility to create achievement lies with the educational institution, not the child. The difference in achievement at grade 12 between the average Negro and the average white is, in effect, the degree of inequality of opportunity, and the reduction of that inequality is a responsibility of the school. This shift in responsibility follows logically from the change in the concept of equality of educational opportunity from school resource inputs to effects of schooling. When that change occurred, as it has in the past few years, the school's responsibility shifted from increasing and distributing equally *its* "quality" to increasing the quality of its *students'* achievements. This is a notable shift, and one which should have strong consequences for the practice of education in future years.

Sources of Resistance to the Coleman Report*

DANIEL P. MOYNIHAN

Harvard University

The author discusses the responses to the Coleman Report of three interest groups from which strong reactions might have been expected—the educational establishment, the reform establishment, and the research establishment. He offers three propositions explaining why these groups responded as they did to the Coleman findings. The author illustrates one of his propositions in some detail by analyzing the Coleman data relating family structure and school achievement.

It is a commonplace in the history of science that the appearance of new information is often followed by an intense struggle to have it accepted. That this should be even more the case in social science is evident enough. Information about human behavior is rarely "neutral," and one can confidently predict that information about the performance of large institutions will almost always be threatening. If a somewhat higher order of rationality is to be introduced into the American educational system, the development of some general understandings about the nature of the response to educational research will be useful and probably nec-

* This article appeared originally in the Winter 1968 issue of the *Harvard Educational Review*. Several footnotes have been slightly altered.

The author gratefully acknowledges the research assistance of Dr. Ying Wang.

Daniel P. Moynihan

essary. The reaction to date to the Coleman Report suggests several possibly important patterns.

The study, *Equality of Educational Opportunity,* was hardly an everyday affair. Commissioned under the Civil Rights Act of 1964, one of the great bills of the twentieth century, sponsored by the United States Office of Education in a period of its most vigorous leadership, and conducted by leading social scientists at just the moment when incomparably powerful methods of analysis had been developed, the study was perhaps the second largest in the history of social science. Its findings were, if anything, even more extraordinary than its genesis. Stodolsky and Lesser summarize these findings with admirable detachment:

> Coleman failed to find what he expected to find, direct evidence of large inequalities in educational facilities in schools attended by children from different majority or minority groups. The study set out to document the fact that for children of minority groups school facilities are sharply unequal and that this inequality is related to student achievement. The data did not support either conclusion. What small differences in school facilities did exist had little or no discernible relationship to the level of student achievement.[1]

The first response to these findings came, of course, from within the Office of Education where Coleman's conclusions caused not consternation but something near to alarm. Clearly this was not information that was going to be well received; the correct bureaucratic instinct was to run to the political executives of the Department of Health, Education, and Welfare for guidance. Consultations were held, reaching all the way to the office of the Secretary, resulting ultimately in a summary report which was a political rather than a professional document. The political instinct was towards obscurity.[2]

In effect, the summary report withheld from all but the *cognoscenti* any suggestion that major, and in effect, heretical findings had appeared. The journalistic "lead" on the report was clearly intended to be that the Federal government had established the existence of widespread racial segregation in the public schools. Not until halfway through a fifty-two page document did the subject of "Relation of Achievement to School Characteristics" appear; and even then, the subject was approached in an oblique, even defensive manner.

"The first finding," it was stated, "is that the schools are remarkably similar

[1] An adaptation of the article by Susan S. Stodolsky and Gerald Lesser, "Learning Patterns in the Disadvantaged," *Harvard Educational Review,* XXXVII (Fall, 1967) from which this quotation (p. 582) is taken appears on pp. 126–138 of this book.

[2] The response of the Office of Education has now been carried to its logical conclusion: the Coleman Report is out-of-print, and there is apparently no intention to reprint.

in the effect they have on the achievement of their pupils." If government prose can be said to be an art, surely this sentence will stand as a consummately artful presentation of bad news as if it were old news. Anyone who might have hesitated a moment in the thought that something unusual was being said was quickly reassured: "The schools *do* differ, however, in the degree of impact they have on the various racial and ethnic groups. The average white student's achievement is less affected by the strength and weakness of his school's facilities, curricula, and teachers than is the average minority pupil's."[3]

The Washington strategy was decisive in the near term. Press accounts, which appeared on the Fourth of July weekend, stressed the seemingly familiar, even over-familiar data about school segregation with only passing reference to the heart of Coleman's findings. The obvious had been elaborated for the edification of any whose inclinations tended in that direction, and there the matter was left.

Only slowly did the report come alive, largely under the influence of persons and institutions at best peripheral to the world of American education. The essential fact is that in those quarters where there might have been the greatest response, there would appear to have been but little, and this largely negative. Three such groups-at-interest might be singled out. In the dictionary-sense of establishment as a "permanent, settled position in life" let these groups be termed the educational establishment, the reform establishment, and the research establishment.

The Educational Establishment

The sluggish response of the educational establishment to Coleman's findings would appear the least exceptional. The report in effect declared that professional practice in a major social institution was not nearly so efficacious as had been thought. Obviously silence is the most effective defense against such a charge, especially when it is embedded in a 738-page government report that almost no one knows about. Defensiveness may be assumed to be the first reaction of any profession under such attack. The traffic-safety "profession," which probably has more extensive contacts with the public at large than does even the elementary and secondary school system, has been under similar charges for several decades, and has more or less successfully followed a "policy" of silence.

[3] James S. Coleman, *et al.*, *Equality of Educational Opportunity: Summary* (Washington: U.S. Government Printing Office, 1966), p. 21.

A related factor is the relative absence of a tradition of basing educational practice on research findings. Writing in *Science* shortly after the appearance of the Coleman report, Robert C. Nichols predicted that the findings would have little influence on educational policy. Members of the American Association for the Advancement of Science, he observed, "may find it hard to believe that the $28 billion-a-year public education industry has not produced abundant evidence to show the differential effects of different kinds of schools, but it has not."[4] On the other hand, he added that in this instance "conservatism may be adaptive. . .because the findings are too astonishing to be accepted on the basis of one imperfect study." Observers such as Peter Rossi would counter that Coleman's findings on the apparent unimportance of pupil-teacher ratio in classroom instruction are matched by similar findings of research going back four decades, none of which have had any apparent influence on educational policy.

A proposition may thus be asserted: the educational establishment is resistant to research findings on institutional grounds, and will probably remain so unless institutional or professional changes occur which change this disposition.

The Reform Establishment

The reform establishment is a more amorphous group, perhaps, than that made up of school administrators, teachers, and such like, but it is not less distinct in its interests and activities. For several decades, a primary concern of this group has been the expansion of educational opportunities for Negro Americans and other minority groups. In the early stages, this concern was directed primarily to the formal segregation of school facilities in the South. Of late, it has turned to the *de facto* segregation in the North and elsewhere, and even more recently to the general fact of low educational achievement among minority groups, and probably also of the white poor.

In effect, the Coleman study was intended to prove beyond further question two central theses of the reform establishment: first, that school facilities available to minorities were shockingly unequal; and second, that this accounted for unequal outcomes. This, of course, was not found. Coleman's findings thus pose two equally difficult choices for the reform establishment. The first would be to conclude that the achievement of equality of educational opportunity—increasingly defined in terms of comparable educational achievement on the part of

---

[4] Robert C. Nichols, "Schools and the Disadvantaged," *Science*, CLIV (December 9, 1966), p. 1314.

minority and majority groups—will require vastly greater expenditures of money and social effort than even they have envisaged. The second would be to conclude that improvement of schools as such should be downgraded in favor of a vast national effort to liquidate the lower class, in Walter B. Miller's phrase, and thereby remove the apparently insurmountable—or at least not likely to be surmounted—restraints on educational achievement among lower-class youth, especially in urban "ghetto" areas. Understandably, the reform establishment chose first of all to concentrate on Coleman's findings, rather than on their implication.

A first reaction was to dispute the data: this was a perfectly respectable, indeed given the issues at stake, an eminently useful response. Other reactions, however, have been less helpful. A considerable body of reform opinion chose to interpret Coleman as having confirmed rather than challenged previous understandings. With but a few exceptions (e.g., pupil-teacher ratio), Coleman found that the effects of what might be termed school input on educational output were in the directions that almost everyone has assumed. However, he found the strength of these relationships to be not nearly so great as had also been assumed. The relationship appeared to be of such a different magnitude as to recede from a primary to a secondary, even tertiary category. That this latter point can, however, be ignored is suggested by a description of Coleman's findings in a forthcoming study:

This study compares the schools attended by and the achievement of various groups of Americans: the white majority, Negroes, and several other ethnic minorities. . . . Although regional differences are marked, the tendency seems to be for Negro children to attend schools with less adequate physical facilities, resources, and curricular and extracurricular programs than do whites. Overall, the teachers of Negroes appear to be less well qualified and Negroes tend to go to school with less able classmates.[5]

At still another level, Coleman's findings have been attacked in the press as "near-racist." His data on the influence of the social class origins of classmates have been interpreted to mean racial origin and caricatured as "the strange equation of the white liberal educators: 'Mix Negroes with Negroes and you get stupidity.' "

This reaction, also, might have been anticipated. There was, however, yet another which was quite new. Coleman's findings appeared almost simultaneously with the rise within the reform establishment of a body of opinion, associated with Negro militancy of the Black Power variety, that repudiates the earlier reform quest for racial integration in the public schools and instead opts for the establish-

[5] Jerome Beker, "Why We Fail," to appear in Paul S. Graubard (ed.), *Readings in the Education of the Disturbed, Delinquent Child* (Chicago: Follett Publishing Co., forthcoming).

ment of "Black" institutions. Coleman's data, however, argue that given the social class status of most Negro Americans, separation by race will have strong counter-productive effects. His report has been correctly interpreted to be the most powerful social science case for school integration that has ever been made. It thus became necessary for those rejecting integration to reject Coleman as well, and this has been done with the customary ill grace of the moment.

A major element in the responses of the reform establishment has been the manifest fact that, heretofore, the public generally has been more willing to consider changes in educational institutions than economic or social institutions. Coleman must be taken to suggest that reform will be considerably more difficult to achieve than has been expected. This is rarely welcome news, and has accordingly been resisted.

A second proposition may thus be asserted: the reform establishment frequently is resistant to research findings on ideological grounds and will probably remain so unless such findings are presented in ways that are responsive to the reform desire to improve the status of minority students.

The Research Establishment

A third participant in the response to the Coleman report has been the research establishment from which the report itself emerged. Although nominally the one most objective, most open to new information, most steadfast in the face of disappointment, the research establishment is nonetheless made up of a distinctive set of persons with distinctive interests and sensitivities that make findings such as Coleman's particularly difficult to assimilate.

American social relations are still significantly affected by characteristics of various ethnic, racial, and religious groups which have the effect of producing quite different levels and patterns of achievement in various fields of endeavor, including education. These influences are separate from those of social class, although presumedly there is considerable interaction. Lesser, Fifer, and Clark were the first to identify the differing patterns of educational aptitude among such groups, revealing distinctive patterns of educational aptitude as between American Chinese, Jews, Negroes, and Puerto Ricans. Levels, but not patterns, of aptitude varied with social class.[6] As Lesser described their findings in a later article:

[6] G. S. Lesser, G. Fifer, and D. H. Clark, "Mental Abilities of Children from Different Social-Class and Cultural Groups," *Monographs of the Society for Research in Child Development*, XXX, No. 4 (1965).

The failure of social-class conditions to transcend patterns of mental ability associated with ethnic influences was unexpected. Social-class influences have been described as superceding ethnic-group effects for such diverse phenomena as child-rearing practices, educational and occupational aspirations, achievement motivation, and anomie. The greater salience of social class over ethnic membership is reversed in the present findings on patterns of mental ability. Ethnicity has the primary effect upon the organization of mental abilities, and the organization is not modified further by social-class influences.[7]

Presumedly, further research would identify comparable distinctions with regard to other characteristics.

Few would dispute that these are sensitive matters, touching as they do on matters of relative success or failure in a highly competitive society in which groups as well as individuals are perceived as being in competition with one another. Although presumedly some part of different achievement patterns arises from different value emphasis, there is nonetheless a generalized value system in American society against which all groups and all individuals can in some general way measure their worth. It is a matter of widely held conviction that until recently, at all events, wealth was one such measure. At present, it is reasonable to posit that educational achievement is another. Sensitivity about research in the field of educational achievement accordingly arises when it is revealed that one group is significantly more achieving, i.e. more successful, than another. This sensitivity might be mitigated were the research conducted by some neutral, or outside, party. This, however, is decidedly not the case. In American society of the present time, research in the field of educational achievement is conducted almost exclusively by members of those groups that have the greatest experience of success. This is nothing more than a secondary consequence of the primary patterns of differential achievement.

The Coleman study is a case in point. It was conducted for the purpose of learning more about the educational opportunities open to "minority" groups, with the clear expectation that such information would be used to enhance these opportunities. However, neither Coleman nor any of the other senior social scientists responsible for the study was Negro, much less Puerto Rican, Mexican American, or American Indian.[8] This may not be a desirable state of affairs—it

---

[7] Stodolsky and Lesser, *op. cit.,* p. 570.

[8] It may be noted that the present discussion of the Coleman Report takes place in a journal, no one of whose editors is Negro, Puerto Rican, Mexican American, or American Indian. This journal is associated with a graduate school no one of whose professors is . . . etc.

assuredly is not—but it is at present the usual one, and this fact requires that its consequences be acknowledged.

One probable consequence is that there arises on the part of social-science researchers a predisposition, confirmed and strengthened by the larger society, to direct attention in education toward the "neutral" strengths and weaknesses of school-related characteristics, rather than student-related characteristics, in ascribing responsibility for inadequate achievement levels. If further research confirms the message of the Coleman Report that student and group-related characteristics are considerably more significant, this predisposition will become an obstacle to doing anything about such achievement levels.

The fact that social scientists from high-status ethnic groups are sensitive as to what kinds of things they can "find out" about low-status groups, is very probably matched by a degree of insensitivity to certain other influences on the lives of lower-class populations. This may be illustrated by the treatment in Coleman of the always sensitive subject of family structure. The influence of such matters on educational achievement has been increasingly discussed and, within limits, demonstrated in recent decades. One of the singular qualities of the Coleman study is that it includes a report by each student as to who is acting as his father: "My real father, who is living at home; My real father, who is not living at home; My stepfather; A foster father; A grandfather; Other relative (uncle, etc.); Other adult; No one."[9] It would appear that this is the first time such information has been collected on such a scale and in such detail. It is but one item in the fascinating range of background data which Coleman and his associates gathered out of apparent impatience with a project designed to demonstrate what everyone knew, namely that schools are unequal in facilities and that such inequalities determine achievement. In assessing the impact of the structural integrity of the home, however, Coleman found very little educational impact for Negroes.

Contrary to much that has been written, the structural integrity of the home (principally the father's presence or absence) shows very little relation to achievement for Negroes. It does, however, show a strong relation to achievement for the other minority groups.[10]

The presumptively wholly objective and innocently curious "scientific mind" should have been intrigued by this finding: if a social condition has strong apparent

[9] James S. Coleman, *et al., Equality of Educational Opportunity* (Washington: U.S. Government Printing Office, 1966), p. 628.
[10] *Ibid.,* p. 302. For similar findings with respect to Negroes, see also: Alan B. Wilson, "Educational Consequences of Segregation in a California Community," *Racial Isolation in the Public Schools,* II (Washington: U.S. Government Printing Office, 1967), 174-9.

influence in one group, but not in another, a process of considerable interest is likely to be at hand. But Coleman went no further. Apart from the fact that he had no time to do so, two further possibilities suggest themselves. The first is the intense sensitivity of this subject in the case of Negro Americans. It is, as it were, a subject best left alone. But there is another possibility, namely that the distance between the experience of upper-status whites and lower-status Negroes has been so great, that whites are *insensitive* to the forces that are narrowing the distance. Specifically, white researchers may not be aware of the extent to which the influences that determined Negro experience in the rural South no longer control that experience in the urban North. Although three-quarters of the Negro population now resides in urban areas, this is a recent development, and it may be assumed that the memories and attitudes of the group are still much influenced by the earlier experience of having been, in effect, a lower caste. It may be hypothesized that one of the central lessons about life learned by persons in a caste situation is that personal characteristics have but little influence on outcomes. In determining status, caste *mutatis mutandis* also determines achievement. (English literature occasionally argues that this is so as much for members of an aristocracy as for less fortunate groups.) Groups such as the Negro Americans of the rural South were (and are) victims of the *institution* of caste. It has been obvious to all involved that the greatest immediate gains any persons in that situation could hope for would come directly from changes in that *institution,* rather than from changes in personal characteristics. It is hypothesized that this fact has led to a predisposition to approach problems of Negro Americans in terms of institutional change, and a corresponding reluctance to pay overmuch heed to problems of personal and individual development.

The accompanying figure, constructed from further analysis of the Coleman data, suggests a variety of influences on white and Negro educational achievement, as well as the changing force of such influences. Verbal scale scores are measured in relation to the structural integrity of the home for whites and Negroes in four different regions. The following influences are to be seen:

First, the influence of race. With but one minor exception, all white averages are above all Negro averages.

Second, the influence of rural-urban residence. With but few exceptions, all city-dwelling groups score above all country-dwelling groups of similar race and region.

Third, the influence of region. With but few exceptions, all Northern groups score above all Southern groups of similar race and region.

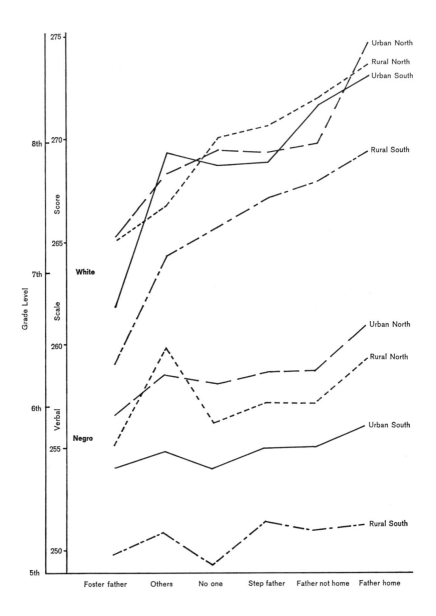

FIGURE 1.

Ninth-Grade Verbal Scale Score in Relation to the Structural Integrity of the Home
(Grade level using metropolitan northeast white as norm)

Fourth, the influence of structural integrity of the home. With but one highly significant exception, almost all groups show a tendency for achievement to decline in homes where the father is not present. The exception is the rural South where, presumedly, a "caste" situation confines almost all Negroes to very low levels of educational achievement, apparently quite independent of personal or home characteristics.

It is further to be noted that the higher one goes on the scale of achievement for persons with father present in the home, the greater becomes the falling-off associated with the absence of the father. This finding holds for Negroes as well as for whites, although the effect is not so pronounced. Table 3.221.5 of the Coleman study also indicates that for both whites and Negroes the background factor of structural integrity of the home has greater influence in the North than in the South.

The well-established fact that structural integrity of the home is an indicator of social class can be seen from Table 1. As parents' education increases, so does the number of fathers present in the home. This increase is especially pronounced in

TABLE 1

Mid-Atlantic Metropolitan Negroes
Ninth-Grade Percentage of Father Home vs. Parents' Highest Education

	25%-50% *Non-white Schools*			75%+ *Non-white Schools*		
	Less than High School	*High School*	*Beyond High School*	*Less than High School*	*High School*	*Beyond High School*
% Fathers home	50.5	54.8	61.2	47.7	54.1	65.4
Total number (N)	(N = 1141)	(N = 952)	(N = 714)	(N = 988)	(N = 788)	(N = 559)

heavily nonwhite schools, where there is a difference of eighteen percentage points in father presence between those whose parents have less than high school education (47.7%), and those with parents educated beyond high school (65.4%). The higher achievement levels of students with fathers present is in part a class effect.

The foregoing data permit the following hypothesis: *As socially-provided opportunities in education expand, student- and group-related characteristics have greater influence on educational achievement.* It may be assumed that white students in the urban Northeast have a comparatively high level of socially-provided opportunities open to them. Their achievement level is also high. As Figure 1 shows, however, that level is markedly affected in the case of individual students who do not

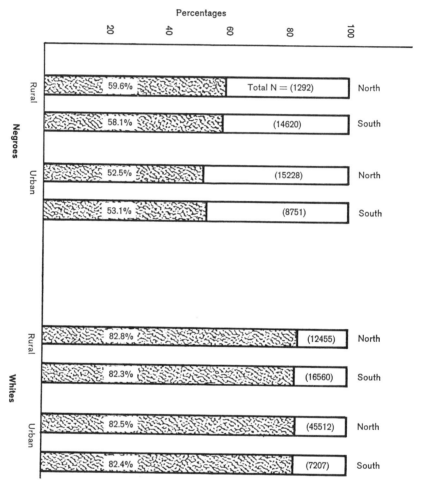

FIGURE 2.

Percentages of Ninth-Grade Students with Father Home

Source: The Harvard Study of the Equality of Education Opportunity Report (Structural Integrity Data).

have the optimum individual or social-class position for taking advantage of such opportunities. Conversely, as socially-provided opportunities in education narrow, student-related characteristics have less influence. This also can be seen from Figure 1.

This hypothesis is relevant to the effort to raise the level of Negro educational achievement, which was the large social purpose behind the study, *Equality of Educational Opportunity*. It would appear that as Negro Americans move further away from the caste condition of the rural South, they encounter wider socially-provided opportunities but also circumstances in which individual characteristics have greater consequences for success or failure. Indeed, it may be argued that not until leaving the rural South do such concepts have any great meaning: caste hardly admits of either. Thus in the urban North, a man may for the first time experience success. Also, for the first time, failure. The significance of this possibility resides in the fact that for Negro Americans of the present period there is a quite marked difference in the incidence of such family characteristics as between the rural South and the urban North. The incidence for Negroes is different from that for whites. (See Table 2.)

The self-reported family situation contained in the Coleman Report confirms this rural-urban trend. Thus barely half of the ninth-grade urban Negro youth reported that their real father was living at home. (See Figure 2.)

But while the incidence of female-headed families varies on the rural-urban continuum, the incidence of poverty among such families does not. Roughly half the number of white children in female-headed families are poor, and three-quarters of nonwhite children are in that situation. Conversely, analyses of unpublished census data by Sheppard demonstrate that in large urban areas roughly one-third of all white poor children and one-half of all nonwhite poor children live in female-headed families.[11]

TABLE 2

Percentage of All Children with Female Family Head, by Residence and Color, 1966

	Rural Farm	Nonfarm out-side SMSA's	SMSA's under 250,000	SMSA's of 250,000 plus
White	2	6	8	8
Nonwhite	14	24	29	29

Source: Special Tabulations by the Census Bureau for the Office of Economic Opportunity. Analysis by H. L. Sheppard, Upjohn Institute, serving as Staff Consultant to the U.S. Senate Committee on Manpower, Employment, and Poverty.

[11] See also Daniel P. Moynihan, "Poverty in Cities," in James Q. Wilson (ed.), *The Metropolitan Enigma*, rev. ed. (Cambridge: Harvard University Press, 1968).

Thus two influences combine to minimize the seeming importance of student-related characteristics for Negro youth: first, that such characteristics had relatively little influence on achievement in the rural South; and second, that the incidence of some such characteristics is much less in the rural South than in the urban North. Considered in the context of the sensitivity of such issues when discussed across racial, ethnic, and religious lines, these data suggest a generalized source of the hesitancy of research workers to pursue such matters more closely.

A third proposition may thus be asserted: the research establishment will be inhibited in its exploration of significant aspects of educational achievement until considerably more social scientists drawn from minority groups are available to take part in such efforts. And this proposition suggests a major national effort to train more such research workers.

Research Issues

School Factors and Equal Educational Opportunity*

HENRY S. DYER

Educational Testing Service

The author surveys three earlier studies of the effects of schooling on achievement and cognitive development in which the conclusions apparently differ from those of the Coleman Report. He suggests that the Report gives an "unfortunate" impression that schools can do little to improve achievement, and then examines certain school characteristics which do seem to influence achievement.

During the years when the separate-but-equal doctrine was in full force, the method of trying to prove or disprove that schools were giving Negroes and whites equal treatment consisted mainly of counting those school characteristics that are easiest to count. Testimony before the courts was full of such matters as the age, size, and location of school buildings; the number of hours in the school day, days in the school year, courses in the curriculum; and the ratios of pupils to basketball courts, drinking fountains, toilets, textbooks, and teachers. In order to make some sense out of these miscellaneous data, the courts translated them into fiscal terms, with the result that assessing the quality of educational opportunity finally boiled down to counting dollars and cents.[1] It was assumed, on the basis of in-

---

* This article appeared originally in the Winter 1968 issue of the *Harvard Educational Review*.

[1] Harry S. Ashmore, *The Negroes and the Schools* (Chapel Hill, N. C.: University of North Carolina Press, 1954), pp. 109-10.

tuition uninhibited by data, that if the schools in a given district were spending as much per pupil for Negroes as for whites, the quality of education for both groups must be equal. The same assumption still has a strong hold on educational thought.

A major contribution of the Coleman survey[2]—possibly *the* major contribution —is its massive challenge to the simplistic notion that counting educational dollars, or the things dollars buy, is a sufficient measure of the equality of educational opportunity. There is no question that the survey has some faults, many of which the authors themselves have conceded: the sample of schools leaves something to be desired; a longitudinal design rather than a cross-sectional design would have made for sounder inferences; there are weaknesses in the measures derived from questionnaire data which make one wonder whether the noise in the information system may not be drowning out some variables that are struggling to be heard; there is too much dependence on a single measure of verbal learning as comprehending the whole of what is meant by academic achievement; and the analysis neglects to show the possible impact of schools on the development of pupil attitudes and outlook.

Despite these flaws, the effect of the Report is to bring us closer to a true national assessment of educational opportunity than we have ever been before. It looks across school district lines and concerns itself with the educational development of minority group children whoever and wherever they may be. In broad terms, it says that the quality of education a school offers is to be measured by reference to those characteristics of a school that bear a known, empirically determined relationship to what pupils learn presumably as a consequence of having gone to school. Basketball courts, teachers' salaries, classroom footage per pupil, and the like may legitimately enter into the assessment of educational opportunity only to the extent that they can be shown to be associated with the intellectual, emotional, and social development of pupils. In the absence of information about such relationships, any attempts to equalize education will of necessity be blind.

I

Following this logic, the Coleman survey, by means of a series of regression analyses, investigates the relationships of pupil achievement with various aspects of pupil background and some forty-five measures that describe the schools the pu-

[2] James S. Coleman, *et al.*, *Equality of Educational Opportunity* (Washington: U.S. Government Printing Office, 1966).

pils attend.[3] These measures fall into three main categories: characteristics of the student body, characteristics of the instructional staff, and characteristics of plant, programs, and finances. Thus, these forty-five measures attempt to characterize the schools as social institutions as well as physical and economic entities.

The logic of the analysis is of course not ironclad. There is no guarantee that the school characteristics that turn up with the largest correlation coefficients or regression weights are the factors that have actually produced the differences among schools in pupil performance, regardless of how elaborate the statistical procedures may be. Even were the analysis to give the teacher salary variable, for instance, a relatively large regression weight in the prediction of pupil achievement, the simple act of a salary increase in the low-achieving schools would be more likely to depress the regression weight than to elevate pupil performance. This line of reasoning is in strict accord with the classical doctrine that correlation does not necessarily imply causation. The doctrine, however, is oversimple. If indeed the data were to yield a relatively large regression weight for teachers' salaries, such a phenomenon *could* be translated into the not unreasonable working hypothesis that if salaries in low-achieving schools are made competitive with salaries in high-achieving schools, then *over the long haul* there is at least a chance that pupil performance in the low-achieving schools will approach that in the high-achieving schools *because* of improved instruction.[4]

As a basis for the appraisal of school characteristics in terms of their relative importance for pupil achievement, the Coleman analyses employ a refinement on the regression model which, though theoretically interesting, may actually be concealing some important factors. The authors of the survey assumed, quite reasonably, that the pattern of relationships between pupil achievement and school characteristics would vary from region to region and, perhaps more importantly, from one ethnic group to another. Some pupils not only need more help than

[3] The regression analyses are given in section 3.2 of the report itself, pp. 290-330; the correlation tables are presented in the *Supplemental Appendix to the Survey on Equality of Educational Opportunity* published separately by the National Center for Educational Statistics (Washington: U.S. Government Printing Office, 1966). For a convenient listing of the variables, see the introduction to the *Supplemental Appendix*, pp. iii-vii.

[4] As far back as 1912, Bertrand Russell was questioning whether the notion of cause had any validity whatever. "In any advanced science," he said, "there is nothing that can be called a cause, and nothing that can be called an effect; there is merely a formula." He conceded, however, that "in daily life and in the infancy of a science," the notion of cause as probable sequence might be useful. Presumably education as a science is still sufficiently infantile and close to daily life to find some uses for the notion of cause. See Bertrand Russell, "On the Notion of Cause," his presidential address to the Aristotelian Society, 1912, reprinted in *Mysticism and Logic* (Hammondsworth, Eng.: Penguin Books, 1954), pp. 171-96.

other pupils, but the kinds of help they need, and consequently the means by which to provide it, will depend on the kinds of pupils they are.[5] On this assumption separate regression analyses were performed on each of ten groups: Mexican-Americans, Puerto Ricans, Indian-Americans, Oriental-Americans, Northern Negroes, Southern Negroes, Northern whites, Southern whites, all Negroes, and all whites. The effect of this grouping is to partial out in some degree the factor of ethnicity and, in the case of Negroes and whites, the factor of geography. From one point of view, the partialling out does not go far enough with respect to ethnicity, region, or other characteristics (social class and religion for instance), and therefore does not take into account the innumerable qualitative differences in the developmental needs of different kinds of pupils, e.g., those in the hard-core poverty areas of the big cities as against those in the rural backwaters. On the other hand, one can also suppose that the subdividing of the sample has gone so far that it has produced groups so homogeneous in respect to schooling and achievement as to conceal many instructive relationships that may in fact exist between the two sets of variables. It would have been illuminating to see what the regression analyses would have produced if all the subsamples had been merged. A re-analysis of some of the Coleman data reported recently by George W. Mayeske takes this tack and provides some useful new insights on what it is about schools that makes a difference in pupils.[6]

II

Some of the problems encountered by the Coleman survey have turned up in at least three earlier studies. The first such study was one carried out by Mollenkopf and Melville in 1953.[7] It took essentially the same approach as the Coleman study, that is, it regressed measures of cognitive development, as measured by tests, on a variety of school, parent, and community characteristics, as measured by questionnaire data. The study involved one hundred high schools that differed with respect to size, region, staff training, percentage of graduates going to college, and financial support. Unlike the Coleman study, which sought a representative cross-

---

[5] Coleman, *et al., op. cit.,* pp. 310-11.

[6] George W. Mayeske, "A Model for School Achievement," paper delivered at U.S. Office of Education Symposium: Operations Analysis in Education (Washington, D. C., November, 1967). (Mimeographed.)

[7] William G. Mollenkopf and S. Donald Melville, *A Study of Secondary School Characteristics as Related to Test Scores,* Research Bulletin 56-6 (Princeton, N.J.: Educational Testing Service, 1956). (Mimeographed.)

section of the nation's schools, the Mollenkopf-Melville study assembled a sample of schools that was as diverse as possible so that those characteristics of schools that are in fact related to pupil achievement would have the best possible chance of emerging from the data. Achievement and aptitude tests were given to some ninety-six hundred pupils at grade 9 and eighty-four hundred pupils at grade 12. The school averages on each of these sets of tests were correlated with thirty-four different school characteristics derived from questionnaire data supplied by the school principals. Four characteristics that showed relatively high relationships with the test scores were geographical location (whether or not the school was in the South), cost of instructional support per pupil, urbanism (whether the school was in an urban, suburban, or rural community), and the number of specialists on the school staff (psychologists, guidance counselors, etc.).

A problem that beclouds this and all later studies of school factors in pupil achievement is the role of socioeconomic variables and family background. The correlation of socioeconomic status with pupil achievement generally runs high— so high indeed that it is difficult to tease out with certainty how much impact the schools *per se* are having on pupils. This first study is no exception. Mollenkopf and Melville caution the reader at length about drawing causal conclusions from correlational data, about illusory distinctions between measures of aptitude and measures of achievement, and especially about the difficulty, if not the impossibility, of disentangling home and community variables from those that might be attributed strictly to the operations of the schools. They nevertheless suggest— almost as it were grudgingly—"that the results support the conclusion that certain characteristics descriptive of the school situation do have a distinct influence on the achievement of students."[8]

The Mollenkopf-Melville study was followed by one undertaken by the New York State Education Department in 1957-58. It was carried out by Samuel M. Goodman and is known as the Quality Measurement Project.[9] Goodman accumulated IQ and achievement test data on some seventy thousand pupils in grades 4, 7, and 10 in 103 school systems which were chosen to be approximately representative of the school systems in the state at large. His report does not explore all the possiblities of his data: correlational results, for instance, focus mostly on grade 7 performance. For this and other reasons—differences in the sample, in the tests, in the school characteristics observed, and in the methods used to observe them—

---

[8] *Ibid.,* p. 37.
[9] Samuel M. Goodman, *The Assessment of School Quality* (Albany, N. Y.: New York State Education Department, March, 1959).

the results of the Goodman study cannot be directly compared with those of the Mollenkopf-Melville study. Even so, the two studies, taken together, begin to give us some notion of how far we can and cannot go in generalizing about school characteristics. Both studies found that per-pupil expenditure and amount of special staffing were associated significantly with achievement. On the other hand, the two differ sharply on how much importance is to be attached to teacher experience. Goodman found this to be the school characteristic most strongly associated with pupil performance; Mollenkopf and Melville found its importance negligible.

TABLE 1

Correlations of Certain School Factors with
Pupil Achievement and Socioeconomic Status[a]

Variable	*Correlation with composite achievement score at grade 7*	
	Raw correlation	*Partial correlation (SES partialled out)*
Teacher experience	.56	.37
Per-pupil expenditure	.51	.31
Special staff per 1000 pupils	.24	.12
Classroom atmosphere[b]	.24	.23
Socioeconomic status of parents	.61	—

[a] Adapted from Goodman, *op. cit.*, Tables 9 and 10.
[b] "Classroom atmosphere" is a measure of the degree to which a school is rated "subject-centered" vs. "child-centered," the ratings being based on an instrument known as *The Growing Edge* by P. R. Mort, *et al.* (New York: Metropolitan Study Council, 1957).

Goodman's study gives a fairly clear-cut indication of the effect of socioeconomic status on the relationship of four school characteristics with achievement. Table 1 summarizes some of his relevant findings. The table contains two bits of information that are of particular interest. First, even though the correlation of socioeconomic status and achievement is of the usual rather high magnitude (.61), partialling out socioeconomic status leaves apparently enough variance in the pertinent variables to suggest that there is still room for the hypothesis that teacher experience and per-pupil expenditure have something to do with how much children learn in school. Secondly, although the ratings on "classroom atmosphere" are only very modestly related to pupil performance, they nevertheless seem to be essentially independent of the socioeconomic factor. The fact that the variable "classroom atmosphere" is based on *direct* observations of what goes on in classrooms may have something to do with this result. While such *indirect* measures as the number of credentials a teacher has accumulated, or the number of years she has been teaching, or the sizes of the classes she teaches have their uses in describing schools, they are likely to be contaminated with so many irrelevancies that the interpretation of any statistics in which they are involved leaves an uncomfortable amount of room for confusion.

The Goodman study, like the Mollenkopf-Melville study before it and the Coleman study after it, was forced by circumstances to rely on cross-sectional rather than longitudinal data. As the authors of the Coleman Report suggest, and as most educational evaluators have been saying for years, the best way to find out what schools are doing to pupils is to observe the pupils before and after the schools have had a chance to influence the way they think, feel, and act. A true definition of achievement must rest ultimately on measures of change. It is not unlikely, therefore, that the school characteristics that are associated with students' *gains* in performance over a particular period could conceivably be quite different from those associated with students' achievement *status* at a given point in time.[10]

A study of cognitive growth in the high school years by Marion F. Shaycoft provides some information on this point.[11] She analyzed data on 6583 students who were tested in Project TALENT in 1960, when they were in grade 9, and were retested in 1963, when they were in grade 12. During the interim they attended 101 nonvocational and 17 vocational high schools. The schools were approximately representative of all such schools; the sample of students, however, consisted only of those who had continued in the same schools throughout their high school years. Another feature that distinguishes the Shaycoft study from the other three is that many of the achievement tests used concentrate on knowledge specific to school subjects. Tests in the other three studies were focused mainly, though not exclusively, on general conceptual development.

The Shaycoft study is concerned, first of all, with a question that seems so obvious that no one has ever before attempted to answer it adequately: Is there in-

[10] Coleman, *et al., op. cit.,* p. 292.
[11] Marion F. Shaycoft, *The High School Years: Growth in Cognitive Skills* (Pittsburgh, Pa.: American Institutes for Research and School of Education, University of Pittsburgh, 1967).

deed a substantial amount of cognitive development in students between grades 9 and 12, and if so, is there any reason to believe that their schooling has anything to do with it? Miss Shaycoft's answer on both counts is strongly in the affirmative. After investigating student gains on the forty-two Project TALENT tests ranging from abstract reasoning and arithmetic to knowledge of such matters as literature, advanced mathematics, mechanics, art, accounting, and electricity, she finds that the gains "are uniformly in the right direction . . . and in the more important areas they are quite substantial in magnitude."[12] By "quite substantial" she means that the average gain on certain measures is as much as a full standard deviation in terms of the grade 9 distribution. She notes further that the larger gains are usually associated with subjects actually taught in school—"curriculum-related" areas of knowledge like literature, mathematics, social studies, and many of the vocational fields like mechanics and accounting.[13]

As to the question whether schools are *differentially* effective, Miss Shaycoft finds statistically significant variation among schools in all but two of the forty-two gains scores[14] and takes this to mean that "students in some schools learn more, or improve their ability more, than in other schools."[15] In other words, it is reasonably safe to conclude that quality of schooling makes a genuine difference in pupil growth, but the Shaycoft data do not tell us how pronounced the differential effects actually are or how far one may go in attributing differences in school effectiveness to variations in the qualities of the schools *per se* (the teaching, the curriculum, the facilities, the general atmosphere) as contrasted to the variation in the quality and character of the communities of people who support the schools and whose children the schools serve. Since, however, many of the most pronounced differences from school to school are in precisely those areas of student growth that are associated with "curriculum-related" content (literature, accounting, etc.), the hypothesis is rather compelling that qualitative differences in the schools themselves account for much, if not all, of the variation in academic and vocational achievement between one school and another. Miss Shaycoft concludes on the cautionary note that "since the sources of these differences among schools resist ready identification, there would appear to be no easy panacea for the problems of education."[16]

[12] *Ibid.*, Ch. 7, p. 8.
[13] *Ibid.*, Ch. 7, p. 8.
[14] *Ibid.*, Tables 7-2a, 7-2b, 7-2c, and 7-2d.
[15] *Ibid.*, Ch. 7, p. 11.
[16] *Ibid.*, Ch. 7, pp. 25-6.

III

None of the three studies preceding the Coleman survey was addressed specifically to the problem of equality of opportunity of minority groups. The main thrust of their results, however, tends to run counter to a salient finding of the Coleman Report, that the differential effects of schools on pupil achievement "appear to arise not principally from factors that the school system controls, but from factors outside the school proper."[17] The Shaycoft study in particular throws doubt on this conclusion by suggesting that it may hold for some kinds of cognitive development but not for others. A serious weakness in the Coleman analysis is at just this point: its criterion of academic achievement is almost exclusively a measure of verbal ability which has long been known to be a slow developing function that for obvious reasons is likely to be far more the product of the child's home than of his school experience.[18] The Coleman study pays scant attention to the kinds of achievement on which the schools have traditionally focused. By contrast many of the criteria of achievement used in the Shaycoft study relate specifically to the subjects pupils actually study in school (literature, mathematics, business subjects, etc.), and it is precisely in these subjects that there appear to be substantial differential effects among schools *even when differences in socioeconomic levels have been accounted for.* The other two earlier studies tend to reinforce this finding. In short, the nearly exclusive use of verbal ability as the measure of pupil achievement in the Coleman analysis probably makes for an underestimate of the importance of factors that school systems do in fact control. As suggested above, this underestimate is further exacerbated by the confining of the analysis to ethnic subsamples in which the schools, pupils, and pupil achievement are likely to be so homogeneous as to prevent important relationships from appearing. *On both counts, then, the Coleman results have the unfortunate, though perhaps inadvertent, effect of giving school systems the false impression that there is not much they can do to improve the achievement of their pupils.*

In light of this situation, it may be useful to consider some other measures, in addition to verbal ability, that are available in the Coleman data as criteria for checking out the importance of school characteristics. These measures include tests in reading and mathematics in grades 3, 6, 9, and 12, and, additionally, a test of general information in grades 9 and 12. The latter encompasses the prac-

[17] Coleman, *et al., op. cit.,* p. 312.
[18] See Coleman, *et al., op. cit.,* pp. 292-5, for the authors' explanation of why they relied so heavily on the measure of verbal ability.

tical arts, natural science, literature, music, art, history, and public affairs.[19] Generally speaking, the zero-order correlations between each of these three measures and measures of the forty-five school characteristics run low. An inspection of the correlation tables in the *Supplemental Appendix* shows that in no case are the correlations over 0.5, and the vast majority are under 0.2. At first glance, this swarm of low correlations would seem to reinforce the Coleman hypothesis that the characteristics of schools *per se* have little or nothing to do with the achievement of pupils. But this interpretation needs a closer look.

In both the Mollenkopf-Melville study and the Goodman study, the relation between per-pupil expenditure and various measures of cognitive achievement was modest but significant. In the Mollenkopf-Melville study, the median of the correlations between instructional cost and seven measures of cognitive performance was .36 at grade 9 and .41 at grade 12. Goodman reported that in his sample of New York State schools the zero-order correlation between instructional cost and composite achievement was .34 at grade 4 and .51 at grade 7. The data from

TABLE 2

Median Correlations Between Per-Pupil Expenditure
and Various Measures of Cognitive Performance
in the Coleman Data

Group	Grade					
	1a	3b	6b	9c	12c	Median
Mexican-American	.09	.00	.08	.07	.09	.08
Puerto Rican	—.24	—.02	.15	.09	—.05	—.02
American Indian	.07	.04	.07	.00	—.10	.04
Oriental-American	.03	.30	.36	.03	.04	.04
Negro North	—.08	—.07	.04	.00	—.01	—.01
Negro South	.07	.01	.19	.11	.20	.11
White North	—.03	.02	.04	.05	.05	.04
White South	.04	.03	.03	.02	.01	.03

[a] Correlation with scores on picture vocabulary test only.
[b] Medians based on correlations with scores on verbal ability, reading, and mathematics tests.
[c] Medians based on correlations with verbal ability, reading, mathematics, and general information tests.

[19] These measures are described with examples on pp. 576-87 of Coleman, *et al., op. cit.*

the Coleman survey are in sharp contrast to these earlier findings. In this case, the medians of the correlations between instructional cost per pupil and various measures of achievement for each of the eight subgroups at each of the five grade levels are, for the most part, scarcely different from zero. (See Table 2.)

The contradiction between the Coleman results and the earlier ones is puzzling, since there is every reason to expect that the amounts of money school systems spend on their pupils *should* bear some positive relationship to the cognitive performance of the pupils in those systems. Even if one is unwilling to grant the not unlikely possibility of a causal connection between the amount of money a school spends on instruction and the amount of learning that takes place in pupils, the relationship should nevertheless be positive if only because the money a community spends on its schools should be a partial reflection at least of the socioeconomic factors normally associated with the pupils' intellectual performance. The data in two of the pre-Coleman studies suggest that there is indeed such an association.[20] But in the Coleman study, the median correlations between per-pupil expense and socioeconomic level are essentially zero at each of the grade levels examined.[21] This result, again, may be explained in part by the homogeneity of the subsample, but it also raises doubts about the credibility of some of the basic data in the Coleman survey. For example, the magnitude of the nonresponse rate for some of the crucial items in the questionnaires, particularly those having to do with socioeconomic status, may be seriously affecting the validity of the measures derived from them. The manner of computing per-pupil expense is also less than adequate since it is based on district-wide figures that may be quite inapplicable to particular schools, especially in slum areas. Regression analyses, no matter how sophisticated they may be, can hardly compensate for, and indeed may inadvertently gloss over, inadequacies in the basic numbers on which they rely. A somewhat cruder approach to the Coleman data may therefore be useful in giving an idea of what is going on behind the numbers.

IV

This cruder approach consists of sorting the forty-five school characteristic variables into correlates and noncorrelates of pupil achievement by simply inspecting the zero-order correlations in the tables of the *Supplemental Appendix*. For this

---

[20] See Mollenkopf-Melville, *op. cit.*, Tables 11 and 12 and Goodman, *op. cit.*, Table 9.
[21] *Supplemental Appendix, op. cit., passim.*

TABLE 3a

Correlates of Pupil Achievement[a] (Grades 6 and 9)

School Characteristics[b]	Mexican-Americans	Puerto Ricans	Indian-Americans	Oriental-Americans	Negroes North	Negroes South	Whites North	Whites South	Total
Student Body Characteristics									
Proportion of pupils with encyclopedia in the home	X	X	X	X		X			5
Proportion of school's graduates in college		X							1
Proportion in college prep curriculum	X	X	X	X		X		X	6
Average attendance as percentage of enrollment	X	X							2
Proportion of pupils who are white	X	X	X						3
Average number of white pupils in preceding year	X	X	X						3
Mean nonverbal test score	X	X	X	X	X	X	X	X	8
Mean verbal test score	X	X	X	X	X	X	X	X	8
Proportion of pupils who think teacher expects their best work	X	X							2
Proportion of pupils whose mothers went to college			X					X	2
Characteristics of Instructional Personnel									
Teacher's estimate of quality of own college	X	X		X					3
Teacher's verbal score	X	X	X	X		X			5
Teacher's race	X	X	X	X					4
Teacher's preference for teaching middle class	X		X						2
Teacher's attitude toward integration	X	X	X						3
Teacher's salary		X		X		X			3
Finances and Program									
Per-pupil expenditure				X					1
Comprehensiveness of curriculum				X	X				2
Mathematics offering	X		X						2
Totals	14	14	12	10	3	6	2	4	

[a] Based on data in the *Supplemental Appendix to the Survey on Equality of Education Opportunity* (Washington: U.S. Office of Education, 1966).

[b] An X in any column indicates that the school characteristic in question correlates 0.2 or higher with one or more achievement test variable at either grade 6 or grade 9 or both.

purpose, a correlate is loosely defined as any school characteristic that correlates 0.2 or better with any one or more of the three achievement measures—reading, mathematics, and general information—in any one of the eight ethnic groups at either grade 6 or grade 9. This may seem like an excessively lenient acceptance criterion, but in view of the probable amount of noise in the basic data, a considerable amount of leniency is needed if one is to identify any school variables at all that might be worth speculating about.

TABLE 3b

Noncorrelates of Pupil Achievement
(Grades 6 and 9)

Student Body Characteristics
Number of twelfth-grade pupils
Pupil mobility (transfers in and out)
Average hours pupils spend on homework
Proportion of pupils who read over 16 books the preceding summer
Teacher's perception of quality of student body
Proportion of students whose mothers expect their best work

Characteristics of Instructional Personnel
Teacher's socioeconomic status
Teacher's experience
Teacher's localism
Teacher's highest degree received
Teacher's absences
Amount of teacher turnover
Availability of guidance counselors
Pupil-teacher ratio

Program, Facilities, Other
Extracurricular offerings
Tracking
Movement between tracks
Accelerated curriculum
Policy on promotion of slow learners
Foreign language offering
Number of days in session
Length of school day
Number of science labs
Volumes per pupil in school library
School location (urban-rural)
Teacher's perception of quality of school

The application of this acceptance test to all forty-five school characteristic items turns up nineteen that pass the test and twenty-six that fail it. The nineteen correlates are shown in Table 3a, and the twenty-six noncorrelates in Table 3b.

Probably the most striking thing about Table 3a is the relatively large number of correlates in some of the minority groups as compared with the small number in the white majority. Fourteen of the functioning items, for instance, are found in the Puerto Rican group; only two in the Northern white group. These differences between groups in the number of functioning school items are, from one point of view, a source of encouragement. For although they can scarcely be regarded as pinpointing the remedies needed to close the educational gaps between the minority and majority groups, some of them may at least provide useful clues about where to begin to look for the remedies.

Another striking feature of Table 3a is that the great majority of the functioning items have to do with characteristics of the *people* who make up the schools—the pupils and their teachers. The proportion of pupils headed for college, the race of the teachers, the racial mix of the student body, the level of verbal ability in both pupils and teachers, the teachers' attitudes toward integration—these are the kinds of school characteristics that appear to be primarily involved with differences in academic achievement.

A comparison of these functional items with the nonfunctional items in Table 3b suggests that closing the educational gap between the white majority and the colored minorities is going to require more social and educational imagination and sustained effort than has hitherto been typical of most school systems. It is fairly obvious that the school characteristics that turn out to be functional are for the most part the *hard-to-change* characteristics, while those that turn out to be nonfunctional are the *easy-to-change* characteristics. As a consequence, over the next decade or two, educators will no doubt be having to fight off pressures from without and temptations from within to try to achieve instant improvement by pouring money and effort into the easy-to-change nonfunctioning features of school systems (the paper credentials, the readily purchasable gimmicks) at the expense of the hard-to-change features that in the long run are more likely to make a real difference in what children become.

Among the easy-to-change items are the things that can be readily bought by spending a little more money here or there or by making a change in administrative or program policy. They include such things as pupil-teacher ratio, the length of the school day, extracurricular activities, and, interestingly enough, such agonizing policy matters as whether slow learners shall receive automatic promotions and whether students shall be assigned to "tracks." These matters, which are much in the minds of educators, are, according to the crude analyses here being applied to the Coleman data, *non*functional school characteristics: their zero-order correlations with academic achievement *never* get as high as 0.2 for any group at grades 6 or 9. Furthermore, they are characteristics that show no appreciable variability across the several regional and ethnic groups, but do show considerable variability within the groups.

By contrast, the school characteristics that tend to be associated with differential levels of academic performance are not the sort that are readily affected by on-the-spot administrative decisions or by the spending of a little more money here or there. Many of them tend to be linked to the socioeconomic level of the pupils' parents and classmates; they tend to be the kind that are deeply rooted in the economic, social, and cultural level of the communities, and no important educational improvements in these schools are likely to take place until changes have occurred in the total community complex in which the schools are embedded.

V

A consideration of the nature of the variables in both Tables 3a and 3b may throw some light on strategies for upgrading schools.

As suggested above, most of the school correlates of pupil achievement are fairly obviously linked to the socioeconomic level of the communities where the schools operate. Clearly, "proportion of graduates in college" is just such an item: students whose families are in the higher income brackets go to college far more frequently than those whose families are in the bottom brackets. There is some tendency among school authorities to stand helpless before this sort of fact, to argue in effect that their schools are either the victims or the beneficiaries of the social environment, and that any efforts to change their fundamental characteristics are almost certain to be exercises in futility.

There is a more hopeful way of looking at the matter. The fact that the student-body characteristics of schools may be strongly linked to socioeconomic factors does not necessarily mean that explicit attention to the more manipulable of such factors may not bear fruit in upgrading pupil performance. No doubt the item "proportion of pupils with encyclopedia in the home" is an item so linked: rich families tend to buy encyclopedias; poor families don't. Nevertheless the item raises a couple of intriguing and presumably researchable questions. First, what would in fact happen to a group of low-achieving pupils if they were actually moved from a school where none of their fellow pupils had encyclopedias at home to a school where all of them had one available? And second, what would happen to achievement levels if, in a district where there are no encyclopedias in the homes, the school authorities supplied one free, or almost free, to every family in the district—accompanied, of course, by the kind of high-powered sales pitch that goes with a normal purchase?

This suggestion that the student-body correlates can be useful in generating hopeful hypotheses to be tested is not to be taken as in any way supportive of the flat assertion in the summary of the Coleman Report that "if a minority pupil from a home without much educational strength is put with schoolmates with strong educational backgrounds, his achievement is likely to increase."[22] Quite the contrary. There is nothing whatever in the Coleman analysis that can justify such an inference. The Coleman study contains no data at all on the effects that might accrue from "putting" minority pupils with different kinds of schoolmates. It is one thing to suppose that a pupil's attitudes and behavior reflect those of the peer group in which, because of innumerable circumstances, including possibly his own predilections, he happens to be; it is quite another thing to infer that if he is moved from one group to another, his attitudes and behavior will change in predictable ways. This is not to say that changing the mix of children in a school will not change the children in the mix; it is merely to call attention to the fact that the Coleman data, by their very nature, are incapable of providing any information at all on what changes will occur or the likelihood of their occurrence.

In a word, the data in the Coleman Report can be a rich source of educational ideas to be tried out—of hypotheses to be tested—but always with the reservation that actual outcomes may be the reverse of expectation. The same data, however, cannot and should not be regarded as sure determiners of educational policy and practice. This is no doubt a hard saying for those who insist that only certainties are acceptable in the conduct of the schools. But until educators and the makers of educational policy can get used to the idea that the management of instruction in all its aspects is of necessity a perpetual trial-and-error process, there is little likelihood that the educational enterprise will ever be liberated from the routines in which it seems now to be frozen.

Some of the "nonfunctioning" items are also instructive, in a negative way, about the kinds of thinking that must go into the development of strategies for change. The item on "tracking" is a case in point. The information on this item at grades 9 and 12 was supplied by the school principals. The questions used to elicit the information asked first whether the school carried out "grouping or tracking according to ability or achievement" for all or some of its pupils and then

---

[22] Coleman, *et al., op. cit.,* p. 22.

asked whether the grouping system, if any, put pupils in a particular group for all their classes or used differing groups for differing subjects.[23] The Report does not make clear how the question was scored, but the mean and standard deviation for each of the eight subsamples in both grades 9 and 12 vary scarcely at all from 2.1 and .6 respectively. The correlations with reading and mathematics scores range from —.07 to +.08 with the median almost exactly at 0. It is as though the responses had been perfectly random.

Such results forcibly raise the question whether it is the item in the questionnaire or the policy concept of tracking itself that is nonfunctional. This is not a trivial matter; it goes to the heart of what may be getting in the way of constructive change in education. The idea of ability grouping or tracking, like many other educational concepts, is not a simple notion; it can mean any number of things in actual practice. There are innumerable ways of placing pupils in tracks and of organizing the activities that go on between teachers and pupils after they have been so placed. All research on the subject has been quite inconclusive for the very reason that the researchers have failed to observe, in any systematic fashion, how teachers actually organize instruction and how pupils actually learn under various conditions of grouping and nongrouping.[24] In short, the negative findings of the Coleman Report with respect to tracking were predictable from past experience and the nature of the question asked. The outcome is hardly surprising inasmuch as tracking and similar concepts, whether used in questionnaires or in the formulation of educational policy, are too semantically soft to penetrate the complexities of the teaching-learning process as it actually operates in classrooms. The same consideration applies with equal if not greater force to more familiar but even less differentiated educational concepts: for instance, reading or writing or arithmetic. The cliché is still good: we are not likely to get meaningful answers until we can figure out how to ask meaningful questions.

VI

So the question remains: What school factors should be considered of primary importance in any effort to equalize educational opportunity for pupils of all

[23] *Ibid.*, p. 667.

[24] For recent reviews of research supporting this point see Ruth B. Ekstrom, "Experimental Studies of Homogeneous Grouping: A Critical Review," *The School Review*, LX, No. 2 (1961), 217-26; Walter R. Borg, *Ability Grouping in the Public Schools* (Madison, Wis.: Dembar Educational Services, Inc., 1966); and Sixten Marklund, "Scholastic Attainments as Related to Size and Homogeneity of Classes," *Educational Research*, VI, No. 1 (1963), 63-7.

kinds and conditions in all parts of the United States? The Coleman study and the three that preceded it have helped to illuminate the question, but they have hardly supplied definitive answers. We strongly suspect that the amount of money spent on instruction can make a considerable difference in the quality of pupil performance, but how the funds are deployed and used probably makes even more of a difference. It seems reasonably clear that the effectiveness of schools is very largely a function of the characteristics of the people in them—the pupils and their teachers—but we are still a long way from knowing in useful detail what specific changes in the people or in the educational mix will produce what specific benefits for what specific kinds of children. Even were the information on this point more firm than it is, there is still much to be learned about how the changes can be brought about. The only thing that is reasonably certain is that they will not be easy to manage, that they will take years rather than months to effect, and that they will require attention to factors in the total environment of the school as well as to those in the school itself. The weaknesses of American education are less likely to be corrected by the rhetoric of educational administration and curriculum development than by closer attention to the realities of the teaching-learning process as they actually are and as they might be.

One of the great unsolved problems of American education, or of education anywhere in the world, is that of providing a continuous flow of dependable information on how well the schools are meeting the developmental needs of children and in what respects they are failing to do so. The Coleman study and its three predecessors are beginnings toward this end; but massive though they seem, they are only beginnings. All four of them have weaknesses that are attributable, in part at least, to the fact that they have had to deal with a vast number of technical, theoretical, and logistical problems that are new and difficult. A weakness common to all of them is their exclusive focus on the purely cognitive outcomes of education. The Coleman study touches on three noncognitive variables—self-concept, interest in learning, and sense of control of the environment—but these are treated as conditions of learning rather than as its goals.[25]

The very great importance of the Coleman Report is that it has highlighted the problems, the possibilities, and the need for an evaluation system that will be cap-

---

[25] Mayeske's re-analysis of the Coleman data, however, (see footnote 6 above) shows a multiple correlation of .59 between sense of control (which he re-labels "attitude toward life") and an optimum combination of 31 school variables, which does not include characteristics of the student body. When the latter are added to the independent variables, the R increases to .64. The result gives some credence to the idea that the characteristics of a school may indeed have an influence for good or ill on how children see their world.

able of informing educational practitioners and policy makers about what is actually going on out there in their schools and what might be tried to improve the situation. Until such information is forthcoming at regular intervals and in large quantities, it is reasonably certain that in spite of large infusions of money and the frenzied innovations that money may bring, the schools will become increasingly inconsequential in helping us toward a viable society.

Academic Motivation and Equal Educational Opportunity*

IRWIN KATZ

University of Michigan

A striking revelation of the Coleman Report is the close tie between Negro academic achievement and the social environment of the classroom. A theory of racial differences in the early socialization of academic motivation is here advanced to account for some of the favorable effect on Negroes of (a) teachers' and classmates' competence, and (b) attendance at predominantly white schools. Unrealistic self-devaluation and strong anxiety are shown by recent research to be common features of Negro behavior in racially isolated institutions. These facts can be related to the educational values and practices of Negro parents, and to the Coleman data on students' academic attitudes.

In some ways the most intriguing data in the Coleman Report are those that reveal the marked sensitivity of Negro pupils to the social environment of the classrooms.[1] Beyond the earliest grades, the scholastic achievement of Negro children when compared with that of whites is much more closely related to the intellectual proficiency of both teachers and classmates. About a year ago I wrote elsewhere about the possible meaning of these findings from the standpoint of what

---

* This article appeared originally in the Winter 1968 issue of the *Harvard Educational Review*.

[1] James S. Coleman, *et al.*, *Equality of Educational Opportunity* (Washington: U.S. Government Printing Office, 1966).

was then known about social-class and racial differences in the early socialization of academic motivation.[2] More recent research has further illuminated the subject.

The earlier paper suggested that in lower-class Negro homes children's language and problem-solving efforts were not adequately encouraged and reinforced so that children failed to acquire the internal mechanisms that were requisite for autonomous achievement striving—namely, realistic standards of self-evaluation and the capacity for intrinsic mediation of satisfaction through self-approval of successful performance. In white middle-class children, on the other hand, internalization of the achievement motive presumably is relatively well advanced at the time of entering school. Therefore, for disadvantaged students but not for their more affluent age peers, the development of the will to learn should depend heavily upon the behavior of social models in the classroom—that is, upon the extent to which teachers and fellow students exhibit suitable standards of performance and reward individual accomplishment with genuine approval and respect. Moreover, in predominantly Negro schools where low attainment levels prevail, most pupils should be largely incapable in the absence of external cues of realistic self-appraisal or intrinsic mediation of achievement satisfaction.

Recent Research on the Motivation of Negro Pupils

To test this last proposition, Reuben Baron, Gloria Cowan, and I recently carried out exploratory research in a northern, *de facto* segregated elementary school.[3] Fourth- through sixth-grade children were taken individually from their classrooms for testing. During a self-evaluation phase, a series of simple tasks (picture assembly, or construction of four-letter words) was presented to each child, who was seated alone at a table and surrounded by partitions. Near the child on the table was a metal box with three buttons which activated small light bulbs of different colors labelled "Good," "Poor," and "Don't Know."

The instructions were in part as follows: "We think you will enjoy doing these things more if you can tell yourself how nice a job you think you did. So after you finish each one you can press the button which shows how you feel about the kind of job you did. . . . No one will know which button you pressed." The experimenter

[2] Irwin Katz, "Some Motivational Determinants of Racial Differences in Intellectual Achievement," *International Journal of Psychology*, II (1967), 1-12.

[3] This research is reported more fully in the following publication: Irwin Katz, "The Socialization of Academic Motivation in Minority Group Children" in D. Levine (ed.), *Nebraska Symposium on Motivation* (Lincoln, Neb.: University of Nebraska Press, 1967).

left the room after explaining the procedure. Hence, the self-evaluations were ostensibly private, unobserved, and for the child's own amusement. But the setup was deceptive: the button pressings were mechanically recorded by counters concealed in the box.

In another phase of the testing, the extent to which the child's self-evaluations had affective consequences was investigated by ascertaining whether the colored lights used in the self-evaluation box had acquired positive or negative incentive value by virtue of being associated with self-criticism or self-approval. Two techniques of assessing acquired reinforcement value were tried at different times. One involved the introduction, after the self-evaluation phase, of a toy-like gadget that the child was permitted to play with unobserved for a few minutes. It had three levers which activated bulbs when depressed. The bulbs corresponded in size, color, and position to those on the self-evaluation box, but were not labelled. The index of acquired reinforcement value was the number of times each lever was depressed as recorded by concealed mechanical counters. The second technique required the child to fill in an outline with colored crayons both before and after the self-evaluation series, from which quantitative measures of the use of critical colors were obtained.

To date we have tested seventy-nine Negro children. Two types of subjects were used: those whom teachers regarded as high achievers and those regarded as low achievers. Of the total sample, only ten were girls. Girls who were good and poor students showed little difference in their self-evaluations; hence they were temporarily dropped from the research. *Among boys, the poor students engaged in more self-criticism and were less favorable in their total self-evaluations than the good students.* That the differences between groups were not created by a few extreme scores is evident from the data on thirty-six boys who evaluated their performance on the picture assembly tasks: only three out of seventeen good students, but fully sixteen out of nineteen poor students, used the "Poor" button at least once out of a total of six self-evaluations. Another male sample of roughly equal size that evaluated their constructions of simple words showed similar differences between high and low academic achievers.

As a check on the possibility that the self-evaluations were reasonably accurate appraisals of actual performance, judges who were unacquainted with the experimental procedures were asked to rate subjects' productions. *They detected no differences in quality of performance associated with academic achievement or self-ratings.*

With respect to mediation of affect, quantitative results did not reach levels of statistical significance, but *there were suggestive tendencies on both the lever-*

pressing and crayon-coloring tests for boys who had been highly self-critical to avoid exposing themselves to the color that had previously been associated with the critical label "Poor."

What are the implications of the foregoing findings? First, it should be explained that the great majority of the children, particularly of the boys, in the school where the testing was done were in the "low achiever" category. The teachers who selected the subjects were hard put to come up with thirty-six boys whom they could call "high achievers"—that is, whom they regarded as clearly competent in school work—and they were drawing on an aggregate pool of about two hundred male pupils. Hence, it is fair to say that the typical boy in the school was both academically weak by teachers' standards, and critical of his own achievement efforts. Yet, relative to pupils in other predominantly Negro schools in the urban North, these boys were no worse than average.

What is intriguing about the results is the suggestion that among northern Negro children academic failure is not necessarily associated with low or unstable standards of self-evaluation. If standards are to be inferred from a predisposition to criticize oneself, then the low-achieving Negro boys had very high standards indeed. Conceivably, their standards were so stringent and rigid as to be utterly dysfunctional. They seem to have internalized a most effective mechanism for self-discouragement. In a sense, they had been socialized to self-impose failure. I use the term socialization deliberately, believing that what is involved is not merely a lack of prior rewards for achievement efforts, but also a history of punitive reactions by socializing agents to such efforts.

The home socialization experiences of subjects were investigated by means of a *Reinforcement History Questionnaire* devised by Reuben Baron. It contained twenty-one items dealing with characteristic reactions of the father or mother to the child in a variety of situations.[4] *We found both low academic achievement and self-criticism related to children's perceptions of low rewardingness and high punitiveness on the part of both parents.*

The Anxiety-reductive Function of Self-criticism

Two theories of children's self-critical behavior point to an anxiety-reductive function. First, consider Aronfreed's model for the socialization of self-criticism as a

---

[4] The *Reinforcement History Questionnaire* is described in Katz, "The Socialization of Academic Motivation in Minority Group Children," *op. cit.*

response to transgressions.[5] Aronfreed is concerned mainly with accounting for the internalization of moral self-control, but his concepts are sufficiently general to apply to achievement situations as well. He defines self-criticism as the most common form of a class of reactions to transgression in which the child imitatively reproduces components of the punishment to which he has been previously exposed. Aronfreed's conception is basically quite simple. *Once a child has had some contact with punishment for a particular type of behavior, he will experience anticipatory anxiety in the intervals which occur between subsequent enactments of such behavior and the occurrence of punishment.* Certain of the stimulus components of punishment can then acquire value as signals for the attenuation of the child's anticipatory anxiety, since they mark the end of the interval of anticipation. Thus, young children can sometimes be observed to verbalize self-criticism aloud and to make the anxiety-reducing function of these responses quite transparent when they show signs of distress following a punishable behavior and then apparent relief after they have overtly censured themselves. Very likely, the extent to which self-criticism is acquired by a child as a technique for reducing anxiety —rather than avoidance, withdrawal, or outwardly-directed hostility—will be governed to some extent by his dependency on adults for emotional security.

A theory of emotional blocks to learning that deals explicitly with the conflict between emotional dependency and hostile impulses has been formulated by Sarason and his associates at Yale in connection with their investigations of test anxiety.[6] Like Aronfreed, the Yale group offers an anxiety-reduction interpretation of self-blame. They regard the test-anxious child as one who typically reacts with strong unconscious hostility against teachers and others whom he thinks are passing judgment on his adequacy as a person. Because of his dependency on adults, the child does not express his feelings openly but instead turns them inward upon himself in the form of self-derogatory attitudes. This is as far as the theory goes with regard to the adaptative function of self-blame. I would simply add that when inward-directed hostility expresses itself as self-criticism, the resultant discharge of the displaced impulses tends to be cathartic, hence anxiety-reducing.

The theoretical linkage between self-criticism and anxiety made it desirable to administer the Yale group's *Test Anxiety Scale for Children* to the Negro boys who were used in our experiments. When this was done, test anxiety scores were

[5] J. Aronfreed, *Conduct and Conscience: The Socialization of Internal Control Over Behavior* (New York: Academic Press, 1968).

[6] S. B. Sarason, *et al.*, *Anxiety in Elementary School Children* (New York: John Wiley & Sons, 1960).

found to be higher among the low academic achievers than among the high achievers, and to be directly related both to propensity for self-criticism and to perception of parents as punitive rather than rewarding. *Thus the likelihood that self-imposed failure operates as an anxiety-reducing mechanism in disadvantaged male pupils is clearly indicated.*

Impressive support for the contention that Negro pupils in racially isolated schools are the victims of inordinately high levels of anxiety has very recently come to my attention through an unpublished report by Sheila Feld and Judith Lewis.[7] These investigators administered the *Test Anxiety Scale for Children* to the entire second-grade population of a suburban school system in the eastern part of the United States. Over eight hundred Negroes and sixty-five hundred whites attending *de facto* segregated schools were tested. Negroes were found to have substantially higher anxiety scores not only on the total scale but also on each of four subscales which were derived by means of factor analysis: test anxiety, remote school concern (e.g., "When you are in bed at night, do you sometimes worry about how you are going to do in class the next day?"), poor self-evaluation, and somatic signs of anxiety. Interestingly, a group of 105 Negro children in racially mixed schools obtained scores about midway between those of the segregated Negro and white samples. However, the meaning of this comparison is not entirely clear, since the Negro children in desegregated schools came from homes of relatively high socio-economic status, a factor found to be associated with low anxiety. Sex differences appeared for white pupils—white boys obtained lower anxiety scores than white girls—but not for Negroes.

The Role of Negro Parents

Paradoxical as it may seem, an important source of school anxiety in Negroes is probably the inordinately high demands for academic achievement that are made by minority-group parents—demands that are higher even than those imposed by white middle-class parents. Several investigators, for example Bell in Philadelphia and Keller in New York City,[8] have found that a majority of Negro parents who have attained an economic status above the very lowest levels of poverty desire a

---

[7] Sheila Feld and Judith Lewis, "The Assessment of Achievement Anxieties in Children," (Mental Health Study Center, National Institute of Mental Health, 1967, MS).

[8] R. R. Bell, "Lower Class Negro Mothers' Aspirations for their Children," *Social Forces*, XLIII (1965), 493-500; Suzanne Keller, "The Social World of the Urban Slum Child: Some Early Findings," *American Journal of Orthopsychiatry*, XXXIII (1963), 823-31.

college education for their sons, and majorities or near-majorities want them to enter professions. These aspirations are so discrepant with the amount of effort lower-class parents actually devote to their children's educational needs (for example, helping with homework), and so unrealistic in view of the typical lower-class child's academic retardation, as to suggest that they are merely empty statements made for the benefit of the interviewer or expressions of fantasies that have nothing to do with real events. In my opinion, the parents' aspirations are indeed in the nature of wishful fantasies, in the sense that the parents do not know how to implement them, but the aspirations have consequences in that they somehow get conveyed to the child as expectations he is supposed to fulfill. This hypothesis helps explain why the low-achieving Negro boys in our study appeared to be harshly over-critical of their own achievement efforts rather than easily satisfied or indifferent. It is also consistent with research that has shown higher educational aspirations among Negro children than among white age-peers of comparable economic levels. In the Coleman survey, Negro twelfth-grade students reported higher levels of academic motivation, interest, and aspiration than whites. For example, when asked about whether they wanted to be good students, a higher proportion of Negroes than any other ethnic group—over half— reported that they wanted to be one of the best in the class. Negroes reported also more studying outside school than any group except Oriental-Americans.

There is, I daresay, a large element of defensiveness or wishful thinking, or both, in the Negro responses. This becomes apparent with regard to college aspirations, for while more Negroes than whites in the Coleman study reported a desire to go to college, lower proportions of Negroes had seen a college catalogue or written to a college. *But having a need to overstate the degree of one's educational interest on an anonymous questionnaire is in itself a fact of much significance. It reveals that one holds achievement values and achievement standards that do not get reflected in actual achievement efforts.* Values and goals have been internalized, but not the behavioral mechanisms requisite for attaining them. The disjunction of cognitions and behaviors is not difficult to understand, for verbal attitudes are relatively easy to acquire through mere imitation of verbalizations observed in adult or peer models. If the attitudes expressed are the "correct" ones, i.e., are held by socializing agents—and I have mentioned research which shows that Negro parents verbalize high educational goals for their children—they will tend to get reinforced either directly or vicariously. But performing the behaviors that are instrumental for attaining the goals is a more difficult feat than the acquisition of verbal attitudes about the goal, especially when there are no models of competency to imitate, and when achievement strivings are not socially recognized and reinforced. Apparently, the typical Negro mother tries to socialize her child for scholastic achievement by laying down verbal rules and regulations about classroom conduct, coupled with punishment of detected transgressions. But she does not do enough to guide and encourage her child's efforts at verbal-symbolic mastery. Therefore, the child learns only to verbalize standards of academic interest and attainment. These standards then provide the cognitive basis for negative self-evaluations.

The foregoing analysis can explain why Negro students do not express *less* scholastic interest than whites, despite lower achievement levels, but it does not satisfactorily account for the finding in the Coleman survey of *greater* scholastic interest in Negro twelfth graders. I suspect that as part of his adjustment to failure, the low-achieving Negro student learns to use expressions of interest and ambition as a verbal substitute for behaviors he is unable to enact. The effect is probably double-edged: anxiety is *reduced* in situations where verbal expressions are enough, yet by emphasizing the discrepancy between real and ideal performance, anxiety is *raised* in actual achievement situations. Hence, as the Negro student falls increasingly behind in his school work, the expression of high verbal standards contributes to a growing demoralization.

Implicit in my analysis is the proposition that *when high standards are adopted, but not the behavioral mechanisms necessary for attainment, the relationship between verbal expressions of the standards and actual performance will tend to be an inverse one.* The Coleman data for Negro students nationally are not inconsistent with the proposition. At the sixth-grade level, the relationship between expressed interest in school work and achievement test scores is very small and positive, at ninth grade it is zero, and at twelfth grade it is extremely small but *negative*.[9] Since I do not contend that Negro students *totally* lack the positive self-reinforcement mechanism, I find the reversal trend with increasing age an encouraging indication that my substitute-value hypothesis may be correct for certain types of Negro students.

Sense of Control and Other Attitudes

In all, Coleman and his associates measured three types of student attitude relevant to academic motivation: interest in school work, self-concept as regards abil-

[9] See Table 3.26.2 in Coleman *et al.*, *op. cit.*, p. 322.

ity, and sense of control of own rewards.[10] For Negro students, sense of control was clearly the most important attitude, contributing at different grades from two to several times as much to the accounted-for variance of verbal achievement as either of the others. Moreover, the relation of Negroes' sense of control to achievement was considerably stronger than that of any family-background factor. Finally, comparing races reveals that among older children sense of fate control accounted for about three times as much test variance among Negroes as among whites.

Since the Coleman findings represent merely empirical correlations, the causal connections between sense of internal control and other variables can only be surmised. Nonetheless, there are strong suggestions in the data regarding the relative importance of home and school determinants. The Report indicates that for Negroes sense of control was little influenced by home factors or objective school characteristics, but one factor apparently affected it strongly: as the proportion of white students in school enrollments increased, Negroes' sense of internality grew stronger. Their self-concept of ability, however, declined as proportion white increased. Since Negro achievement in fact was higher in majority-white schools, it would appear that *a modest self-concept is not detrimental to Negro academic performance, provided children can depend upon the environment to dispense rewards in a fair and equitable way.*

Thus, a fascinating implication of the Coleman Report is that relatively realistic perceptions of one's ability relative to classmates of higher ability need not produce discouragement in the disadvantaged pupil—indeed, it may have the opposite effect—provided the child has a secure awareness of opportunities for social and material reward commensurate with his own efforts and capabilities. The research described earlier in this paper on-self-criticism and anxiety provides support for the above interpretation of the Coleman findings—that is, debilitating anxiety in minority-group students may be more a function of perceived isolation and exclusion from the main American opportunity structure than of awareness of one's intellectual limitations relative to classmates. Future research should be addressed to this question.

---

[10] To assess sense of control, students were asked to respond to three statements—that "good luck is more important than hard work for success"; that "every time I try to get ahead something or somebody stops me"; and that "people like me don't have much of a chance to be successful in life."

Race and Equal Educational Opportunity*

THOMAS F. PETTIGREW

Harvard University

After reviewing several studies that support the Coleman finding on the significance of the social-class climate of the school's student body, the author considers effects which can be attributed specifically to racial-composition factors. He distinguishes between a "desegregated" school and an "integrated" school, and discusses the explanatory power of this "crucial distinction." The author concludes with an examination of questions concerning the dynamics of the interracial classroom suggested by the Equality of Educational Opportunity survey data. Two processes are considered in some detail: "fate control" and "social evaluation."

In racial terms, the complex concept of "equal educational opportunity" translates into *effective integrated schooling.* That anything less than this has not proven to be truly equal opportunity for Negro American children is a demonstrably harsh fact of the current scene—and there is reason to believe that the same holds true for white American children as well. There are many reasons for this translation, a number of which receive considerable support from the extensive Coleman

* This article appeared originally in the Winter 1968 issue of the *Harvard Educational Review*. It was written as part of Contract No. OEC 1-6-061774-1887 from the U.S. Office of Education.

data. This brief summary will utilize analyses of the data from the 1966 Coleman Report itself[1] and the 1967 U.S. Commission on Civil Rights report, *Racial Isolation in the Public Schools*.[2]

The Social Class Climate of the School

The most significant school correlate of achievement test scores uncovered by the Coleman study is the social-class climate of the school's student body. This variable is measured by the social-class origins of all of a school's students; and it appears most critical in the later grades and somewhat more important for Negro than white children. Put bluntly, children of all backgrounds tend to do better in schools with a predominant middle-class milieu; and this trend is especially true in the later grades where the full force of peer-group influence is felt. This basic finding of the Coleman Report has been vigorously challenged by a number of methodological critics, none of whom seem aware that the identical finding had been attained by four other studies which employed sharply different measures and samples from those used by Coleman. Interestingly, three of these replications were in print several years before the appearance of *Equality of Educational Opportunity* in 1966.

The importance of this key Coleman conclusion warrants further mention of these supporting studies. In a research paper published in 1959, Alan Wilson demonstrated the special significance of school social class in determining college aspirations in eight high schools in the San Francisco–Oakland Bay area of California.[3] He found higher percentages of college aspirants in higher-status schools even after controlling for other determinants of college aspirations: father's occupation and education, mother's education, median academic grade, and intelligence-test score. For example, among those boys whose fathers and mothers were high-school graduates and whose fathers held manual occupations, 60 per cent in upper-status schools wanted to go to college compared to 54 per cent in the medium-status schools and only 32 per cent in the working-status schools. Likewise, among those boys with a modest "C" academic grade record, 72 per cent from upper-status schools aspired to college in contrast to only 55 per cent from medium-status schools and 41 per cent in working-status schools. Finally, for those in the 100 to

[1] James S. Coleman, *et al., Equality of Educational Opportunity* (Washington: U.S. Government Printing Office, 1966).

[2] (Washington: U.S. Government Printing Office, 1967), I.

[3] A. B. Wilson, "Residential Segregation of Social Classes and Aspirations of High School Boys," *American Sociological Review*, XXIV (1959), 836-45.

119 I.Q. test range, 93 per cent in the upper-status schools, 72 per cent in the medium-status schools, and 51 per cent in the working-status schools aimed for college.

Differential college aspirations are not the only outcomes of school social class uncovered in this Wilson study. Controlling for father's occupation, he found that both occupational aspirations and political party preferences are also influenced. Hence, among boys whose fathers occupied manual positions, 44 per cent in the upper-status schools wanted to be professionals and 50 per cent preferred the Republican Party compared with 31 per cent and 32 per cent in the medium-status schools and 27 per cent and 24 per cent in the working-status schools, respectively.

A second early attack on the problem was mounted at Harvard University, though it substituted the social-class level of nine Boston suburbs for a direct measure of the schools' social-class levels.[4] Controlling for father's occupation, the researchers found that boys from the higher-status communities were more likely to go to college. In addition, community status, which determined the status level of the schools, had its crucial impact only at the high-school level, the level at which Wilson was working. Consequently, community status predicted neither primary-school grades nor entrance into the college preparatory courses in high school from junior high school, a finding that resembles the Coleman result that the social status of schools gained in predictive value in the secondary-school grades.

The most definitive early study was conducted by John Michael.[5] He analyzed the aptitude test scores (on a test not unlike those used by Coleman) as well as the career and college plans of 35,436 seniors in a nationally representative sample of 518 American public high schools. Michael classified the students on an index of family social class using such information as the father's occupation and education and whether older siblings had attended college. Further, he classified the high schools into five status ranks according to the percentage of seniors in each school who fell into his two top family-status classifications, a method similar to the school social class measures of Coleman.

The first finding showed that with family status controlled, the higher the status of the school, the higher the average score on the scholastic aptitude test. Further analysis revealed that the variation in the percentages of students scoring above the national average on the test was roughly equally attributable to the individual

[4] Stuart Cleveland, "A Tardy Look at Stouffer's Findings in the Harvard Mobility Project," *Public Opinion Quarterly*, XXVI (1962), 453-4.

[5] John A. Michael, "High School Climates and Plans for Entering College," *Public Opinion Quarterly*, XXV (1961), 585-95.

and school social class indices. But the variation in the percentages scoring in the top quarter was considerably more related to individual social class than school social class—a result directly in line with Coleman's finding that school social class is most important for the more deprived students and in line with the Commission's re-analysis finding that among whites in the metropolitan Northeast, school social class was least important for the highest-status students.[6] The little-known Michael research, then, provided early evidence for most of the major Coleman Report conclusions.

On the matter of plans to attend college, the Michael study, like the Wilson and Harvard investigations, demonstrated that school social class makes a difference. But Michael's larger sample allowed deeper analysis and, as did the Coleman analysis, revealed that these effects are strongest for students from lower individual class backgrounds. Consider first those seniors who score in the top quarter of the aptitude test distribution. Among these talented youngsters from the lowest individual social class group, only 44 per cent who attended the lowest-status high schools planned to go to college compared with 57 per cent who attended the highest-status high schools. By contrast, among the talented seniors from the highest individual social class group, 80 per cent who attended the lowest-status high schools planned to go to college compared with 86 per cent who attended the highest-status high schools. In other words, the high-status school exerts a far greater influence on college plans among talented lower-status than talented higher-status children.

Much the same phenomenon is true for Michael's entire sample. The percentage differences in college plans between individual social class groups is essentially the same at each type of school; but the percentage differences in college plans between scholastic aptitude test levels is far higher in the high-status than the low-status high schools. Put simply, attendance at a low-status school does not deter seniors from upper-status families in planning for college, but attendance at a high-status school is an important aid to able seniors from lower-status families.

These three early investigations, however, suffered from two interrelated methodological weaknesses that also limit the Coleman survey: the results are neither longitudinal nor corrected for initial achievement and aspirations upon entering school in the primary grades. These limitations open the studies to the possibility that their findings are merely the result of special selection biases. That is, lower-class children in predominantly middle-class schools may achieve more and aspire

---

[6] U.S. Commission on Civil Rights, *op. cit.,* I, 85.

higher not because of the school climate but only because they are as a group brighter and more ambitious to begin with than lower-class children in general.

Robert Nichols has been a particularly vehement critic of the social-class climate finding of the Coleman Report on precisely these grounds of possible selection biases.[7] He and other critics apparently choose to ignore a fourth replication of the Coleman result reported at length in the U.S. Commission on Civil Rights report.[8] Wilson, in a follow-up to his earlier research, studied the social-class climate variable on a probability sample of junior- and senior-high-school children in California's Bay area. He had the advantage of longitudinal data and initial scores upon entering school, thus overcoming Nichols' objections. In this study, Wilson finds a strong effect of the social-class context at even the elementary-school level. After carefully "allowing for individual differences in personal background, neighborhood context, and mental maturity at the time of the school entry," he notes that the social-class level of elementary schools has a significant effect upon subsequent academic success at higher grade levels.

The Racial Composition of the School

The racial significance of this social-class climate finding of the Coleman Report becomes obvious as soon as we recall that, at most, only about one-fourth of the Negro American population can be accurately described as "middle-class." Apart from strictly racial factors, then, extensive desegregation is necessary to provide Negro pupils with predominantly middle-class school settings. On these class grounds alone, Negro children in interracial classrooms would be expected to achieve more than similar Negro children in all-Negro classrooms, and these expectations are supported in the Coleman data. Negro children from "more than half" white classrooms score higher on both reading and mathematical achievement tests than other Negro children; and this effect is strongest among those who began their interracial schooling in the early grades.[9] In addition, Negro students in "more than half" white classrooms yield as a group higher standard deviations in test scores than Negroes in classrooms with fewer whites—that is, desegregated Negroes reveal a wider spread in test performance.[10]

[7] Robert C. Nichols, "Schools and the Disadvantaged," *Science*, CLIV (Dec. 9, 1966), 1312-4.

[8] U. S. Commission on Civil Rights, *Racial Isolation in the Public Schools* (Washington: U.S. Government Printing Office, 1967), II, 165-206.

[9] Coleman, *et al.*, *op. cit.*, p. 332.

[10] *Ibid.*, p. 333. The scores of the few Negroes with all white classmates have the highest SD's of all, though smaller cell sizes are involved.

But are these achievement benefits of the interracial classroom *completely* a function of the social-class climate factor? Or are racial composition factors independently related *in addition?* The text of the Coleman Report is equivocal on this point; it speaks of the desegregation effect being "largely, perhaps wholly, related to," or "largely accounted for by," other student-body characteristics.[11] The Civil Rights Commission's re-analysis of these data, however, focuses further attention upon this particular question and finds that there *is* indeed a critical racial composition correlate. The re-analysis uncovers relatively large and consistent differences in favor of those twelfth-grade Negroes who are in "more than half" white classrooms even after the two major factors of the Coleman analysis have been controlled—family social class and school social class.[12] The apparent benefits of interracial classrooms are not linear; in other words, Negroes in predominantly-white classrooms score higher on the average, but those in classrooms with "less than half" whites do no better than those in all-Negro classrooms. Once again, this effect of improved performance appears greatest for those Negro children who begin their biracial training in the early grades. Moreover, this is not a zero-sum game; that is, white performance in predominantly-white classrooms does not decline as Negro performance rises. The achievement scores of white children in biracial classes with "more than half" white students average just as high as those of comparable children in all-white classes.[13]

The Commission Report also makes a crucial distinction between a merely desegregated school and an integrated one. Desegregation involves only a specification of the racial mix of students—preferably, more than half white. It does not include any description of the *quality* of the interracial contact. Merely desegregated schools can be either effective or ineffective, can boast genuine interracial acceptance or intense interracial hostility. In short, a desegregated school is not necessarily a "good school." Recall the greater spread of test scores of Negro children in desegregated classrooms. Many of these children are doing extremely well, but others are not doing nearly as well. What accounts for the difference? The Commission's re-analysis of the Coleman data suggests that the explanatory intervening variable is *interracial acceptance.* In the schools which can truly be described as "integrated," where most teachers report no racial tension whatsoever, Negro students evince higher verbal achievement, more definite college plans, and more positive racial attitudes than comparable Negro students in tense, merely "desegregated"

[11] *Ibid.,* pp. 307 and 330.
[12] U.S. Commission on Civil Rights, *op. cit.,* I, 90.
[13] *Ibid.,* p. 160.

schools.[14] Desegregation, then, is a necessary but not sufficient condition for integration, for integration involves in addition to racial mix a climate of interracial acceptance.

While important, high achievement-test scores are surely not the sole goal of education. Indeed, many advocates argue for integrated education only in terms of the nonacademic benefits of diverse contacts. Preparation for the interracial world of the future, they insist, demands interracial schools today for both white and Negro youth. The Coleman data speak to this issue, too. The Coleman Report itself shows that white students who attend public schools with Negroes are the least likely to prefer all-white classrooms and all-white "close friends"; and this effect, too, is strongest among those who begin their interracial schooling in the early grades.[15] Consistent with these results are data from Louisville, Kentucky on Negro pupils. In an open-choice situation, Negro children are far more likely to select predominantly-white high schools if they are currently attending predominantly-white junior high schools.[16]

A Civil Rights Commission survey of urban adults in the North and West suggests that these trends continue into adulthood. Negro adults who themselves attended desegregated schools as children tend to be more eager to have their children attend such schools and do in fact more often send their children to such schools than comparable Negro adults who attended only segregated schools as children.[17] They are typically making more money and are more frequently in white-collar occupations than previously-segregated Negroes of comparable origins. Similarly, white adults who experienced as children integrated schooling differ from comparable whites in their greater willingness to reside in an interracial neighborhood, to have their children attend interracial schools, and to have Negro friends.[18] For both Negro and white adults, then, it appears that desegregated schooling does in fact prepare its products for interracial living as adults.

Two Psychological Processes

Most discussion to date of these results has centered upon their immediate implications. But of greater psychological significance are the questions they raise con-

[14] *Ibid.,* pp. 157-8.
[15] Coleman, *et al., op. cit.,* p. 333.
[16] U.S. Commission on Civil Rights, *Civil Rights USA: Public Schools, Southern States, 1962.* (Washington: U. S. Government Printing Office, 1963).
[17] U. S. Commission on Civil Rights, *op. cit.,* I, 111-3.
[18] *Ibid.*

cerning the actual dynamics of the interracial classroom and the precise individual processes which undergird these crude aggregate findings. A number of fascinating clues concerning these psychological processes are provided in the Coleman Report, two of which deserve special mention: "fate control" and "social evaluation." The former is essentially Rotter's "internal-external control of reinforcement" variable;[19] while the latter refers to the cross-racial comparisons made possible by the interracial classroom.[20]

Student personality variables are surprisingly strong independent correlates of test performance in Coleman's data for all groups of children, though different measures predict white and Negro achievement. An "academic self-concept" variable (measured by such items as "How bright do you think you are in comparison with the other students in your grade?") proves more significant for white performance. But a brief scale of "fate control" (indicated, for example, by disagreeing that "Good luck is more important than hard work for success") is much more important for Negro performance. Not surprisingly, this sense of internal control among Negroes tends to be greater in desegregated schools—a vital finding that contradicts those who would distort the "fate control" results as evidence for separate all-Negro schools under "black control."

Clearly, these personality-achievement findings result from tapping into a complex process involving a two-way causal pattern. Not only do those Negro children with a sense of internal control subsequently do better in their school achievement, but those who do well in school achievement undoubtedly begin to gain a sense of internal control. Nevertheless, it is tempting to speculate with Coleman that each child faces a two-stage problem: first, he must learn that he can, within reasonably broad limits, act effectively upon his surroundings; and, second, he must then evaluate his own relative capabilities for mastering the environment. The critical stage for white children seems to be the second stage concerning the self-concept, while the critical stage for Negro children seems realistically enough to involve the question of manipulating an often harsh and overpowering environment. In any event, more detailed experimental work along the lines of Rotter's research and Coleman's speculation appears warranted.

A number of theoretical considerations from social psychology suggest a broad social evaluation hypothesis: *Many of the consequences of interracial classrooms*

[19] J. B. Rotter, "Internal versus External Control of Reinforcement," *Psychological Monographs,* LXXX (1966), Whole No. 609.

[20] Thomas F. Pettigrew, "Social Evaluation Theory: Convergences and Applications," in D. Levine (ed.), *1967 Nebraska Symposium on Motivation* (Lincoln, Neb.: University of Nebraska Press, in press).

for both Negro and white children are a direct function of the opportunities such classrooms provide for cross-racial self-evaluation. It follows from such an hypothesis that the more opportunities for cross-racial self-evaluation a school provides, the greater the consequences. And it also follows that those children for whom peers of the other race become referent should evince the largest changes.

These predictions are consistent with the analyses of the Coleman and Commission reports and with the conceptual framework and experimental results on biracial performance of Irwin Katz.[21] Hence, the repeated indications of the special potency of desegregation in the early elementary grades fit well with the self-evaluation view. Young children have less rooted self-conceptions and have not yet adopted uniracial school cliques as their chief peer referents. So, too, do the Coleman conclusions that the most significant school correlate of test scores is the social-class climate of the school's student body; and that this factor is especially important for Negro children. Schools with a middle-class milieu furnish higher comparison levels for achievement and aspirations; and these higher levels will be especially influential for disadvantaged Negro youngsters whose referents otherwise might well have lower levels. And the special efficacy of "more than half" white classrooms and schools, particularly those characterized by cross-racial acceptance, is also consistent with these predictions. The integrated class and school are unique in the range of opportunities they provide Negro children for maximal self-evaluation against higher comparison levels.

The inclusion in Coleman's student schedules of a question about cross-racial friendships makes possible direct tests of the social evaluation hypothesis. All students tested in the sixth, ninth, and twelfth grades were asked: "Think now of your close friends. How many of them are white? None, less than half, about half, more than half, all." Assuming "close friends" to be referent, the social evaluation hypothesis predicts that the major consequences of interracial schools for both Negroes and white will be found among those who report "close friends" of the other race.

The published analyses employing the "close friend" variable confirm this hypothesis. Thus, with the family and school social-class variables controlled, Negro children with close white friends far less often prefer all Negro friends and an all-Negro school than other Negro children regardless of the racial composition of their classrooms.[22] Classrooms with half or more white students relate strongly to

[21] Irwin Katz, "Review of Evidence Relating to Effects of Desegregation on the Performance of Negroes," *American Psychologist,* XIX (1964), 381-99.
[22] U. S. Commission on Civil Rights, *op. cit.,* II, 97-9.

these interracial preferences solely because Negroes in them more often have close white friends.[23] In addition, Negroes who participate in extra-curricular activities more frequently report close white friends.[24]

Negro achievement scores and college aspirations present a slightly different picture from the attitude data. Having close white friends is related neither to higher scores nor aspirations in all-Negro classrooms. But in "more than half" white classrooms, Negro students with close white friends tend to have both higher achievement scores and college aspirations.[25]

Friendship operates in a similar fashion for white students. Hence, with father's education controlled, having close Negro friends is strongly and positively related to white preference for an interracial school.[26] And, as noted, white pupils who begin their interracial schooling in the early grades are more likely to have close Negro friends when they reach the ninth and twelfth grades.[27]

In short, integrated education in the early grades seems to have important benefits for both Negro and white children in terms of improved interracial attitudes and preferences—not an unimportant consequence in a nation torn by racial strife and bigotry. And if social evaluation processes during interracial contact are as critical contributors to these benefits as they appear in these data, even the most academically-successful "compensatory program" in ghetto schools cannot rival genuine integration.

A Final Word

Let it be clearly stated that Coleman and his associates achieved a landmark contribution in an amazingly short span of time. Though not without its problems of sampling, non-response, and analysis, this massive and ambitious study should influence educational research and practice for years to come. It is of necessity a broad-gauged, aggregate survey of what exists now in American public schools. It could neither detail precise learning processes nor test what American public schools could potentially become in the future. Similar to the naked eye compared with an electronic microscope, the Coleman Report outlined the gross facts of American public education today, while the precision of the limited experiment is now needed to detail

---

[23] *Ibid.,* p. 103.
[24] *Ibid.,* p. 102.
[25] *Ibid.,* pp. 100-1.
[26] *Ibid.,* p. 141.
[27] Coleman, *et al., op. cit.,* p. 333.

the undergoing processes that go unseen by the survey. From fate control to social evaluation, the results of the Coleman Report are rich and suggestive for fruitful experimentation. In the meantime, the racial implications of the Coleman Report for practical school policy are reasonably clear: equal educational opportunity for both Negro and white children requires socially and racially integrated, not merely desegregated, schools.

Social Class and Equal Educational Opportunity*

ALAN B. WILSON

University of California, Berkeley

After reviewing briefly the influence that the ideology of equal educational opportunity has had on the development of public education, the author considers the relationships between the "aggregative characteristics" of schools and the development of individual students attending these schools. In particular, he considers the relevant findings presented in the Coleman Report and in related studies. He discusses several levels at which the Coleman inference with respect to the effect of student body characteristics on academic achievement has been questioned, and uses related studies where possible to eliminate ambiguities. The author concludes by considering the problem of a theoretical rationale adequate to account for the empirical findings of the Coleman study.

On an inscription found in the Old Kingdom of Egypt,[1] an anonymous father admonishes his son to study hard so that he may become a revered scribe rather than a peasant who "always sweats" or a miner who "stinks like a fish." Such worldly motives for learning have characterized all societies where literacy qualifies one for desirable occupations. The most frequent response to any inquiry into why one should do well in school is in terms of future socioeconomic attainment. The widespread belief that mobility may be achieved, or status maintained,

---

* This article appeared originally in the Winter 1968 issue of the *Harvard Educational Review*.

[1] Reported by Stanislaw Andrzejewski, "Vertical Mobility and Technical Progress," *Social Forces, XXIX (October, 1959), p. 49.*

through educational attainment is paralleled in sociological and political theory, wherein education is perceived as a social mechanism permitting "meritocracy" and ameliorating the inheritance of social position.[2]

The ideology of equal social opportunity permeates the history of the growth of public education. The provision of public secondary schools was a deliberate extension of the "educational ladder," providing the opportunity for upward mobility. Thomas Huxley, serving on the Board of Education in London, declared, "I conceive it to be our duty to make a ladder from the gutter to the university along which any child may climb."[3] This same apt metaphor was used by the Royal (Bryce) Commission's Report on Secondary Education which led to the Education Act of 1902. Josiah Quincy, mayor of Boston at the time of the establishment of the first public high school in the United States, commented: "In 1820, an English classical school was established, having for its object to enable the mercantile and mechanical classes to obtain an education adapted for those children, whom their parents wished to qualify for active life, and thus relieve them from the necessity of incurring the expense incident to private academies."[4]

Although the rapid growth of the secondary school in this country was consequent on the shifting composition of the labor force,[5] its rationale as a public institution was to provide for social mobility on the basis of universalistic criteria. Step after step has been taken in all western societies enabling the able and ambitious to climb the educational ladder and to circumvent obstacles due to particular ascribed circumstances. The Kalamazoo decision of 1874 marked an important milestone and precedent in the growth of public secondary education in the United States. The argument of the jurist, Thomas M. Cooley, expresses the ethos of the time and the interests of the advocates of public education:

We supposed it had always been understood in this state that education, not merely in the rudiments, but in an enlarged sense, was regarded as an important practical advantage to be supplied at their option to rich and poor alike, and not as something pertaining merely to culture and accomplishment to be brought as such within the reach of those whose accumulated wealth enabled them to pay for it. . . .[6]

[2] The literature is very extensive. An early statement is made by Pitirim Sorokin, *Social Mobility* (New York: Harper & Brothers, 1927).

[3] Ellwood P. Cubberley, *The History of Education* (Boston: Houghton Mifflin Co., 1920), p. 648.

[4] Josiah Quincy, *A Municipal History of the Town and City of Boston* (Boston: Charles C. Little and James Brown, 1852), pp. 21-2.

[5] See, for example, Warren S. Thompson, *Population Problems* (4th ed.; New York: McGraw-Hill Book Co., 1953), p. 390.

[6] Quoted in Elmer Ellsworth Brown, *The Making of Our Middle Schools* (3rd ed.; New York: Longmans, Green, and Co., 1910), pp. 357-8.

That public sentiment on the practical values of schooling has not altered in subsequent years is reflected in the language of the Supreme Court of the United States in its decision of 1954 on the issue of racial segregation in the schools:

> In these days, it is doubtful that any child may reasonably be expected to succeed in life if he is denied the opportunity of an education. Such an opportunity, where the state has undertaken to provide it, is a right which must be made available to all on equal terms.[7]

Not only had it been hoped that public education might make a reality of the Alger legend, but also that it would enhance social harmony by a process of cultural homogenization and through the teaching of intergroup tolerance, understanding, and respect. Not only equality but also fraternity was to be fostered by the schools.[8] "Bringing together the children of the rich and poor will benefit both, by removing from one any disposition to arrogance and self-will, and from the other the spirit of envy and jealousy."[9]

Although the assertion that public education should promote equal opportunity commands widespread assent, there is little consensus on the meaning of the phrase "equality of educational opportunity." The traditional liberal view of equality of opportunity which motivated the extension of public elementary and secondary education in this country would, as far as possible, remove legal and economic handicaps to the acquisition of education by intelligent and industrious youths whose parents sought their social advancement. The more radical conception calls for the provision of experiences which generate intelligence and arouse interest even where the influence of the home and neighborhood may be impoverished or hostile.[10]

While the schism between liberal and radical views of opportunity lead to different boundaries around public responsibility for the intellectual development of the child, and may reflect differing presuppositions about the salience of environmental variation for intellectual development, they share a common mini-

---

[7] *Brown et al. v. Board of Education of Topeka et al.,* 347 U.S. 5 (1954), p. 493.

[8] See, for example, Herbert G. Espy, *The Public Secondary School* (Boston: Houghton Mifflin Co., 1939), pp. 116-23.

[9] Mattie Crouch Kneece, *The Contribution of C. G. Menninger to the Cause of Education* (Bulletin of the University of South Carolina, No. 177, February 15, 1926), p. 25. The continuing objective of inter-class cohesion is described by Bernard Mehl, "Political and Social Cohesion in Secondary Education in the United States," in George Z. F. Bereday and Joseph A. Lauwerys (eds.), *The Year Book of Education: 1958* (London: Evans Brothers Ltd., 1958), pp. 129-38.

[10] Martin Trow applies this contrast between "liberal" and "radical" views of opportunity to a discussion of the education of the gifted and the disadvantaged in "Two Problems in American Education," in Howard S. Becker (ed.), *Social Problems* (New York: John Wiley & Sons, 1966).

mum mandate that circumstances of wealth, race, and geography should not affect the quality of public education which is available to an eligible pupil.

Thus, while programs of compensatory education, preschool training, parenthood training, and remedial curricula compete for scarce resources by trying to demonstrate their educational effectiveness, the equality of the educational experience enjoyed by equally eligible pupils at different facilities is claimed as an acknowledged right. While the obligation—or even propriety—of teachers trying to modify parent-child relationships for the educational benefit of the child is hotly contested, offering demonstrably unequal educational experiences to students having similar educational needs is taken as an injustice.

The effects which differences between schools may have upon students' academic development acquires special public salience, then, even though this effect may be much smaller than the effects upon achievement of family socialization or the differences between pupils within schools. The gross disparities in educational attainments of students attending schools with contrasting racial or socioeconomic composition have been repeatedly documented and publicized during the past several years. Schools in depressed areas are stigmatized; the avoidance of such schools by parents in a position to choose reflects their belief that schools do provide unequal educational opportunities.

Clearly, however, the gross disparities in achievement between children attending different schools are to a large extent—or perhaps entirely—due to prior differences between students aggregated in separate attendance areas: differences in native ability; contrasting preschool socialization and continuing family influences; and diverging extra-school, peer-group and neighborhood influences. Pupils from disadvantaged homes and depressed neighborhoods are behind their compeers at the time of school entry, and do more poorly than their more privileged fellows within the same schools.

Since the 1954 decision of the Supreme Court requiring racial desegregation of schools, there has been a growing accumulation of social research exploring the relationships between aggregative characteristics of schools and the development of individual students attending these schools. The great majority of these studies has documented the thesis that the school environment has an independent effect molding the educational aspirations and orientation of students.[11] Until the publication of the Coleman Report, however, there was little available

---

[11] See, for example, Alan B. Wilson, "Residential Segregation of Social Classes and Aspirations of High School Boys," *American Sociological Review*, XXXIV (December, 1959), 836-45; John A. Michael, "High School Climates and Plans for Entering College," *Public Opinion Quarterly*,

evidence about the effects of school characteristics upon measured academic achievement.[12]

A central thesis of the Coleman Report,[13] subsequently elaborated in the U.S. Commission on Civil Rights report, *Racial Isolation in the Public Schools*,[14] which is particularly pertinent to the issue of whether *de facto* segregation jeopardizes equal opportunity, is the claim that attributes of other students in a school have a substantial impact upon the achievement of individual students who are enrolled, independent of their own background. That is, the academic achievement of initially similar students—and, by inference, the same student— depends in part upon the modal characteristics of the other students at the school he may attend. Moreover, the purported effect of student body characteristics has a greater impact upon members of minority groups than upon white "Anglo" students.[15]

There are several levels, however, at which the warrantability of this inference from the data presented may be questioned. At a technical level, many have questioned the precision of estimates in this report because of the high nonresponse rates and the procedures for estimating missing data. At a methodological level, the adequacy with which the contextual characteristics of the student body have been disentangled from the influences of the family is unclear. The logic of the problem requires that factors affecting achievement which are prior to the hypothesized effect of the school context should be "held constant" in order to isolate any effect of school context. Finally, at a theoretical level, the empirical generalizations which are affirmed are not explained. The greater sensitivity of minority groups to interschool variations, for example, is claimed on the basis of the regression analyses, but the reader is provided with no clues as to why this should be so. Hence, the finding lacks the *a priori* plausibility which would facilitate its acceptance.

XXV (Winter, 1961), 585-95; Ralph H. Turner, *The Social Context of Ambition* (San Francisco: Chandler, 1964); Richard P. Boyle, "The Effect of the High School on Students' Aspirations," *American Journal of Sociology*, LXXI (May, 1966), 628-39.

[12] In an earlier study, I dealt with effects of *de facto* segregation upon the reading test scores of sixth-grade students. The article, "Social Stratification and Academic Achievement," appears in A. Harry Passow (ed.), *Education in Depressed Areas* (New York: Columbia University, Teachers College Press, 1963), pp. 217-35. Other studies, including James S. Coleman's *The Adolescent Society* (New York: Free Press, 1961) and my study cited in n. 11, deal with contextual effects upon teachers' grades.

[13] James S. Coleman, *et al.*, *Equality of Educational Opportunity* (Washington: U.S. Government Printing Office, 1966), pp. 302-12.

[14] (Washington: U.S. Government Printing Office, 1967), pp. 81-108.

[15] Coleman, *et al.*, *op. cit.*, pp. 297, 304-5.

Among these several levels of criticism, the technical criticisms, while the most obvious, are the least serious. In most instances, the practice of estimating missing scores at the population mean is conservative in its effects. This practice will tend to attenuate the intercorrelations among variables. The estimates which were made for those schools and districts which failed to cooperate with the survey—based upon similar schools in the same strata—are reasonable if not optimal. Criticism of this procedure should show how it would lead to bias, not merely point to the possibility that biases might exist. In any event, criticism at this level must cope with the fact that independently conducted studies, using different measures and samples, have confirmed the empirical generalizations of the Coleman Report at many points.[16]

A more serious problem in the Coleman Report is the methodological difficulty of disentangling personal from contextual effects in a nonexperimental study.[17] In comparing how students fare academically in contrasting school environments, it is clearly necessary to compare students who are similar in all relevant ways—students who would presumably perform identically if they were in the same environment—if differences are to be attributed to the contrasted schools which they attend. In a field experiment, we might make random assignments of matched pairs to attend differing schools (assuming that the number of people in the experimental group was not so large as to seriously affect the school composition) and compare their academic gains. In trying to approximate such comparisons in nonexperimental observations, it is necessary to control statistically the nonschool characteristics which might lead to variations in achievement.

The most conspicuous determinant of achievement which is not controlled in the analysis presented in the Coleman Report is "ability." In fact, a verbal-ability test is used throughout as the criterion of achievement upon which schools have their supposed effect.[18] This bold move, however, does not meet the argument that children attending more favored middle-class schools are likely to be more intellectually developed—and perhaps better endowed—than their compeers in more depressed schools. Making additive allowances for differences in parents'

[16] In addition to the studies mentioned in n. 12, above, see Alan B. Wilson, "Educational Consequences of Segregation in a California Community," in *Racial Isolation, op. cit.*, II, 165-206. Edward L. McDill, Edmund D. Meyers, Jr., and Leo C. Rigsby, "Institutional Effects on the Academic Behavior of High School Students," *Sociology of Education*, XL (Summer, 1967), 181-99, also show that Project Talent achievement test scores are affected by characteristics of other students in the school setting.

[17] Arnold S. Tannenbaum and Jerald G. Bachman discuss this problem in "Structural versus Individual Effects," *The American Journal of Sociology*, LXIX (May, 1964), 585-95.

[18] Coleman, *et al., op. cit.*, pp. 292-5.

education and selected social characteristics of the home through multiple regression analysis will not sufficiently allow for these differences.[19]

Nevertheless, the reasons for not controlling for differences in performance on a concurrent ability or IQ test score when examining effects of environmental variations upon performance are compelling. Standard intelligence and ability tests are measures of specific knowledge and problem-solving skills which have been acquired by the testee at some time prior to the test situation. The validity of the IQ test score as a measure of learning "potential" depends upon the assumption of equal exposure to and practice with the kinds of knowledge and skills that the test calls upon. Since the tests were designed to predict performance in school, they call upon the kinds of knowledge and cognitive skills that are required in school. Thus the hypothesis under investigation must be assumed to be false in order for this control to be valid.

One alternative design to circumvent this difficulty would be to undertake a longitudinal study comparing children with similar measured abilities early in their school careers who are subsequently exposed to contrasting school experiences. A study using this strategy was conducted in one community after the publication of the Coleman Report and substantially confirmed the finding that interschool differences do affect student achievement.[20]

However, it remains true that the hypothesis of a contextual effect, where the relevant context is determined by aggregative characteristics of the members, is always vulnerable to the counter-hypothesis of self-selection. It is easy to suppose that parents with the strongest economic, social, and personal resources both place their children in schools of high reputation and influence their children's school performance in ways we have not adequately measured.[21] The Coleman Report, while strengthening the hypothesis, certainly does not close the argument.

Because of the haste with which this study was assembled, and the limited mandate under which it was executed, the theoretical rationale and implications of the empirical findings are not thoroughly elaborated. Most prior investigations of the differential impact of school contexts upon aspirations and achievement

---

[19] Sets of socioeconomic indices rarely account for more than 30 per cent of the variance in IQ test scores. A more extensive set, including race and neighborhood status, accounted for only 15 per cent of the variance in primary grade IQ test scores in Wilson, "Educational Consequences," *op. cit.*, p. 176.

[20] Wilson, "Educational Consequences," *op. cit.*, p. 171.

[21] While unreliability of measures and disparities between indices and theoretical concepts ordinarily exert a conservative effect against an hypothesis, in this case the opposite is true. The less we control for a personal attribute, the more that personal attribute will be confounded with the contextual variable.

have been based upon some variant of reference-group theory—expectations, values, norms, and sanctions vary between schools and impinge upon the individual student. Also teachers' standards, the time spent in instruction as opposed to behavioral control, and teacher-characteristics vary from school to school. The image conjured up by reference-group theory suggests a process of homogenization.

The empirical finding that Negro students are affected more than white students by the quality of the school staff and student body is certainly a happy observation from the point of view of advocates of school integration. It suggests that privileged students will not suffer academically from integration—at least not commensurately with the gains to be enjoyed by the disadvantaged. Yet the finding seems anomalous from the point of view of reference-group theory.

If we focus upon the learning of cognitive skills, however, rather than upon the motivational and normative effects of the social group, this finding makes more sense. It is only among those students who do not acquire the verbal and cognitive skills which are tested through home experiences that variations between schools make a difference.[22] Since there is a higher proportion of educationally disadvantaged students among Negroes than whites, variation between schools is more salient for Negroes. This line of interpretation would suggest an interaction between environmental deprivation and the importance of school context for each racial and ethnic group. Severely disadvantaged white students, also, should benefit from attending excellent schools.

[22] Jensen's finding that the correlation between IQ and learning ability measured in a controlled laboratory setting is much higher among middle-class children than among lower-class children supports this interpretation. Among the disadvantaged, there are larger reservoirs of undeveloped talent; among the advantaged the talent that exists is manifest. See A. R. Jensen, "Learning Abilities in Mexican-American and Anglo-American Children," *California Journal of Educational Research*, XII (1961), 147-59; and "Learning Abilities in Retarded, Average, and Gifted Children," *Merrill-Palmer Quarterly*, IX (1963), 123-40.

Policy Issues

Policy for the Public Schools: Compensation and Integration*

DAVID K. COHEN

*Joint Center for Urban Studies of the Massachusetts Institute of
Technology and Harvard University*

*This article is concerned with the implications of research for national policy. As
a consequence, the discussion centers upon only a few of the many changes which
are generally advocated for urban education. The focus is upon those few basic
aspects of urban public education which probably could be reached and fundamentally changed by the relatively limited instruments of national policy. Although
they have enormous potential for creativity, these instruments—the law, money,
and administrative requirements—also have limitations. The limitations are a
good deal more acute in matters of educational opportunity than in, say, voting
rights. It is in large part for these intrinsic reasons, and owing to certain historic
limitations (we do not have a national school system, and thus cannot have a
national policy on curriculum) that policy implications assessed here may seem
to some rather narrowly circumscribed. It is not my view that unique programs
and personalities, engaged creatively in education under what are often very trying
conditions, are not important or significant. They are, and there is much to be
learned from them.*

*But for our time the learning may not be directly relevant to national policy.
The sources of racial inequality in educational opportunity are very deeply em-*

* This article appeared originally in the Winter 1968 issue of the *Harvard Educational Review*.

David K. Cohen

bedded in the social structure of cities and their school systems. Remedy for these conditions lies in changing those structural features of urban education which produce and sustain inequity. It is therefore a bit wide of the mark to focus attention—as is too often done—on unique personalities and programs which flourish in the face of severe adversity; this can become an exotic form of tokenism. Policy is required which (1) will effect those changes most likely to allow most students, teachers, and principals to function systematically at a higher level, and (2) is not outside the reach of the present instruments of national policy.

For nearly a decade, urban education has been the focus of national attention, and problems of race always have been prominent. Although some civil rights groups have shifted their demands from desegregation to school improvement, race still is the leading issue. As in past years, the leading public policy question currently appears to be whether to take students and school attendance patterns as they are and seek to improve Negro achievement by improving educational quality in the existing schools, or to desegregate schools and thus improve educational opportunities for Negro students.

Although the debate goes on at all levels, there is less ambiguity the further one recedes from the Federal scene. Most urban school systems are firmly committed to compensation as the remedy for Negro students' under-achievement; this commitment seems to be more uniformly true the larger the cities. The Federal position never has been quite this clear. To judge by the various speeches and statements of officials in the Department of Health, Education, and Welfare, there is a general view that school segregation is harmful to all children, that it does Negroes specific educational damage, and that it should be eliminated. But Federal practice, most clearly embodied in Title I of the 1965 Elementary and Secondary Education Act, reflects local priorities; the act provides unprecedented funds to improve education in the existing segregated schools.

Although there is every sign that this effort will continue and be expanded, the speeches and statements decrying segregation continue. More funds are directed to segregated schools, but the public position against such segregation remains. It is likely that—all other things being equal—come the end of the Vietnam war, a Democratic or liberal Republican administration would seek legislation to substantially increase existing expenditures on ghetto schools. One easily can imagine the maintenance of an anti-segregation public posture while, in response to Federal and local pressures, increasingly large amounts of Federal funds are channeled into ghetto schools. Since the Congress might well allocate these new funds for school construction—thus fixing more segregation upon the existing ghettoes—and since a whole new bureaucracy with a vested interest in certain approaches to "cultural deprivation" is being created, the stakes are considerable. If, as it seems, a policy exists or has been very nearly created, it will have major consequences for some time to come. The issues involved merit careful consideration.

The arguments for assigning high priority to compensation and low priority to desegregation rest upon three related judgments:

(1) For the time being at least, the political climate is unfavorable to any efforts to desegregate schools;

(2) Desegregation—especially in the older and larger cities—also is unfeasible from a demographic, fiscal, and administrative point of view. The intergovernmental arrangements, and the costs of busing and/or school construction simply would not be supported;

(3) In any event, desegregation is not really appropriate. The problem of racial disharmony is not nearly so acute as the problem of Negro under-achievement; the latter is a result of cumulative environmental deprivation which requires improved education, not racial mixing.

For one or more of these reasons it is argued that major efforts should be directed at improving the academic competence of Negro students in existing schools. Compensation is advanced as an alternative policy to desegregation, one which is more appropriate educationally, more likely to be accepted politically, and probably cheaper and easier to implement. It is put forward as a practical short-range policy which can provide immediate, workable remedies for Negro under-achievement. Desegregation is regarded as a visionary and long-range solution, a policy which will have to wait for more funds, more intergovernmental flexibility, and a greater likelihood of white acceptance.

It is on the basis of these claims that existing programs are justified or attacked, and new approaches recommended. To further complicate the matter, conclusive data are not available on some of the major questions. But policy exists and is being made; on the basis of these claims and what data there are, therefore, the alternatives must be evaluated. Is compensation a more appropriate, and politically more likely remedy for unequal educational opportunity?

School Quality and the Improvement of Academic Competence

Programs of compensatory education typically proceed on the assumption that children who experience academic retardation do so mainly because their prep-

David K. Cohen

aration for school is seriously deficient. Poor children, it is said, come to school with less well-developed verbal skills, lower motivation, and less family support for academic success. They begin badly and do progressively worse.

Programs based on such a definition seek to make up for children's individual deficiencies by intensifying schools' educational services. A quick review of compensatory program descriptions, or for that matter the criteria for Title I ESEA eligibility, leaves little doubt that most educators and public men regard the children's deficiency as the major educational problem.[1] Notwithstanding the many unimaginative compensatory programs, the underlying idea is in the tradition of liberal social reform: to make of the schools an instrument for removing the educational consequences of social and economic inequities which society gratuitously imposes upon small children.

Some critics object to the view that children are deficient and must be adjusted to schools, arguing that there is at least an equal deficiency on the part of the schools. If children can be defined as "culturally deprived," they say, then schools must be described as institutionally deficient. But whether the deficiency is alleged to be the quality of the children or the quality of their schools, the basis of social reform is seen to lie in improving the schools.

After a few years of experience with such efforts, what have the results been? By now the existing evidence is fairly well known: compensatory programs in schools isolated by race and social class have resulted in no substantial or lasting improvement in students' academic competence. Evaluations have been undertaken in a number of different school systems, on programs with different emphases, under varying conditions of expenditure for school improvement. The data are scarce and very imperfect, but the uniformity of results cannot be ignored.[2]

---

[1] U. S. Department of Health, Education, and Welfare, *The First Year of Title I, ESEA: The States Report* (Washington: U.S. Government Printing Office, 1966). "In practice, the goal of Title I is to provide 'compensatory education' for the millions of schoolchildren whose crippling background offers them little hope for successful schooling" (p. vii).

[2] The largest number of compensatory program evaluations was brought together by the U. S. Commission on Civil Rights (hereafter cited as U.S.C.C.R.), in *Racial Isolation in the Public Schools* (Washington: U.S. Government Printing Office, 1967), I 120-37. After reviewing the evaluations of various programs, none of which seemed to show any sustained academic improvement, the Commission concluded:

... the compensatory programs reviewed here appear to suffer from the defect inherent in attempting to solve problems stemming in part from racial and social class isolation in schools which themselves are isolated by race and social class (p. 139).

The Commission report, however, noted proposals to double expenditures in city schools, and said that "short of such steps" compensation was unlikely to work (pp. 139-40).

What accounts for this rather poor record? The evaluations—and recent research—suggest two basic problems. First, compensatory programs misconceive the sources of academic failure, locating them exclusively in individual children's "cultural deprivation." Second, there has not been a clear definition of "compensation," nor of the required changes in the schools' programs and the magnitude of the effort involved.

With respect to the first problem, if we agree that poor children typically experience difficulty in school, does this imply that "cultural deprivation" is the main cause? Does it imply that improved instruction alone will eliminate the children's academic deficiencies? Not unless there also is a covert assumption that the only critical elements in children's formal education are the processes of interaction between parent and child, and between teacher and child.[3]

But there is strong evidence that this assumption is unwarranted. Everything we know, from research and as a matter of common experience, suggests that there is a third set of processes—those involving social and academic interaction among students—which have a powerful cumulative influence upon the development of academic competence.

For Negro students in urban areas the impact of these processes is apparent in the relationship between the racial and social-class composition of student bodies and achievement. *Equality of Educational Opportunity, Racial Isolation in the Public Schools,* and a variety of other studies show that the racial and social-class composition of student bodies is very closely related to student achievement.[4]

The lack of sound evaluation and the lack of results are exemplified by and attested to by the California State Department of Public Instruction report, *The First Year of Title I,* ESEA (Washington: U.S. Department of Health, Education, and Welfare, 1966). The report assessed the success of projects conducted in 1044 school districts in the state. If only those projects which definitely require quantitative evaluation (reading improvement) are included, the report shows that only 2.6 per cent showed "substantial" (statistically significant) gains in student achievement. If all projects are included, 2.3 per cent showed "substantial" gains in student achievement. See also D. J. Fox, *Expansion of the More Effective Schools Program* (New York: Center for Urban Education, 1967), pp. 120-4.

[3] This assumption underlies the current practice of compensatory education. It is perhaps best illustrated in a sentence from a joint publication of the U. S. Office of Education and the Office of Economic Opportunity, *Education: An Answer to Poverty* (Washington, n.d.).

If a three- or four-year-old child can be stimulated in a prekindergarten to learn the simple things he does not learn from his parents . . . he may get a headstart on later success in school. (p. 20)

[4] The relationship between school social class and achievement persists when the social class background and race of students is controlled. There are two studies which impressively document this relationship between school social class and student achievement: J. S. Coleman, *et al., Equal-*

David K. Cohen

The "average" poor child who attends school with a substantial majority of children from more advantaged homes performs at a higher academic level than a poor child—similarly situated in all other respects—who attends school with a majority of poor children.[5]

In addition to the negative effects of attending schools whose populations are lower-class, Negro students suffer from the special effect of the racial composition of their schools. Even when their social-class origin and the social-class level of their schools are taken into account, those Negroes in school and class with a majority of white students perform at a higher level than those in school and class with a majority of Negro students.[6]

Most Negro children, of course, attend schools which are predominantly Negro and predominantly poor, and thus they experience a double disadvantage. The consequences, viewed at the end of the children's school careers, are devastating— the overwhelming majority are academically crippled. The average Negro student in the Metropolitan Northeast enters twelfth grade reading below the level of ninth-grade whites.[7] But the Negro student who is in school with a majority of advantaged children, and who has attended class with whites since the outset of his school career, experiences less than half this disadvantage.[8] Only a tiny fraction of Negro students are in this last group.

Not all of the specific processes by which schools' social-class and racial com-

---

ity of Educational Opportunity (Washington: U.S. Government Printing Office, 1966), show that the educational background of students' classmates accounts for more variation in achievement than any other school-related factor (pp. 302-12). Even when teacher and school quality are allowed to "explain" as much variance as possible first, student-body factors still account for a very substantial proportion of the total variance in achievement (Table 3.25.3, p. 319).

Some objections have been raised to the cross-sectional character of the Coleman report on the grounds that students' initial abiliy could not be measured and controlled. Alan Wilson, in "Educational Consequences of Segregation in a California Community," (U.S.C.C.R., *op. cit.*, II, 165-206), had the required longitudinal data; controlling for first-grade I.Q., he found that by the sixth grade the cumulative social-class composition of schools was as closely related to achievement as individual social class (Table 17, p. 181).

[5] The social-class composition of schools affects children regardless of color, but it has particular implication for Negroes. A far greater proportion of urban Negroes than urban whites are poor. As a result, Negro children are much more likely than whites to attend school with a majority of poor children, and therefore are more often exposed to the handicapping effect of a "disadvantaged" student body.

[6] U.S.C.C.R., *op. cit.*, I, 90. For a discussion of the measurement and analysis problems associated with this "racial-composition effect," see II, 35-47.

[7] U.S.C.C.R., *op. cit.*, II, Table 4.2, 67. This also is true of other regions; Coleman, *et al.*, *op. cit.*, pp. 242-3.

[8] Because the appropriate variable in the Coleman survey data was mis-coded for grade 12 (see U.S.C.C.R., *op. cit.*, II, 37, note 6), this measurement is possible only for grade 9; for those data, see U.S.C.C.R., *op. cit.*, II, Table 2.2, 50.

position affect achievement have been established. But whatever they may be, *none have been recognized as barriers to learning in the design and execution of compensatory education programs.* Can the theory and practice of compensatory education programs be so adjusted as to take account of the effects of student environments upon student achievement?

Some have said that the studies cited earlier show that the only way to deal with the effects of social class and racial segregation on achievement is to eliminate the segregation. None of the studies say this; indeed, it would be absurd to argue that under no circumstances could the effects of a weak student environment upon the development of academic competence be remedied in segregated situations. The lackluster results thus far are no basis for such a view. The question is not *whether* student performance could thus be improved, but rather *how*: with what programs, under what circumstances, at what level of investment, and with what major second-order effects?

This is not the place to discuss in detail all the specific program elements which will produce successful compensation; to do so would require a wide variety of successful programs, and they simply do not exist. But the research just discussed and experience with some programs do permit a few inferences about the elementary structural changes which probably would be required to provide the conditions for effective compensation.

Most important, it would be necessary to abandon the widespread educational practice based upon the naïve idea that the only major barrier to effective learning lies in the individual student's cultural deprivation. The student body is the immediate medium in which instruction and learning occurs; its educational strength or weakness can facilitate or impede intellectual growth. One change in school organization consonant with this view would be the implementation of very drastic reductions in the number of students assigned to every teacher. As long as each teacher must divide himself over twenty or thirty students, the low academic level of the class impedes effective learning. A weak student environment is a non-conductor inserted in the learning process. Until it is eliminated, the problems of individual children cannot be reached and remedied. The logical conclusion would be the tutorial situation—completely individual attention—where the teacher alone constitutes the student environment.[9]

[9] The experience of Project Headstart, which has small class size and even lower pupil-teacher ratios, suggests this change as does the apparent success of some tutoring programs, notably the Homework Helper Program in New York City. Furthermore, Federal officials appear to be moving toward this position. The Advisory Committee on Follow-Through, U.S.O.E., *Preliminary Report* (Washington: U.S. Office of Education, 1967) lists as its second major criterion for Follow-Through programs a pupil-staff ratio of 7-9:1 (p. 6).

Such a policy might draw support from one of the major findings of the Coleman survey: disadvantaged students exhibit a substantially greater sensitivity to variations in their educational environment than advantaged students. Presumably, changes in school and classroom organization of the sort suggested here would make it possible for teachers to take greater advantage of this differential sensitivity.

The More Effective Schools Program in New York City is the only compensatory program known to have made serious efforts in this direction. This program sharply reduced the number of students per teacher so as to intensify substantially the attention which could be devoted to individual students' needs. It cut the number of students per professional by more than half (from 28.3 in 1963 to 12.3 in 1965), and as a result raised per-pupil expenditures for instruction by a similar factor (from \$457 in 1964 to \$946 in 1965).[10]

The MES Program was a significant departure in compensatory education. No other program so dramatically intensified the instructional attention to individual children. If MES were to be made national policy, it would require roughly a nine-fold increase in the annual Title I ESEA outlay for instruction—from about sixty to about five hundred dollars per pupil. This appropriation would increase the total annual Title I instructional outlay from \$.5 billion to \$3.5 billion.[11]

But such a drastic reduction in pupil-teacher ratios would require an equally drastic increase in the supply of teachers. The national supply of qualified teachers, as estimated by recent studies, may be as little as 50 per cent of existing demand.[12] Each September the major urban school systems open with less than thir required complement of teachers, and each day their slum schools are short-staffed. The cost of college training required to generalize present MES staffing levels to a national scale (provide one teacher for every twelve ESEA children), would be about \$2.3 billion.[13]

[10] Fox, *op. cit.*, Appendix A, pp. A2-A3 and A8-A10.

[11] This figure is arrived at by multiplying the total ESEA population (eight million), by the total MES increment per pupil over prior expenditures, which was roughly five hundred dollars. The ESEA information was derived from *The First Year of Title I, ESEA, op. cit.*, p. v. This understates the cost, since New York City spends more per pupil than the national average on instruction.

[12] National Education Association, *Teacher Supply and Demand in Public Schools* (Washington: National Education Association, 1966), Table 25, p. 50. This estimate is based on the "number of new teachers needed to immediately achieve a standard for minimum quality in the staffing of public-school classrooms" (p. 29).

[13] This figure was computed by first figuring the number of additional teachers required to cover classes at 12:1. Eight million (ESEA) students ÷ 12 = 0.67 million teachers total, minus 0.27 million (at 30:1) = 0.4 million teachers. The U. S. Office of Education (*Projections of Educational Statistics to 1975*, Washington, 1966, p. 66), estimates the direct cost of producing an A.B. degree to

In addition, although the MES program reduced pupil-teacher ratios drastically, it reduced average class size to only twenty, from twenty-eight. Further reductions in class size would require the provision of additional classroom space through new school construction. Although national surveys reveal a serious shortage of classroom space, let us assume that class size could be reduced by half for the Title I ESEA target population (to the level MES in fact calls for), by building classrooms for only slightly more than one-third of these students. This construction would cost roughly $6 billion.[14]

Thus the cost of generalizing the main elements of the existing MES program to a national scale would be quite substantial. If it were to be accomplished in five years, the bare minimum average annual cost would be between five and six billion dollars.

But there is no evidence that such a policy would change the relative position of advantaged and disadvantaged students. Students in the MES schools—after two years—exhibited the classical pattern of increasing academic retardation.[15] If a pupil-teacher ratio of 12:1 produces no improvement in academic competence, how closely must pupil-teacher ratios approach the tutorial situation before basic improvements would result? Let us assume that if pupil-teacher ratios reached 6:1, a point midway between the tutorial situation and present MES levels, substantial improvements in academic competence would become possible. This would require doubling the instructional cost per pupil of the MES program over present levels. Generalized to the present Title I ESEA pupil population, the resulting cost for teacher salaries would raise annual ESEA expenditures for instruction from $0.5 billion to about $8.6 billion.[16] And it would require that at least $5.8 billion be spent upon the production of new classroom teachers.

---

be $5800. The total was computed by multiplying this cost figure by the 0.4 million teachers required. Although it may seem unreasonable to suppose the need to train all these teachers, the NEA (*op. cit.*, p. 51) estimates suggest a continuing tendency for teacher supply to fall well below demand, even at existing pupil-teacher ratios.

[14] This assumes a need for two hundred thousand classrooms, and a construction cost per classroom of $30,000. *School Management* (July, 1966) estimates that the average construction cost per classroom in 1965 was $43,700; this cost figure per classroom was arbitrarily reduced about 30 per cent, to $30,000, to take account of smaller class size, and this cost figure was multipled by the needed number of classrooms. No account was taken of rising construction costs, classrooms needing replacement, or classrooms needed to reduce class size nationally to twenty-four. The Office of Education (*Projections, op. cit.*, p. 40) estimates the cost of meeting these needs by 1974-75 will be $29.5 billion. It seemed reasonable to assume that any construction beyond that would have to be financed by nonlocal sources.

[15] Fox, *op. cit.*, p. 63.

[16] The total was computed as explained in note 11, above.

David K. Cohen

These estimates are very rough, but they suggest the rather substantial costs of reducing pupil-teacher ratios. The increase in annual expenditures for instruction alone would raise what presently is being spent annually on salaries for poor childrens' teachers from about $1.7 billion to about $8.6 billion, or from 8 per cent to 43 per cent of present total annual public school instruction expenditures for *all* children.[17]

But drastic reductions in pupil-teacher ratios are only a necessary, not a sufficient condition of effective compensation. To improve academic competence, not only the conditions of instruction but also its quality must be improved. The final evaluation of MES pointed out:

Despite the . . . organizational changes, little has happened in the way of innovation or restructuring in the basic teaching process. Observers noted that a majority of lessons they saw could have been taught to larger classes with no loss in effectiveness. . . . All levels of staff noted that the basic weakness of the program, or their major disappointment with it, centered about the functioning of teachers, which they attributed to inexperience and lack of preparation.[18]

A more general way of putting this criticism is that compensatory education programs have concentrated heavily upon the deficiencies of children, and neglected to give serious attention to the deficiencies of schools. So much has been made of the deprivations children are supposed to have inflicted upon the schools that hardly any serious thought has been given to the institutional deficiencies of schools which regularly are inflicted upon children.

The best evidence available seems to show that one of the critical deficiencies involves teacher quality. For disadvantaged students, the quality of the teaching provided is closely related to their academic performance. In the Coleman survey, three teacher characteristics which showed very close relation to student performance were teachers' social class origin, their verbal ability, and the quality of their education.[19]

Our concern is with the prospects for change in the distribution of teacher quality; it therefore is important to note that inequity in the distribution of these

[17] There is no analysis of teachers' salary by students' socio-economic status, so the $1.7 billion figure was computed by dividing the ESEA pupil population (eight million), by the national pupil-teacher ratio (25:1) (U. S. Department of HEW, *Fall 1965 Statistics of Public Schools*, p. 3), and multiplying that quotient by the average 1966-67 salary ($7119) (NEA, *Estimates of School Statistics, 1966-67*, Washington: National Education Association, 1966, p. 14).

[18] Fox, *op. cit.*, p. 122.

[19] Coleman, *et al.*, *op. cit.*, p. 317, note; for a fuller definition of these three variables, see pp. 316-7.

characteristics is an integral feature of the structure and status of schools, and of recruitment to and within the teaching profession. Change is not likely to be produced by brief workshops, or other such familiar programs of in-service training.

If the usual superficial efforts to improve teaching for the disadvantaged are not likely to yield substantial results, what would improve the quality of teachers' training? As we have just seen, estimating the cost of improving education is very difficult. Let us assume the best: that college students in general and future teachers in particular are more sensitive to improvements in school quality than public school students, and that only a 50 per cent increment (about six hundred dollars more per student per year) in existing expenditures for college education would very substantially increase the skills of future teachers.[20] If this increased expenditure was allocated to the education of the number of new teachers required to reduce ESEA pupil-teacher ratios to 6:1, it would cost about $2.4 billion.[21]

But in some respects the more difficult question is how such improved teachers could be better distributed, so as to create a massive resource inequality in favor of ghetto schools. The existing suggestions for achieving such a redistribution illustrate the lack of serious thought which has been given to this basic aspect of effective compensation.

The suggestions fall into three categories: those which propose some system of salary incentives to attract teachers to "inner-city" schools; those which propose to capitalize on the so-called "Peace Corps spirit" of existing or potential teachers to attract highly motivated individuals to ghetto schools; and those which assume

[20] The order of magnitude of this effort is about the same as the National Science Foundation's estimate of the cost of improving the quality of science teachers; the N.S.F. seems to believe that a full year of intensive retraining is the best and most productive approach. The National Science Foundation is the only Federal agency which has made a serious effort to improve teachers' competence—albeit in special subject areas—and it is important to note that they invest only about 9 per cent of their total annual budget for teacher training ($3.5 million out of $36.5 million) in school-year, in-service programs. Nearly 70 per cent ($23 million) is invested in intensive summer institutes, and the remaining $10 million (about 20 per cent) is invested in full-year, full-time training. The cost per teacher of each is, respectively, $250, $1200, and $6500. One of the main goals of the summer institutes is to provide teachers with an M.S., for which four summer institutes ($4800) are required. This seems to be a reasonable model for improving teachers' competence in other areas. (The information was obtained in a telephone interview with Dr. Russell Phelps of the Teacher Education Section, National Science Foundation, October 18, 1967.)

[21] This figure was computed by multiplying the one million new teachers needed (see note 13, above for the method of computing this figure of one million) by the cost of a four-year, 50 per cent improvement ($2400), a very conservative estimate as the preceding data on NSF show. The figure represents a gross underestimate of the cost, since it is figured only for the additional teachers needed, and thus does not take into account any attrition or market factors.

that inequities in the distribution of teacher resources can be redressed only by improving the conditions of teaching in deprived schools.[22]

The first two proposals rest on the view that either the profit motive or missionary idealism will overcome racial and social-class prejudice, and what are perceived as poor working conditions, and thus reverse the present maldistribution of competent teachers. With respect to missionary idealism, there are no precedents for the hope that it will be widespread. It exists in limited quantities, and although one must applaud and encourage dedication which is not patronizing, it simply is not an everyday quality. Wise policy cannot be made on the assumption that most people will be heroic.

The situation is no more encouraging with respect to the profit motive. The idea that, of itself, receiving more money effectively stimulates improved teaching has no basis. It seems dubious that children's learning could be improved by offering "combat pay" to attract teachers to, or hold them in deprived schools when, all other things being equal, the teachers prefer to be elsewhere. After all, it is the children who constitute the "combat" condition for which the special pay is offered; utilization of such incentives would be a poor basis for a productive student-teacher relationship. On the whole, there seems to be little hope for either a missionary or a mercenary approach to improving the distribution of teachers to slum schools.

The third proposal is more to the point. Present inequities in the distribution of teacher quality can be reversed only if the status of schools is raised by dramatically improving working conditions. At a minimum, this proposal recognizes that the problem of teacher maldistribution will not be solved by the voluntary action of individuals. But the available evidence on its potential efficacy is not very encouraging. The evidence suggests four major difficulties.

First, improving working conditions—for instance, reducing class size—for teachers in low-status schools deals with only one aspect of these schools' perceived status. There also is the matter of their students' color and class. Although we know little about the changes in job preferences which might be associated with improved working conditions, something is known about teachers' racial and social-class preferences. Even under very favorable conditions, only a tiny proportion of teachers express a definite preference for teaching in all or predominantly Negro schools. Negro and white teachers in predominantly Negro schools

---

[22] This last is manifested in the inclusion of MES programs as a main demand of the A.F.T. in collective bargaining, along with more traditional items.

are a good deal less likely than those in predominantly white schools to want to remain in their present assignment. And the higher the teachers' verbal ability the less likely they are to want to remain in predominantly Negro—or predominantly working-class—schools. High-ability Negro teachers in predominantly Negro schools are—of all teachers—the group *most likely* to be dissatisfied with their present teaching position.[23] In general, *the better teachers are least likely to prefer teaching in predominantly Negro, or blue-collar schools.*[24]

Second, the status of schools is ascribed not only on the basis of class and color, but also on the basis of students' performance; this too is reflected in teachers' preferences. Teachers typically prefer to teach in academic schools oriented toward college preparation. Again, the higher a teacher's verbal ability, the more likely he is to prefer such schools; the best qualified teachers are the least likely to prefer teaching in those schools which Negro children are most likely to attend.[25] The desired end result of improved teaching—high student performance—appears to be an important condition for recruiting better qualified teachers to schools in the first place.

Third, there is no evidence that there will be basic change in these preference patterns in the future. College students who plan to teach are no more likely to prefer teaching in predominantly Negro schools than experienced teachers. More than half of the whites express a preference for teaching *only* white students, a preference as prevalent among high-ability as among low-ability students. Furthermore, over half of the college students—Negro and white—express a preference for an academic school, oriented toward college preparation. But perhaps most important, these preference patterns are as true of college freshmen as of college seniors.[26] If changed recruitment patterns are required to improve the quality of teaching in predominantly Negro schools, the existing data offer little promise.

This state of affairs, and recent developments in some cities and some civil rights organizations, have prompted suggestions for a policy of recruiting only Negroes to teach in ghetto schools. This policy, it has been argued, would remedy the problems which arise from white teachers' preferences. In fact, this proposal represents nothing new in most of the older and larger cities; in these cities there

[23] Coleman, *et al., op. cit.,* Table 4.8.1, p. 350.
[24] *Ibid.*
[25] *Ibid.*, Table 4.10.1, p. 350. For the ability control (which in this case was used only for future teachers), Tables 4.11.6, p. 362; 4.11.8, p. 364.
[26] These are data on the attitudes and preferences of non-Southern, Negro and white college students (*Ibid.,* Tables 4.11.6, p. 362 and 4.11.8, p. 364).

already is substantial racial matching of teachers and students, and as city-wide student enrollments grow progressively more heavily Negro, so will the teaching staffs. Most Negro students, it seems, will attend school with predominantly Negro faculties.[27]

Unhappily, this trend may have the effect only of perpetuating the closed and inferior educational system which now exists in urban Negro ghettoes. The effects of segregation are cumulative; its impact upon past generations is visited in a variety of ways, and with a vengeance, upon those of the present. Negro students who are taught by predominantly Negro faculties—whose education was segregated and inferior—now and in the foreseeable future are likely to be taught by faculties of relatively low verbal ability.[28]

The trend is unmistakable. As Table 1 shows, over two-thirds of Negro teachers fall below the mean verbal ability score of white teachers; only one-third of white teachers fall below that mean score. This comparison is not weakened when older or

TABLE 1

Teachers' Verbal Ability, by Race and Experience†

Teachers' experience	% who scored below white mean	
	Negro	White
10 years' or more experience	75.8	37.8
5-9 years' experience	69.7	31.6
5 or less years' experience	74.8	36.1
Future teachers: College seniors	75.5	46.7
Future teachers: College freshmen	85.4	43.5

†Source: Coleman, *et al., op. cit.,* Table 4.5.1, p. 345.

more experienced teachers are contrasted to younger or less experienced teachers, nor is there any improvement for future teachers. These data offer little support for the idea that increased teacher-pupil racial matching will improve the quality of education in ghetto schools. They suggest rather that the cumulative effects of segregation will not be eliminated as long as the closed system from which they arise exists.

[27] *Ibid.,* p. 126; U.S.C.C.R., *op. cit.,* II, Table A-2, 8-10.
[28] Although verbal ability is by no means the only important attribute of teachers, it seems to be an important one.

The data presented here do not show that changed patterns of teacher distribution to and within school systems are impossible. Indeed, the limited changes undertaken by the MES program did appear to improve teacher morale, and undoubtedly such programs would therefore change teachers' preferences and job choices to some extent.[29] But there is a difference between changing some teachers' preferences and job choices, and the basic change in preferences and assignments which would be required before school systems could select the best candidates from an oversupply of applicants, all of whom wanted to teach in predominantly Negro schools. Merely stating the problems suggests the enormous barriers to basic change. It is likely that no program designed to reverse existing teacher distribution patterns can be effective unless it changes the major factors —in addition to working conditions—which determine school status and teacher preferences: the schools' color, class, and achievement composition.

This analysis does not exhaust discussion of effective segregated compensation— it merely suggests some of the leading problems. The cost for the first ten years of an effort such as that outlined above would probably be between 100 and 160 billion dollars. The calculations on which these figures are based are not precise, but are intended only to suggest in a very rough way the order of magnitude. They suggest that a major reallocation of national social and budgetary priorities, and therefore of political priorities as well, would be required.[30] There are other problems, illustrated by teachers' preferences, which would not as easily yield to fiscal formulation or economic solution.

---

[29] Fox, *op. cit.*, pp. 120-1.

[30] The Table below shows the method of computation for these figures.

Item	Cost (in billions)
Construction: 200,000 classrooms x $30,000. *10 years total*	$ 6.0
Teacher training (1 million teachers needed at 6:1 x $5,800). *10 years total*	$ 5.8
Teacher salaries ($7.1 billion per year at pupil-teacher ratio of 6:1). *10 years total*	$71.0
Improving teacher qualifications. *10 years total*	$ 2.4
	$85.2

That this is a very conservative estimate can be seen by comparing this total with the total based on the annual per-pupil cost of Headstart, which is roughly $1000-$1200. If a ten-year total using Headstart standards as a base is computed, the grand total would be $95-$110 billion. And, if— as is almost sure—the estimates of teacher-retraining and training were much too low (as note 20 above suggests), and the construction estimates were too low (as note 14 above suggests), the total could easily be $20 or $30 billion higher. Passow, in the summary of his report on the Washington, D. C. public schools, estimates the cost of effective compensation to be three or four times what presently is spent in advantaged school districts (pp. 25-6). His estimates would about double my estimates. See A. H. Passow, *Summary,* (New York: Teachers College, Columbia University, 1967.) (Mimeographed.)

David K. Cohen

Effective compensation in schools segregated by color and class is not impossible. But fundamental changes in the organization of schools and the production and distribution of educational resources would be required to realize such a policy. The discussion here suggests that little serious attention has been given to the elements of such a policy, or to its economic and social costs. Most policy discussions and formulations seem to have been carried out on the assumption that segregated compensation would provide a relatively easy remedy. There is no evidence that this is so.

Limitations of the Segregated Compensatory Approach

In addition to the above limitations there are a few basic objections to a policy of segregated compensation. First, whereas there is direct and indirect evidence that integration will improve achievement, there is little such evidence at hand for segregated compensation. Second, there is direct evidence that segregated compensatory programs will compound other major educational problems.

With respect to the first, it is not unfair to say that if policy were made only on the basis of available data, American schools would be desegregated. A fair amount of data shows a substantial performance increment associated with racial and social-class desegregation.

The Equality of Educational Opportunity survey data show the Negro students who attended school with whites for most of their elementary school career exhibited, on the average, about half the academic disadvantage of those Negroes who attended school only with Negroes.[31] In addition, studies of elementary school desegregation in a number of cities show higher achievement gains for Negro children placed in majority white schools than for Negro children remaining in predominantly Negro schools. Not all the studies show gains, but most do, even though the majority are only single-year studies. In particular, the evaluation of Project Concern in Hartford, Connecticut can be fairly described as a careful study, with an effort to take the main variables into account. It concludes:

> Youngsters who were placed in suburban schools and received supportive assistance clearly outperformed the [segregated] subjects.... The differences are statistically significant and are found across the full range of grades.[32]

[31] U.S.C.C.R., *op. cit.*, II, Table 2.2, 50.

[32] T. W. Mahan, *Project Concern* (Hartford, Conn.: Project Concern, 1967). (Mimeographed.) p. 47. See also Buffalo Public Schools, Buffalo, N.Y., *Study of Achievement of Pupils Transferred to Achieve a More Desirable Racial Balance*, March, 1967; and Philadelphia Public Schools, Philadelphia, Pa., *The Effect of Bussing on Achievement*, December, 1966.

The question of whether this improvement is an effect of racial or of social-class integration, given the present American social structure, is academic. There are so few middle-class Negroes that social-class desegregation for Negro children could not be accomplished without racial desegregation.

Moreover, there is pretty convincing evidence that these school performance differences for Negro students *are* in fact related to specifically racial contexts and conditions. For example, students' higher performance in interracial class-rooms[33] is specifically related to the schools interracial climate; Negro and white students in schools with little or no reported interracial tension perform at high-er levels than similarly-situated students in schools where considerable tension is reported.[34]

Another bit of evidence along the same lines is the association between inter-racial acceptance and performance. Negro students in desegregated classrooms who report no interracial acceptance achieve at a lower level than those, in the same and similar classrooms, who do report such acceptance.[35] Similarly, white students who are accepted in predominantly Negro schools perform at lower levels than those who are not.[36] Just as acceptance in a predominantly white school facilitates Negro performance, acceptance in a predominantly Negro milieu has a de-pressing effect upon white performance. This evidence points to specifically racial conditions which affect achievement.[37]

There is no question, of course, that a larger proportion of variance in achievement is explained by social class than by racial composition. But for policy purposes, the general implications are the same: (1) racial desegregation is the necessary concomitant of social-class desegregation for Negro students, and social-class desegregation is required to produce the fullest academic benefits; (2) in-terracial acceptance, classroom desegregation, and minimal tension seem to be the specifically racial conditions for academically sound desegregated situations.

The second basic objection to segregated compensation rests upon the fact that the crucial outcomes of education are not restricted to the development of aca-demic competence: there is good evidence that the racial composition of schools

---

[33] U.S.C.C.R., *op. cit.*, II; Tables 4.1-5.7, 66-92, suggest that even with very rigorous controls, the effect of racial composition remains.

[34] U.S.C.C.R., *op. cit.*, II; Tables 6.1, 93; 6.2, 94; and 8.12, 142.

[35] U.S.C.C.R., *op. cit.*, II, Table 6.9, 100.

[36] Thomas F. Pettigrew, "Race and Equal Educational Opportunity" (paper presented at the annual meeting of the American Psychological Association, Washington, D. C., September 3, 1967).

[37] As the Tables cited in notes 34 and 35 above show, desegregation will probably not have a positive effect unless at least certain minimal interracial conditions also are met.

shapes the racial preferences and interracial behavior of children and adults. Consider the attitudes and associations of Negro and white adults as they relate to the racial composition of the schools they attended as children. Those who attended racially isolated schools are likely to express fear, distrust, and hostility concerning members of the other race. White adults who attended racially isolated white schools are more likely than those who attended desegregated schools to oppose measures designed to secure equal opportunity for Negroes. They are more likely to live in segregated neighborhoods, and to express a desire to continue living in such neighborhoods. Their children are more likely to attend all-white schools, and they are more likely than "desegregated" whites to reject the idea of their children attending desegregated schools.

Likewise, Negroes who attended segregated schools not only are likely to fear and distrust whites, but they also are quite likely to express the idea that they would like to "get even" with them. There are manifestations of that feeling in the cities every summer now. Negroes who attended segregated schools are much less likely than Negroes who attended desegregated schools to live in desegregated neighborhoods, and they are more likely to oppose sending their children to desegregated schools.[38]

These differences are independent of the particular neighborhoods in which these adults lived as children, and independent of their relative economic status; we see here the racial effect of schools. A dramatic illustration of this effect is that high-status (college-educated) Negroes who attended segregated schools are *less likely* to live in integrated neighborhoods than lower-status (high-school-educated) Negroes who attended integrated schools.[39] American race relations being what they are, racial experience often carries more weight than economic status in such critical areas as school and housing decisions.

As racially isolated public schools shape children's values and attitudes, they also set the mold for adult associations. As they create and reinforce preferences for association only with persons of one's own race in the school years, they also build the foundation for adult housing and school decisions. Efforts to eliminate residential segregation are blocked by Negro and white attitude barriers created in racially segregated schools. Those who argue that school desegregation should wait until housing is desegregated support the very school segregation which

[38] This entire analysis is derived from the results of a survey published in U.S.C.C.R., *op. cit.*, I, 112-3; and II, 211-41.

[39] Only the Negro adult survey data permitted control of neighborhood racial composition. This comparison is found in U.S.C.C.R., *op. cit.*, I, Table 11, 113.

shapes racist and separatist attitudes, and thus continues to delay housing integration. In effect, they advocate the continuance of segregation in both areas. Governmental support of segregated schools—through compensatory education —creates and compounds residential segregation, and governmental efforts to eliminate residential segregation will be impeded by the barriers created in racially isolated schools.

This evidence on the adult effects of the racial composition of schools also bears on the effectiveness of programs which seek to improve education in segregated schools. Let us assume that compensatory programs will make substantial improvements in Negro achievement. There remains a stronger relationship between students' interracial experience and their racial attitudes and preferences than between their academic performance levels and racial preferences. Students with high levels of academic competence who attend isolated schools are less likely to express acceptance of desegregated schools and friends of the other race than those who do less well academically, but attend desegregated schools.[40] Improvements in academic competence are not likely to reduce the schools' contribution to increasing segregation and racial friction. Even if programs of compensatory education could substantially improve academic competence in schools isolated by race and social class, the schools would continue to compound segregation, and thus intensify the specifically racial damage it generates for white and black Americans. Negro achievement is no more a remedy for the racism and separatism that segregation produces than white achievement has been in the past.

All of this suggests again that any educational policy-making agency seeking to decide logically between integration and segregated compensatory education would choose integration. Yet, in another sense, this crude juxtaposition is unfair; discussions of national policy must take account of two additional considerations.

First, although desegregation reduces the gap between the distribution of achievement for Negroes and whites, it does not eliminate it by any means.[41] Desegregation is a very important element in eliminating inequality of opportunity, but it is clearly not all that is required. Racial and social-class desegregation have a facilitating effect upon Negro students' performance; indeed, it does not seem unreasonable to speculate that in some respects they may be almost a precondition for improvement. But they are not a sufficient condition for eliminating in-

[40] D. Singer, "Interracial Attitudes of Negro and White Fifth-Grade Children in Segregated and Unsegregated Schools" (unpublished doctoral dissertation, Columbia University, 1966), Ch. 3 and 4.
[41] The best available evidence for this is presented in the following Table, derived from

equities. A good deal of educational improvement also will be required. More investigation is needed, but it is worth noting that the Project Concern evaluation found consistent positive results only from a combination of integration *and* compensation. A similar result has been reported for Greenburgh District #8, in New York. Very substantial educational improvements probably will be required, along with desegregation, to eliminate existing achievement disparities for Negro students.

Second, the racial and social-class demography of the older and larger cities compels a metropolitan approach to school desegregation. There are not enough suburban Negroes to desegregate schools outside these central cities, and not enough affluent urban whites to desegregate schools within them. The distribution of educational quality follows roughly these same suburban-urban lines; this offers another reason for making substantial improvements in the quality of education in desegregated schools; without such improvements, it is dubious that suburban districts would become involved in large-scale cooperative arrangements with the central cities.

Thus for rather different reasons, it seems that very substantial improvements in educational quality would be required—for both white and Negro students —in desegregated schools. The schools most likely to meet the requirements for substantially improved education and for metropolitan attendance are education parks. Such larger schools—by consolidating pupil attendance and educational resources—would permit both improvements in the quality of education and desegregation. Plans and proposals for education parks are so diverse as to suggest

U.S.C.C.R., *op. cit.*, II, Table 2.2, 50. It presents ninth-grade Negro verbal-achievement scores (in terms of grade levels relative to whites), for the metropolitan northeast.

Parent's education	School average Parent's education	Earliest grade in class with whites	Percentage white in class	
			None	Most
less than high school	less than high-school graduate	1, 2, 3	—3.2	—2.1
		Never	—3.4	——
	high-school graduate or more	1, 2, 3	—2.1	—1.3
		Never	—2.8	——
high-school graduate or more	less than high-school graduate	1, 2, 3	—3.0	—2.0
		Never	—3.3	——
	high-school graduate or more	1, 2, 3	—1.6	—1.8
		Never	—2.6	——

only a common set of educational principles, not a specific sort of school. The group of principles includes resource consolidation, desegregation, and preservation of small educational units within a larger cosmopolitan setting. While individual plans vary greatly on almost everything else, they contemplate in common a change in the structure of attendance and in resource allocation, thereby providing the conditions for improved educational opportunities.

Studies suggest that the direct savings on construction-associated costs alone would be 15-20 per cent over neighborhood schools, and that the educational benefits of consolidation would be manifold. Chief among them would be greater individual attention to students, and greater occupational specialization and diversification for teachers. Any educational institution which offers these two things in the context of a majority-advantaged student body is likely to have few problems attracting and holding competent teachers.[42]

How does such a policy compare with the costs of segregated compensation? The first ten years' cost, the cost of building education parks (including in the estimate twice as many advantaged children), of providing all with daily transportation, and of increasing per-pupil expenditures by five hundred dollars (about double present levels), might be as much as 20 per cent more than the first ten years' cost of segregated compensation.[43]

These comparisons are quite rough and some of the data are not very good. But public schools and public policy go on; despite limitations of the data, they suggest a few conclusions. First, it seems possible that the academic competence of Negro students can be improved—without desegregation—if certain structural features of their present school environment are radically altered. These changes, which probably would have to include very sharply reduced class size and pupil-teacher ratios, and very sharply improved teachers, would center upon compensa-

---

[42] For a collection of papers on this subject, and a good brief bibliography, see U. S. Commission on Civil Rights, *Education Parks* (Washington, 1967).

[43] The following table presents the cost figures and the methods of computation involved.

Item	Cost (in billions)
Cost of construction: at current classroom costs, for 20 million children (ESEA population x 2.5)	$34.4
Cost of transportation for 20 million students (average per-pupil cost, 1964-65, $43; U.S.O.E., Digest of Educational Statistics, Washington, 1965, p. 29). *10 year total*	$ 0.9
Increase per-pupil instructional expenditure for 20 million students by $500 per year = 10 billion. *10 year total*	$100.0
Total	$135.3

tion for the barriers to learning which educationally weak student environments pose. They would represent a basic revision in the theory and practice of educational compensation; school organization would have to be structurally changed to provide substitutes for the academic stimulation deriving from educationally rich student environments.

Second, such changes would be very costly in terms of fiscal and social effort. From a fiscal point of view, they would probably require an expansion of present ESEA instructional allocations by a factor of at least twenty or thirty, to between $100 and $160 billion in the first ten years of such an effort. Even half of this amount would require a major reallocation of national budget priorities. And the required changes would be difficult to accomplish in other ways as well. The barriers to changing the entire system of educational resource allocation—typified in the problem of teacher quality discussed above—are formidable as long as segregation remains; there are no plans on the horizon or programs in operation which seem likely to overcome these obstacles.

Third, there may not be a very substantial difference in the order of magnitude of the costs involved for school desegregation. It seems that either policy would require very serious revisions, not only in the structure of schools and classrooms, but also in the organization of schools and the levels of investment in education. Whether we consider the matter from an educational or social perspective, the required investment will be much more than presently is allocated to the education of Negro children. Either policy would require far-reaching and fundamental change.

Given this rough fiscal parity, it is of particular importance that discussion of and choice between the two policies *not* be based simply on immediate fiscal or educational considerations. Policies often are implemented or rejected, and work or fail to work, for other than purely educational or fiscal reasons. Two questions are directly relevant. First, what are the major second-order effects—those not directly related to academic competence—of each policy likely to be? Second, what social and political considerations bear upon the likelihood of either policy working?

With respect to second-order effects, there is little doubt that desegregation is the more desirable alternative. Compensatory programs institutionalize segregation, and therefore compound racism in a number of important ways. By definition, compensation maintains segregation in schools, and thus maintains institutions which produce racist and separatist attitudes and behavior. Second, such programs create ever larger bureaucracies with a vested interest in the maintenance of compensation—and thus segregation. Third, existing compensatory programs support a local tendency to build more segregated white and Negro schools. If large quantities of new Federal funds are made available for compensation—even in the unlikely event that none are allocated specifically for construction—they would lend enormous support to this local tendency toward neighborhood school replacement, and thus huge capital investments in segregation. As a result, what is now a difficult discussion would, for all practical purposes, become entirely academic.

It is typically argued, however, that these considerations are outweighed by the simple fact that a policy of segregated compensation is more workable—that is, politically and socially more practical and acceptable. But this argument neglects the likelihood that effective compensation will be very nearly as expensive as a policy of desegregation and educational improvement. The same legislators who oppose desegregation have in the past, do now, and probably would in the future oppose programs of massive, sustained, superior treatment for Negro children, or for the children of the poor. Perhaps more to the point, there is little reason to believe that many legislators who represent Caucasian sections of metropolitan areas would be willing or politically able to support such massive unequal treatment. The probable costs of effective compensation throw a somewhat different light on its political feasibility.

This brings to mind the historic and political experience out of which the integration strategy evolved. The experience, in brief, was that even in crude, tangible respects separate never was equal; an entire series of commitments to enrich the ghetto went unmet. The conclusion drawn from this experience was that the only politically feasible way to gain access to the same resources as those available to whites was to be with them. This principle applies as well—or perhaps with even more political force—to the problem of establishing massive inequalities in favor of segregated Negroes.

The corollary of this principle is that desegregation is not a process in which every Negro gain implies a corresponding white loss. In the case of education, this means that every desegregated school should provide concrete and apparent improvements in educational quality for both whites and Negroes. Education parks, for example, promise very substantial improvements in the quality of education for all children. If such a system of schools were built in a metropolitan area, whites who refused to send their children would have to reject better and higher status education in order to reject desegregation. This principle applies to their legislators as well. But as long as educational improvement is only a matter of ghetto improvement, whites can reject it, or maintain it at minimal levels, at no apparent or immediate cost to themselves. That has been the case for time out of mind, and in all probability will be the case with future programs of ghetto improvement.

When everything else is said, then, and all the educational and fiscal evidence is in, the most compelling reason for a policy of improved and integrated schools is that only this policy will make it politically feasible for the destinies of America's two separate nations to become bound up together. A policy of segregated compensation cannot provide that binding tie and, therefore, can promise only the continuance of a segregated, closed, and inferior system of education for Negro Americans.

Towards Equality of Educational Opportunity?*

SAMUEL BOWLES

Harvard University

In this article, the author argues that a number of changes are necessary if equality of educational opportunity is to be achieved: the allocation of unequal amounts of resources for educating Negro as compared to white children and poor as compared to rich children, the rejection of the notion that the educational system alone can and should bear the responsibility for achieving equal opportunity, and a major redistribution of political power within our society.

I have been billed in some quarters as a critic of the Equality of Educational Opportunity survey, and the Coleman Report.[1] For many years to come, however, all of us, both critics and supporters (and even those hardy few who simply want to find out how our educational system works) will repeatedly return to the Coleman data. This is our great debt to Professor Coleman and his co-workers.

I will concentrate here on the problem of achieving equality of educational opportunity. Because the evidence contained in the Coleman Report is central

* This article appeared originally in the Winter 1968 issue of the *Harvard Educational Review*. It is based on remarks made at the Conference on the *Equality of Educational Opportunity* Report sponsored by the Colloquium Board of the Harvard School of Education, October 21, 1967. One footnote has been slightly altered.

[1] James S. Coleman, *et al.*, *Equality of Educational Opportunity* (Washington: U.S. Government Printing Office, 1966).

to this question, I will focus on a number of the important aspects of the Report and the underlying survey. I suspect that much of the interest in the Coleman Report has been aroused by concern for gaining a greater measure of equality of opportunity for Negroes. For this reason, I will emphasize the achievement of equality of educational opportunity between races. However, let me urge you not to lose sight of the gross inequalities of educational opportunity among social classes, i.e., between rich whites and poor whites, and between rich Negroes and poor Negroes.[2]

I intend to show:

(1) that while the Coleman Report understates the effectiveness of devoting more resources to the education of Negro children, equality in the resources devoted to the education of children of different racial groups will not achieve equality of educational opportunity;

(2) that equality of educational opportunity implies major changes in society at large and, in fact, cannot be achieved by the efforts of the educational system alone; and

(3) that the achievement of equality of educational opportunity will require changes in the distribution of political power between races and among social classes.

Equality of Educational Opportunity through Equal Schools?

My first point is that the achievement of equality of educational opportunity requires inequalities in the amounts of resources devoted to the education of black children and white children, and of rich children and poor children.

There is nothing new about compensatory education; programs designed to give Negro children a higher level of school resources than whites have been in existence for years. Some of these programs have been investigated, and a number of studies have reported their ineffectiveness. A recent evaluation of the More Effective Schools Program in New York, for example, showed that the very large increase in per-pupil expenditures was associated with a comparatively minor increase in grade level achievement on most tests.[3] Moreover, the findings in the

[2] Cf. William Spady, "Educational Mobility and Access in the U.S.: Growth and Paradoxes," *American Sociological Review*, XXXII (November, 1967), and *Project Talent, One Year Follow-up Studies* (Pittsburgh, Pa.: School of Education, University of Pittsburgh, 1966), p. 96ff. Also *U.S. Census of Population 1960, PC (2) 5A, School Enrollments,* Table 5.

[3] (New York: Center for Urban Education, 1967).

Coleman Report itself have been taken by some as an indication that the level of school resources devoted to the education of children of any race has very little effect on the level of achievement. Professor Coleman has written that the evidence in the Report revealed that "the physical and economic resources going into a school had very little relation to the achievement coming out of it," and that "variations in teacher salaries (and a number of other resource measures) had little relation to student achievement when the family backgrounds of the students were roughly equated."[4]

These findings have raised difficult questions for the nation's educators, for if increases in per-pupil expenditures, higher teacher salaries, and a number of other conventional remedies for low scholastic achievement in fact have virtually no effect on achievement, what grounds are there to press for the allocation of increased funds to education? And, if the conventional remedies don't work, what new educational policies are required?

I believe that the evidence does not support the hypothesis that school resources are ineffective in increasing achievement levels. I intend to show that the inference that per-pupil expenditure, teacher salaries, and other measures of school resources have very little relationship to student achievement is open to serious question and that, in fact, the evidence of the Equality of Educational Opportunity Survey itself suggests that student achievement is sensitive to the level of resources devoted to the school. At the close of this section I will suggest that while the effect of additional school resources on Negro student achievement could be substantial, a sizeable racial deficiency in achievement scores would remain even if we were to equate the presently measured characteristics of the quality of schooling of white and of nonwhite children. Let me make it entirely clear that in suggesting the importance of school resources as a determinant of educational achievement in the schools, I do not intend to denigrate the importance of peer-group influence and the social backgrounds and attitudes of students.

We cannot hope to measure the effects of school resources on achievement without developing adequate measures of the school resources themselves. Yet the measurement of school resources in the survey appears to me to be highly inadequate.[5] Consider first the treatment of instructional expenditure per pupil. This measure would appear to be a rough index of the amount of instructional re-

[4] James S. Coleman, "Towards Open Schools," *The Public Interest*, No. 9 (Fall, 1967), 20-7.
[5] For a more complete discussion of the data collected for the Report and the statistical methods used, see Samuel Bowles and Henry M. Levin, "The Determinants of Scholastic Achievement—An Appraisal of Some Recent Evidence," *Journal of Human Resources*, II (Winter, 1968).

sources devoted to each student. However, the measure used in the analysis in the Report was not a school-by-school per-pupil expenditure, but rather an average of instructional expenditures per student within an entire school district. School-to-school differences within a district (even differences between secondary and elementary schools) were simply ignored. Even those inputs which were measured on a school-by-school basis are subject to some of the same measurement errors because the use of these measures necessarily ignores differences in the amount of resources devoted to children in different tracks within the same school.

A further problem arises because students who attend schools characterized by high levels of educational inputs, more often than not, come from higher social-class backgrounds and have attitudes conducive to educational achievement. The authors of the Report were obviously faced with the difficult statistical task of disentangling the effects of achievement associated with these overlapping characteristics of students. The method of statistical analysis adopted in the Report, however, is incapable of distinguishing among the overlapping effects of family background, attitudes, and school resources.

The inference that school resources are relatively ineffective in increasing achievement levels is based on the finding that when the social background of the students is controlled first, the level of school resources adds very little predictive power to the analysis. Recent reanalysis of the data shows that controlling the level of school resources first, produces radically different results. For example, the amount of variance in achievement scores of twelfth-grade Negro students explained by the variable "teachers' verbal ability" more than doubles if this variable is brought into the analysis first, rather than after the social background variables.

Both approaches, however, give misleading results. Let me try to explain why this is so. Assume that we want to predict the weight of children on the basis of knowledge of both their age and their height. Because heights and ages of children are closely associated, we can predict a child's weight if we know only his age nearly as well as when we know both his height and his age. If we ran the analysis the other way around, i.e., first controlled for height and then investigated the additional predictive power associated with the variable age, the results would of course be reversed. We would find very little additional predictive power associated with age.

A similar statistical difficulty arises in the Coleman analysis because the level of resources devoted to a child's education and the child's own social background are not independent. When we control for the social class of the student, we implicitly control also for some part of the variation in school resources. The additional predictive power associated with the explicit addition of school resources to the analysis thus represents a downward-biased estimate of the real relationship between school resources and achievement. There is no rigorous statistical or compelling theoretical reason for controlling first for social background. In particular, it is not relevant that much of the effect of family background is felt first, prior to a child's entry into school, for the Coleman analysis is cross-sectional and does not take into account in any way the time sequence of the explanatory variables. By choosing to control first for social-background factors, the authors of the Report inadvertently biased its analysis against finding school resources to be an important determinant of scholastic achievement.

Fortunately for us, we do not have merely to speculate about the importance or direction of these biases, for the data which form the basis of the relevant portion of the Report have kindly been made available to me for re-analysis; and they reveal that school resources have a statistically significant relation to scholastic achievement, particularly for Negro children. Let me explain the apparent contradiction. When we talk about the effectiveness of a school input or a social background factor on scholastic achievement, we may talk either about the closeness of the association between the variable and achievement or about the magnitude of a change in achievement associated with a change in the variable. For purposes of educational policy-making, we clearly want to use the second approach; that is, we want to know how much change in achievement is associated with change in, say, class size, teacher quality, or student attitudes. Although the material was not published in the Report, the authors did in fact estimate what I believe to be the relevant quantities: namely, how large an effect on achievement do changes in school resources and other variables have?

Their decision not to publish this material was unfortunate, because the closeness of association measures which they did publish not only fail to shed much direct light on the educational policy issues at hand, but they are also subject to a number of statistical shortcomings such as those previously mentioned. The unpublished estimates avoid the most serious of these shortcomings.

Preliminary analysis of the computer runs which form the basis of the section of the Report on the effects of school resources indicate that the achievement levels of Negro students are particularly sensitive to the quality of the teaching staffs assigned to them.[6] The survey employed a number of measures of teacher

---

[6] I am currently using the Coleman data and other sources to generate new estimates of the relationship between school inputs and achievement.

quality; not surprisingly, the one most closely associated with student verbal achievement appears to be the teacher's score on a verbal facility test.

While these results must be subjected to further scrutiny, the implication is that, contrary to the Coleman conclusion, significant gains in Negro students' achievement levels can be made by directing additional resources to their education. Research currently in process[7] indicates that the cost of major changes in the quality of the teachers of Negro students would not be prohibitive; in fact, the cost would be far below the per-pupil expenditure increases involved in many of the existing compensatory education programs. I do not minimize the practical difficulties involved in making improvements in the quality of the teachers of Negro students, nor do I intend here to endorse any particular form of compensatory education. There are no simple answers to these questions. What I seek to emphasize is that the evidence of the Coleman study itself, far from documenting the ineffectiveness of increased school resources, indicates that teacher quality is a major determinant of scholastic achievement among Negro students and that feasible changes in the level of quality of the teachers of Negro students would bring about significant changes in the achievement levels of these students.

Let me make my position clear: the type of compensatory educational program I am talking about does not involve simply spending more money on Negro than on white students, although more money will be necessary. We must go beyond the measure of money resources and concentrate on those school inputs which appear to have the greatest effect; i.e., on the basis of present data, teacher quality. Of course, in developing programs of compensatory education, we must not exclude consideration of other programs, such as the social-class or racial integration of the school, which may also have significant effects on achievement. Moreover, our present knowledge of the relationship between school inputs and achievement is still too rudimentary to justify much confidence in policies designed directly from the quantitative estimates of the effects on achievement of any particular school inputs. Many of the proposed solutions to our current educational problems imply increases in school resource levels considerably beyond our present range of observations, and therefore beyond the applicable range of our present statistical estimates.

More generally, the intelligent formulation of educational policies requires not only a more adequate theory of the learning process under various school and community conditions, but a far more complete description of the school, includ-

[7] This research, using the Equality of Educational Opportunity Survey data, is being carried on at the Brookings Institution under the direction of Henry Levin.

ing such aspects as the atmosphere of the classroom and more exhaustive measurement of teacher attitudes. Detailed longitudinal case studies hold out some possibility of capturing the dynamic process of the development of cognitive skills, at least in the particular cases to which they apply.

After this lengthy statistical excursion, let me return to my first main point. The same evidence mentioned earlier suggests that were we merely to raise the quality of the teaching resources devoted to the education of Negroes to the level of that currently devoted to whites, we would significantly improve Negro achievement. Nevertheless, we would reduce the gap in Negro and white verbal achievement at grade 12 by only a little more than a quarter.[8] This estimate may be on the low side, since I have been able to estimate the impact of equating only a limited number of imperfectly measured teachers' characteristics. For example, we probably do not equalize the educational levels of teachers when we equate the degree levels that the teachers of Negro students have to those of teachers of whites, since the teachers of Negroes are more likely to be Negroes who have suffered serious deficiencies in their own education.[9] Even with more nearly ideal measures of teacher quality, however, a substantial gap would certainly remain. Equal school inputs will not produce equal school outputs.

Equality of Economic Opportunity through Education?

Let me move on now to my second point, which is that the burden of achieving equality of educational opportunity should not, and cannot, be borne by the educational system alone. The achievement of some degree of equality of opportunity depends in part upon what we do in the educational system but also, to a very large degree, upon what we do elsewhere in the economy, in the polity, and in the society as a whole.

First, given the importance of student attitudes and social-class background in the learning process, it may well be that no feasible program of compensatory education could overcome the educational disabilities imposed upon Negro children by racial discrimination and, in addition, upon poor Negro children by their lower-class origins. Closing the achievement gap may require changing student

[8] This result is based on the regression equations underlying Table 3.25.2 in Coleman, *et al., op. cit.*, and evidence in the Report on differences between the means of the teacher quality variables for whites and Negroes. Naturally these calculations are subject to some error, although probably not enough to alter the substantive point being made here.

[9] Cf. Coleman, *et al., op. cit.*, Ch. 4.

121

attitudes towards schooling and towards themselves; this can hardly be accomplished except through, or at least in conjunction with, an all-out social assault on racism and on the poverty and the powerlessness of the poor.

But closing the educational gap is not enough. Let me follow Professor Coleman in suggesting that equality of educational opportunity has to do with the effects of education rather than the inputs into education.[10] I will broaden the concept of the effects of education to include some of the crucial determinants of the distribution of economic well-being in our society, namely, the effects of education on jobs and the effects of education on income.

Education is obviously only one of the many influences on earnings and its effects differ considerably between racial groups. Differences in years of schooling appear to explain less than a third of the variance of earnings among individuals after account has been taken of race, region, sex, and age.[11] On the basis of U.S. Census returns, we find that Negroes gain considerably less from an additional year of education than do whites.[12] Discrimination in the labor market, as measured by the ratio of expected lifetime earnings of whites with a given level of schooling to the expected lifetime earnings of Negroes with a similar level of schooling, rises with increasing years of education through the completion of college. For example, the estimated lifetime earnings of nonwhite males with eight grades of education is 64 per cent of that for whites with a similar level of schooling; the analogous fraction for those with 12 years of schooling is 60 per cent.[13] This means that with each additional year of education, short of postgraduate study, Negroes benefit less, both absolutely and relatively, than whites in terms of increased income. This situation obtains in the North as well as the South. Indeed, one competent piece of research using U.S. Census data suggests that for Negroes in the North, the economic gains associated with additional years of education beyond the eighth grade are comparatively minor, and that at a number of points in the educational career of a Negro youth staying in school for an additional year results in an actual reduction in the present value of expected lifetime earnings.[14]

[10] This position is advanced by Professor Coleman in the article which appears earlier in this book.

[11] G. Hanoch, "Personal Savings and Investment in Schooling" (Unpublished doctoral dissertation, University of Chicago, 1965), 42-7. (Mimeographed.)

[12] See *U.S. Census of Population 1960, PC (2)7B, Occupation by Earnings and Education,* Table 1. See also Stephan Michelson, "Equating Racial Incomes: On the Efficacy of Employment and Education Policies" (Washington: The Brookings Institution, 1967). (Mimeographed.)

[13] Based on 1960 Census returns for workers aged eighteen to sixty-four; H. Miller, *Income Distribution in the United States.* U.S. Census Monograph, 1966, p. 165.

[14] G. Hanoch, *op. cit.,* p. 90 ff. The present value of lifetime earnings is the sum of expected earnings over an individual's working life with future earnings discounted at some interest rate. Present values were computed with a variety of discount rates, ranging from 2 to 20 per cent. A

In part, these depressing results arise from the fact that the labor market rewards additional education in white children with a much lower probability of
unemployment. This is not nearly as true in the case of Negroes. Let me give you
two examples. For Negroes and whites with the lowest level of education, only one
to four years of schooling, the rates of unemployment among males twenty-five years
of age and above were roughly equivalent. For high school graduates, the Negro unemployment rate was fully two times as large as the white unemployment rate.[15]
Moreover, in 1964 the unemployment rates for male high school drop-outs under
twenty-four years of age was 25 per cent higher for nonwhites than for whites. By
comparison, for high school graduates, the nonwhite unemployment rate was
more than twice that of whites.[16]

Of course, these differences in the gains from education reflect, among other
things, differences in the quality of education received by the different races. It is
extremely difficult to measure the economic impact of this quality difference, but
the available evidence suggests that the economic gains from additional education
would differ substantially for Negroes and whites even if the two racial groups had
equal achievement scores. For example, the Coleman Report indicates that the
mean Negro verbal-achievement score in the metropolitan Northeast is roughly
one standard deviation behind the whites at grades 1, 3, 6, 9, and 12; a constant
fraction of the whites score above the Negro mean achievement level at all grade
levels.[17] Yet the fraction of whites earning more than the Negro mean by years
of schooling shows a general rise from grade to grade. For example, among males
with eight years of schooling, 66 per cent of the whites earn above the Negro mean.
Among high school graduates, the figure is 74 per cent.[18] Thus, while Negro
achievement levels are by this measure no further behind the whites' at the higher than at the lower grades, Negro income levels fall increasingly far below the

---

recent study of 2500 draft rejects aged 17 to 25 indicated low returns to schooling of the poor generally. Among that group an additional year of schooling contributes only an additional $37 to ex-
pected annual earnings. See W. Lee Hansen, B. Weisbrod and W. Scanlon, "Determinants of
Earnings: Does Schooling Really Count?" (Unpublished, preliminary paper.)

[15] *U.S. Census of Population 1960, PC (2) 5B, Educational Attainments.* These figures refer to
1960. Similar figures are reported in the *Monthly Labor Review* (March 1966), "Educational Attainment of Workers in March 1965" for 1962, 1964, and 1965.

[16] "Employment of High School Graduates and Drop-outs in 1964," Table A (U.S. Department
of Labor, Bureau of Labor Statistics, Special Labor Force Report, No. 54, June, 1965).

[17] Coleman, *et al., op. cit.,* p. 273.

[18] The figures refer to workers aged twenty-five to sixty-four in the North and West (*U.S. Census
1960, PC [2] 7B*). If only workers in the age category twenty-five to thirty-four are considered, or
if Southern workers are included, the same general picture emerges.

income of whites with each additional year of schooling. Or to use a slightly different measure, we know that by grade 12, Negro achievement levels are approximately three years behind the whites. Yet mean earnings of nonwhite twelfth-grade graduates fall far short of the earnings of whites with eight years of schooling.[19] The earnings gap considerably exceeds the learning gap.[20]

Let me state two conclusions. First, the achievement of equality of educational opportunity, if this concept is measured only by equivalent achievement scores, would take us only a small part of the way towards the achievement of equality of opportunity in the society at large, but it will take us some of the way.

Secondly, if we choose to define equality of educational opportunity in terms of the economic results of education, then in addition to equalizing achievement in school, we must tackle the problem of racial discrimination in the job market directly.

Equality of Educational Opportunity: Who Wants It?

This brings me to my third and last point, namely that the achievement of equality of educational opportunity in our society will probably require major changes in the distribution of political power. Decision-making in the educational system is a sensitive barometer of the power relations within a society. The selection processes, the promotion probabilities, and the formulation of educational policy reflect who really counts and who really governs.

Professor Coleman and his co-authors have made it painfully clear to us that, left to the benevolence of those who presently count, our system of education does not achieve equality of educational opportunity. There is ample evidence that we have not arrived at equality of educational opportunity; there is very little evidence that we are moving closer to its achievement.[21] Let me suggest that this situation has not come about by accident.

Raising Negro achievement levels confers definite benefits on those directly involved, and on many not so directly involved. But if we view the individual gains from education in relative rather than absolute terms, equality of educational opportunity is a two-way street. Some stand to benefit by it and others stand to

---

[19] The figures refer to male workers twenty-five to sixty-four years old in the North and West (*U.S. Census 1960*, PC [2] 7B).

[20] In a recent study of white-nonwhite income differentials, Stephan Michelson concludes that equating both the quantity and quality of schooling between races would reduce the racial income disparity by less than half. Cf. S. Michelson, *op. cit.*

[21] Cf., for example, W. Spady, *op. cit.*

lose. The competition for places in good colleges and the competition for good jobs must cause many white parents to regard the narrowing of racial discrepancies in educational opportunity with mixed feelings, or worse.

Those who stand to gain are the objects of my attention here. Yet we must recognize that the achievement of equality of educational opportunity involves very real conflicts of interest. More specifically, it will involve favoring the interests of the poor and the powerless to the detriment of the interests of those better endowed with wealth and influence. Are we ready to take this road? Is Congress? Is City Hall?

If I am correct in suspecting that in most cases the answer is no, then we are faced with a choice. We can, of course, continue to make recommendations directed towards particular causes of low achievement among Negro children, ignoring the underlying dynamics of the system which produces these results. Or we may broaden our attack and attempt to increase the degree of participation in educational decision-making and to transfer power to groups presently excluded from influence.

Many of our policy decisions in education can have little effect on the distribution of political power. But I believe that many options open to us could have the effect of mobilizing poor communities, particularly of mobilizing Negro communities to exert their interests more effectively in the making of educational policy. For example, greater parental involvement in school decisions could have the effect of developing political and organizational skills in the ghetto, and building a political base which may allow the Negro community to make felt its claims for a larger share of educational and other social resources. The immediate effects of such programs on the scholastic achievement of children in school is of course unknown. But if the above analysis is correct, the immediate effects on scholastic achievement must be considered along with the long-run effects on the distribution of political power, on the attitudes of parents and students, and on the degree of racial discrimination in employment.

Let us continue to ask *what* school policies should be adopted. But let us also ask *who* should decide, and *how*. We must, of course, attempt to right the particular wrongs which we observe today; but we must attempt as well to understand why our system of decision-making in education has worked so consistently to the disadvantage of Negroes and the poor. Let us first understand it and then let us change it.

Equal Opportunity
for Maximum Development*

GERALD LESSER

Harvard University

SUSAN S. STODOLSKY

The University of Chicago

The authors discuss the meaning of equal educational opportunity in the light of the research on diverse patterns of mental ability in children. They take issue with James Coleman's contention that equal opportunity should imply equal test-score averages between different racial and ethnic groups, holding that such a definition underestimates the role that diversity should play in education. They argue that, beyond the acquisition of certain basic skills, children should be provided with an opportunity to maximize their strongest mental abilities.

James Coleman and his associates failed to find what they expected to find, direct evidence of large inequalities in educational facilities in schools attended by children from different majority and minority groups. The study set out to

* This article is an adaptation for the purposes of this book of the longer paper on "Learning Patterns in the Disadvantaged" by Lesser and Stodolsky which appeared in the Fall 1967 issue of the *Harvard Educational Review*.

document the fact that for children from minority groups school facilities are sharply unequal and that this inequality is related to student achievement. The data did not support either conclusion. What small differences in school facilities did exist had little or no discernible relationship to the level of student achievement.

Starting with these facts, Coleman develops an argument concerning the goals of education which we shall outline below in order to clarify the points at which our own thinking, based on the study of the diversity of mental abilities in children, departs from his. Inequality of educational opportunity still prevails, he says, because white and Negro (and other minority-group) students do not display equal levels of educational achievement when they complete high school. *Ipso facto,* the schools are unequal, despite the absence of direct evidence of such inequality.

Coleman's argument starts with the premise that the proper function of the schools in a democracy is to produce equal achievement levels among different groups in our society. Arguing from this premise, the demonstrated fact that Negroes and whites are unequal in level of educational attainment testifies to the inequality of educational opportunities provided by the schools. That is, by definition, schools are designed to make groups equal. They do not do so. Therefore, schools are unequal in the educational opportunities they provide. Indeed, following this argument, the single decisive criterion for judging equal educational opportunity is that the mean school performance of all groups be equal.

Coleman makes his position clear by saying that the role of the schools is to "make achievement independent of background" and to "overcome the differences in starting point of children from different social groups."[1] This position is shared by much research on the "disadvantaged," where the objective is to seek means to reduce the discrepancy in achievement levels between "deprived" and "nondeprived" children.[2]

[1] James S. Coleman, *et al., Equality of Educational Opportunity* (Washington: U.S. Government Printing Office, 1966), p. 72.

[2] The counterpart to Coleman's reasoning about equal educational opportunity exists in the history of "culture-free" test construction, another topic of great relevance to the education of the disadvantaged. Early developers of "culture-free" tests (for example, K. W. Eells, *et al., Intelligence and Cultural Differences* [Chicago: University of Chicago Press, 1951]) argued that only tests which eliminated items distinguishing among groups were free of "bias." The parallel to Coleman's argument is apparent: (1) the proper function of a "culture-free" test is to produce equal test scores for different social-class and ethnic groups; (2) if equal scores are not obtained,

Gerald Lesser, Susan S. Stodolsky

The "Equal-Footing" Basis of Coleman's Argument. At one level—the "equal-footing" level—Coleman's line of reasoning seems to epitomize logic, common sense, and compassion. It seems to ask only that we give children from "disadvantaged" backgrounds a fair shake—that through the educational system, we educate all children to a point of equality in school achievement so that all groups can compete on equal terms for jobs or future educational opportunities.

However, it is our contention that Coleman's analysis does not go far enough, does not tell the whole story or consider all the evidence, and therefore is misleading and perhaps destructive. It fails to consider either the role of diversity and pluralism in our society or several alternative definitions of the function of schooling.

The important role that the notions of diversity and pluralism should play in the discussion of educational goals is illuminated by the results of our investigations of the patterns of mental ability in children of different ethnic groups and social classes, which are outlined below.

The Original Study

Aims: Our goal was to examine the patterns among various mental abilities in six- and seven-year-old children from different social-class and ethnic backgrounds. We accepted the definition of intelligence which postulates diverse mental abilities and proposes that intelligent behavior can be manifested in a wide variety of forms, with each individual displaying certain areas of intellectual strength and other areas of intellectual weakness. A basic premise of this study is that social-class and ethnic influences differ not only in degree but in kind, with the consequence that different kinds of intellectual skills are fostered or hindered in different environments.

Design: Hypotheses were tested regarding the effects of social-class and ethnic-group affiliation (and their interactions) upon both the level of each mental

---

the fault is that the test (or some kinds of test items) produce the difference. Difference in test scores, *ergo,* bias in test items. The logical fallacy of this argument is now well-documented (for example, Anne Anastasi, *Differential Psychology* [New York: Macmillan, 1958]; and I. Lorge, "Difference or Bias in Tests of Intelligence," in Anne Anastasi (ed.), *Testing Problems in Perspective* [Washington: American Council on Education, 1966]), but the sample and surface persuasiveness of the argument stalled progress for many years in the study of cultural influences upon intelligence.

ability considered singly and the pattern among mental abilities considered in combination. Four mental abilities (verbal ability, reasoning, number facility, and space conceptualization) were studied in first-grade children from four ethnic groups (Chinese, Jewish, Negro, and Puerto Rican). Each ethnic group was divided into two social-class components (middle and lower), each in turn being divided into equal numbers of boys and girls.

Thus, a 4 x 2 x 2 analysis-of-covariance design included a total of sixteen subgroups, each composed of twenty children. A total sample of 320 first-grade children was drawn from forty-five different elementary schools in New York City and its environs. Three test influences were controlled statistically: effort, responsiveness to the tester, and age of the subject.

Ethnic Group

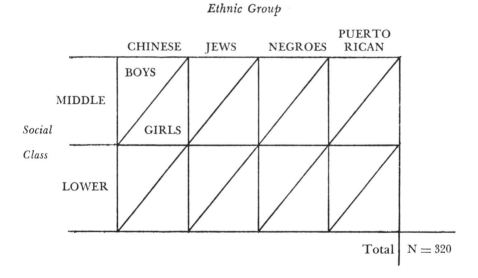

The selection of four mental abilities (verbal ability, reasoning, number facility, and space conceptualization) is described in detail elsewhere.[3] To obtain a first approximation to the assessment of intra-individual profiles of scores for the various mental abilities of children, these skills were assessed:

[3] For a description of the original research project, see G. S. Lesser, G. Fifer, and D. H. Clark, "Mental Abilities of Children from Different Social-Class and Cultural Groups," *Monographs of the Society for Research in Child Development*, XXX, No. 4 (1965), pp. 32-43.

Gerald Lesser, Susan S. Stodolsky

Verbal—The skill is defined as memory for verbal labels in which reasoning elements, such as those required by verbal analogies, are reduced to a minimum. Verbal ability has long been regarded as the best single predictor of success in academic courses, especially in the language and social-science fields. It is involved to a marked degree in the work of all professions and in most semiprofessional areas.

Reasoning—Reasoning involves the ability to formulate concepts, to weave together ideas and concepts, the central element of aptitude for intellectual activities and, therefore, is of primary importance in all academic fields and in most vocations.

Number—The ability is defined as skill in enumeration and in memory and use of the fundamental combinations in addition, subtraction, multiplication, and division. It is of great importance in arithmetic in elementary schools and in mathematics in secondary schools.

Space conceptualization—The ability refers to a cluster of skills related to spatial relations and sizes of objects and to visualizing their movements in space. It is involved in geometry, trigonometry, mechanics, and drafting; in elementary-school activities, such as practical arts and drawing; and in occupations such as mechanics, engineering, and architecture.

Of course, many procedural issues are raised by an attempt to measure such skills in children from diverse backgrounds. These include the identification of the children for the study, the design of tests, and the control of influences on student performance such as the degree of identification with the tester. A detailed discussion of the procedures developed to deal with these problems is outlined in the original research report.

Some Findings: Hypotheses were tested regarding the influence of social class and ethnicity (and their interactions) upon the levels of the four mental-ability scores and upon the patterns among them. The results are summarized in Table 1.

TABLE 1
Summary of Results

Source of Influence	Effect upon Mental Abilities	
	Level	Pattern
Ethnicity	Highly Significant*	Highly Significant*
Social Class	Highly Significant*	Nonsignificant
Social Class x Ethnicity	Significant**	Nonsignificant

* $p < .001$
** $p < .05$

Distinctive ethnic-group differences: Ethnic groups are markedly different ($p < .001$) *both* in the absolute *level* of each mental ability and in the *pattern* among these abilities. For example, with regard to the effects of ethnicity upon the *level* of each ability, Figure 1 shows that:

(1) on verbal ability, Jewish children ranked first (being significantly better than all other ethnic groups), Negroes second, Chinese third (both being significantly better than Puerto Ricans), and Puerto Ricans fourth.

(2) on space conceptualization, Chinese ranked first (being significantly better than Puerto Ricans and Negroes), Jews second, Puerto Ricans third, and Negroes fourth.

But the most striking results of this study concern the effects of ethnicity upon the *patterns* among the mental abilities. Figure 1 (and the associated analyses-of-variance for group patterns) shows that these *patterns* are different for each ethnic group. More important is the finding depicted in Figures 2-5. Ethnicity does affect the pattern of mental abilities *and, once the pattern specific to the ethnic group emerges, social-class variations within the ethnic group do not alter this basic organization.* For example, Figure 2 shows the mental-ability pattern peculiar to the Chinese children—with the pattern displayed by the middle-class Chinese children duplicated at a lower level of performance by the lower-class Chinese children. Figure 3 shows the mental-ability pattern specific to the Jewish children—with the pattern displayed by the middle-class Jewish children duplicated at a lower level of performance by the lower-class Jewish children. Parallel statements can be made for each ethnic group.

The failure of social-class conditions to transcend patterns of mental ability associated with ethnic influences was unexpected. Social-class influences have been described as superseding ethnic-group effects for such diverse phenomena as child-rearing practices, educational and occupational aspirations, achievement motivation, and anomie. The greater salience of social class over ethnic membership is reversed in the present findings on patterns of mental ability. Ethnicity has the primary effect upon the organization of mental abilities, and the organization is not modified further by social-class influences. (Many other findings are described in our full report of the original study.)

Since our early results were both surprising and striking in magnitude, our next step was to conduct a replication[4] and extension with first-graders in

---

[4] This replication study was conducted under the direction of Dr. Jane Fort, Laboratory of Human Development, Harvard University.

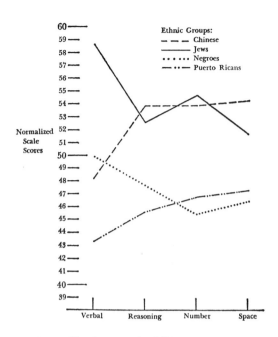

Fig. 1. *Pattern of Normalized Mental-Ability Scores for Each Ethnic Group*

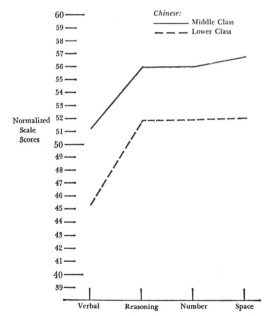

Fig. 2. *Patterns of Normalized Mental-Ability Scores for Middle- and Lower-Class Chinese Children.*

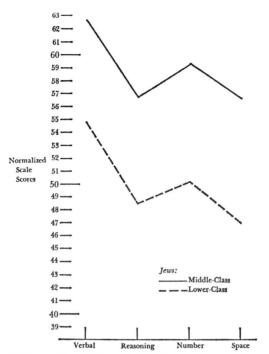

Fig. 3. *Patterns of Normalized Mental-Ability Scores for Middle- and Lower-Class Jewish Children.*

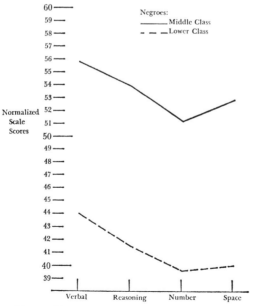

Fig. 4. *Patterns of Normalized Mental-Ability Scores for Middle- and Lower-Class Negro Children*

Gerald Lesser, Susan S. Stodolsky

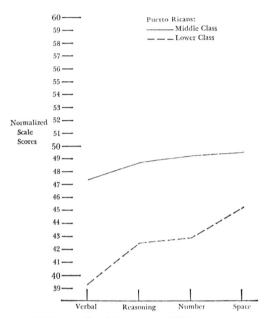

Fig. 5. *Patterns of Normalized Mental-Ability Scores for Middle- and Lower-Class Puerto Rican Children.*

Boston. The replication was conducted with middle and lower class Chinese and Negro children (the samples of Jewish and Puerto Rican children who fit our social-class criteria were not available). Once again, the results were both striking and surprising. The replication data on Chinese and Negro children in Boston duplicated almost exactly our earlier data on similar samples in New York City.[5]

An Alternative to Coleman's Argument

Equal Opportunity for Maximum Development: Returning to Coleman's argument regarding equal educational opportunity, we believe that our data on patterns of mental ability clarify two alternative and perhaps complementary assumptions regarding the function of education: (1) to provide equal opportunity for *equal* development, or (2) to provide equal opportunity for *maximum* development of each group or individual, whether or not group differ-

[5] For a more detailed description of this study, see Susan S. Stodolsky and Gerald Lessser, "Learning Patterns in the Disadvantaged," *Harvard Educational Review*, XXXVII, No. 4 (Fall 1967).

ences remain, enlarge, or disappear as a consequence. These positions are apparently incompatible but need closer examination in the light of empirical evidence.

a) Data on social class: From our mental-ability data, what would we predict would happen if we modified the social-class characteristics of all our lower-class families—elevating the jobs, education, and housing of the lower-class families in all ethnic groups? Within each ethnic group, we would expect to elevate the mental abilities of the lower-class children to resemble those of the middle-class children in that ethnic group, making them more similar to their middle-class counterparts in that ethnic group in level of ability. In this sense, we would be making groups of children more similar, removing the differences in mental ability associated with differences in social-class position.[6]

If we elevated the social-class position of lower-class families, we might produce still another effect which increases the similarity among groups. The interaction effect between social class and ethnicity showed that the mental-ability scores of middle-class children from various ethnic groups resembled each other more than the scores of the lower-class children from these ethnic groups. This interaction can be described as a convergence effect: the scores of the middle-class children across ethnic groups converge to a greater extent than the scores of lower-class children.

Thus, by elevating the occupations, educations, and neighborhoods of our lower-class families, our data would lead us to expect an increased resemblance of mental-ability levels for children within each ethnic group and, in addition, a convergence of scores of children across ethnic groups. To the extent that level of performance on mental abilities predicts school achievement, these convergences would narrow the range of differences in school achievement among social-class and ethnic groups.

b) Data on ethnic groups: To this juncture, our analysis supports the argument for equal educational opportunities for *equal* development: our data on level of mental ability suggest that elevating social-class characteristics of lower-class families would contribute to a greater degree of equality of development in level of intellectual functioning. Now, what of the alternative conception

[6] We noted earlier that social-class position produces more of a difference in the mental abilities of Negro children than for the other groups. From this finding, it is possible to speculate that elevating the social-class characteristics of lower-class Negro families would produce a more dramatic increase in the level of the Negro children's abilities than would a comparable change in social-class position affect children from other ethnic groups.

that the proper function of education is to provide equal opportunity for *maximum* development no matter what the consequences for the absolute magnitude of group differences? Since the data on pattern of intellectual functioning indicate that once the mental-ability pattern specific to the ethnic group emerges, social-class variations within the ethnic group do not alter the basic organization associated with ethnicity, this finding suggests that lower-class children whose social-class position is elevated would still retain the distinctive mental-ability pattern associated with their ethnic group. The implication is that no matter what manipulations are undertaken to modify the social-class positions of children within an ethnic group, the distinctive pattern of abilities will remain.

From this set of observations, the question then arises: how can we make maximum educational use of the distinctive patterns of ability the child possesses? We do not have definitive answers to this question, which has led us to undertake a line of research that seeks to match instructional strategies to patterns of mental ability. For example, in teaching mathematical functions to children strong in space conceptualization but weak in numerical facility, we use graphical presentation; in teaching the same concept to a child strong in number facility but weak in space conceptualization, we rely on the manipulation of numbers in a tabular form. What seems needed at this point is a research program to identify and explore the mental attributes of children and the instructional methods that could be matched most effectively to these attributes in order to produce successful learning. In the simplest case, we can conceive of successful matching producing equal levels of achievement for children; such an outcome would be consistent with Coleman's argument. We think that at least for basic skills (for example, literacy) the achievement of equal levels by all children is desirable.

Two possible contradictions to Coleman's argument remain, however. Beyond deploying all necessary resources to achieve minimal equality in essential goals, further development of students may well be diverse. A continuous utilization of student strengths and weaknesses may well lead to diverse development beyond a minimal set of achievements. To the extent that past experience, interests, and achievements of students are regularly related to subcultural membership, educational outcomes may differ. Second, we do not know what effects the matching procedure will have over time. We start, let us say, by using suitable alternative routes to identical educational objectives. Assuming we successfully achieve these outcomes, what else have we done? Have we, perhaps, reinforced and strengthened abilities, interests, or personality characteristics which are in fact associated with subcultural membership? In the long run, will we develop more diverse students than we started with?

Let us take a specific, if partially hypothetical, case. Our evidence indicates (see Figure 1) that young Chinese children have their strongest skill in space conceptualization and their weakest in verbal ability. Conversely, young Jewish children are strongest in verbal ability and weakest in space conceptualization. Following our principle of matching instruction and ability, we incidentally may enhance the initial strengths which each group possesses. For example, through the incidental enhancement of the space-conceptualization skills of the Chinese children, we may produce proportionally more Chinese than Jewish architects and engineers. Conversely, through incidental enhancement of verbal skills of the Jewish children, we may produce proportionally more Jewish than Chinese authors and lawyers. We will not have put members of these two ethnic groups on an "equal footing" for entering a particular occupation. But can we say that we have produced a socially-destructive outcome by starting with the knowledge of differences in ability patterns and adapting our instructional strategies to this knowledge to produce a maximum match for each child, even if this process results in inequality of certain educational and professional attainments? We are willing to accept, then, one possible consequence of arranging instruction to capitalize maximally on distinctive patterns of ability: that, in certain areas of intellectual accomplishment, rather than reducing or bringing toward equality the differences among various groups, we may actually magnify those differences.[7]

A Summary: We challenged Coleman's "equal-footing" argument on the grounds that it did not tell the whole story or use all known data. Some of these data, mainly the effects of social class upon level of mental ability, testify in favor of the argument for equal educational opportunity for *equal* development. Other data, namely the effects of ethnicity upon patterns of mental ability, testify to the importance of providing equal educational opportunities

---

[7] At this point in the argument, the counterpart topic is that of the difference between "compensatory" and "supportive" educational programs for "disadvantaged." "Compensatory" programs aim to compensate, to make amends, to eradicate symptoms and causes—to give "disadvantaged" children what they need to make them like everyone else. In contrast, the aim of what might be termed "supportive" education is to give disadvantaged children what they need and can use maximally in order to learn to cope with and change their particular environments, even if they are made more different from everyone else in the process.

for the *maximum* development of groups and individuals, even if inequality of groups occurs as a consequence.

Are equalization and diversification necessarily incompatible goals? We do not believe so. If accelerating the feasible gains in jobs, education, and housing of lower-class families accelerates the gains in intellectual development of their children and reduces the difference in intellectual performance between social-class groups, we can all agree on the desirability of this outcome. On the other hand, if recognizing the particular patterns of intellectual strengths and weaknesses of various ethnic groups and maximizing the potential power of these patterns by matching instructional conditions to them makes the intellectual accomplishments of different ethnic groups more diverse, we can all accept this gain in pluralism within our society. Thus, if lower-class children now perform intellectually more poorly than middle-class children—and it is clear that they do—and lower-class status can be diluted or removed by a society truly dedicated to doing so, this gain in equalization seems to be one legitimate aim of education. If the maximum educational promotion of particular patterns of ability accentuates the diverse contributions of different ethnic groups, this gain in pluralism seems another legitimate aim of education.

Our main point is that the study of mental abilities suggests that there may be patterns of attributes (cognitive, personality, motivational, and so forth) which are related in some regular way to ethnic-group membership. School-based research has not as yet identified the particular patterns of attributes which are educationally important and which (when matched with the appropriate instructional strategies) will maximize school achievement. Thus, we do not yet know if attribute patterns associated with ethnic-group membership will, in fact, be identified as educationally important. We believe, however, that data such as those derived from the current mental-abilities study must be considered since their implications may in fact require revisions of Coleman's position. We raise the issue because we are committed to a program of research on matching individual differences and instructional strategies; whether or not ethnic-group differences are in fact minimized, held constant, or inflated, we believe it important to pursue these programs nonetheless.

Perhaps our position asks no more than to change what is bad and change-able in education and society (resulting perhaps in greater equalization) and to use maximally what is good in education and society (resulting perhaps in increased diversity). Logic—and the empirical evidence—endorses both conclusions.

The Poor, the Schools, and Equal Protection*

DAVID L. KIRP

Harvard University

This article is the first in a projected series on Law and Education, which will deal with both legislation and court decisions relevant to education.

The article considers the state's duty to afford equal educational opportunity in light of (1) the Coleman Report and its progeny, and (2) landmark judicial decisions of the past decade concerned with the meaning of "equal protection," where "fundamental rights" are at stake. The article develops a set of standards for identifying fundamental rights and applies this fundamental rights analysis to public education. Based on that analysis, the article asserts that the state has a vastly greater constitutional obligation to its schoolchildren than it presently accepts. It proposes judicial tests of the implications of that expanded obligation.

While educators have long spoken of equality of educational opportunity, it has been tacitly understood for at least as long that the quality of education that a schoolchild received depended in large part on the community in which he happened to grow up. Suburban towns have had sufficient financial resources to afford the finest facilities and the best qualified teachers; their students have come almost exclusively from upper middle-class backgrounds. In contrast, at least since World War II, the big cities have been poor cities, poor both in money available to spend for facilities and teachers, and in vitally important human resources. This disparity between rich suburbs and poor cities (and rural poverty areas in

* This article appeared originally in the Fall 1968 issue of the *Harvard Educational Review*. All cross-references to the Winter 1968 issue have been altered to the appropriate pages in this book.

David L. Kirp

places such as Appalachia) has, through longevity, acquired the aura of inevitability. Yet from a constitutional standpoint, the inevitability of the status quo is far less clear.

The pertinent constitutional provision upon which poor cities might pin their hopes in challenging the status quo is the equal protection clause of the Fourteenth Amendment. That provision, addressed to the states, is brief and seemingly unambiguous: "No state shall . . . deny to any person within its jurisdiction the equal protection of the laws." The meaning of that requirement has, however, varied when tested in different contexts by the courts.

Traditional constitutional analysis has left the state ample leeway to adopt social legislation that benefited different segments of the community unequally. In certain areas, however—notably criminal process and suffrage—the Court has read the requirement of equality more literally, as imposing an affirmative duty on the state to overcome inequalities caused by economic happenstance.

This essay moves from an examination of the rationale of these new equal protection decisions to a consideration of public education, concluding that criminal process, suffrage, and public education all bear so directly and fundamentally on the nature of our society that they require judicial analysis differing radically from traditional equal protection analysis. The state owes a vastly greater responsibility to all of its schoolchildren than it presently accepts. It is constitutionally obliged, not merely to open its doors to all comers, but to provide *effective* equality to all. A reconsideration of effective equality in the light of recent and extensive educational research studies, such as the Coleman Report, suggests that the state's obligation to provide an equal educational opportunity is satisfied only if each child, no matter what his social background, has an equal chance for an equal educational outcome, regardless of disparities in cost or effort that the state is obliged to make in order to overcome such differences.

The essay proceeds to a discussion of recent landmark cases which espouse this position, and suggests other lawsuits that could conceivably be brought (some of which are in fact in the preliminary trial stages) to test the implications of the expanded requirement of equal educational opportunity. The final section poses questions about the appropriateness, and the necessity, of judicial involvement in these complex, confounding, and critically important issues.[1]

[1] I wish to acknowledge, and to express my gratitude, for considerable assistance that I received in thinking through this paper from Professor Adam Yarmolinsky, Professor Arthur Sutherland, Professor Frank Michelman, and Mr. Maurice Ford of the Harvard Law School; and Professor Daniel P. Moynihan, Professor Robert Binswanger, and Dr. David Cohen of the Harvard Graduate School of Education. Patricia Marschall and Sidra Stich assisted in editing this paper.

140

I

Courts have long recognized that the equal protection clause could not be read literally to compel all legislation to have equal and universal impact. "From the very necessities of society, legislation of a special character ... must often be had in certain districts .... Special burdens are often necessary for general benefits."[2] The judicial wisdom has usually deferred to legislative expertise in discriminating between—classifying—persons affected. Courts have been satisfied if some rational relationship between a legitimate legislative purpose and the classifying principle could be established; they have not required a showing that the relationship be the *most* rational that could be conceived, that the alternative chosen be somehow the wisest.[3] Such questions, it has been felt, are "political," and thus inappropriate for judicial examination.

Only infrequently has legislation run afoul of the equal protection clause.[4] Where the classification appears to be based on pure hazard or caprice, where *no* reasonable classification relates the legislation to the persons affected, statutes have been struck down. "The equal protection clause prevents States from arbitrarily treating people differently under their laws."[5]

Statutes have also been overturned if they classify "in a way which is on its face rational, but which nonetheless proves on closer examination to include within a single classification some members not like others in the same group, or fails to include some that are like those in the group selected for favored or disfavored treatment."[6]

When a legislative classification bears on a vital personal right of anyone, regardless of his identity, that classification is scrupulously examined for reasonableness.[7]

When the legislature relies on certain traits, notably race and creed, in making classifications, courts have erected a presumption of unreasonableness. "All legal restrictions which curb the civil rights of a single racial group are immediately

[2] Barbier v. Connolly, 113 U.S. 27, 31 (1885).
[3] See, for example, Skinner v. Oklahoma, 316 U.S. 535 (1942); Tigner v. Texas, 310 U.S. 141 (1940); Heath & Milligan Mfg. Co. v. Worst, 207 U.S. 338 (1907); Bell's Gap R.R. Co. v. Penn. 134 U.S. 232 (1890).
[4] Tussman and ten Broek, "The Equal Protection of the Laws," *California Law Review* XXXVII (1949), 341, provides a cogent and carefully reasoned equal protection analysis.
[5] Harper v. Virginia Board of Elections, 383 U.S. 663 (1966) (Harlan, J., dissenting).
[6] McKay, "Political Thickets and Crazy Quilts: Reapportionment and Equal Protection," *Michigan Law Review*, LXI (1963), 671.
[7] See, for example, Carrington v. Rash, 380 U.S. 89 (1965) (right to vote); Skinner v. Oklahoma, 316 U.S. 35 (1942) (sterilization).

suspect. That is not to say that all such restrictions are unconstitutional. It is to say that the courts must subject them to the most rigid scrutiny."[8]

In the last decade, however, the Supreme Court has read the guarantee of equal protection more broadly, striking down state statutes which conditioned the exercise of certain rights upon the payment of a sum of money. Thus, where adequate appellate review of a conviction could be had only if a transcript was provided, the Court in *Griffin v. Illinois* found a denial of equal protection in the State's refusal to provide all indigent defendants with free transcripts.[9] In *Douglas v. California,* the state guaranteed appellate review of a criminal conviction. Those who could afford counsel had received a full hearing automatically; those who could not afford counsel had been provided free counsel only if, after an examination of the trial record, the appellate court concluded that counsel would be of particular value to the defendant or to the court. This provision was overturned by the Court.[10] In *Harper v. Virginia Board of Elections,* Virginia's poll tax, which conditioned the right to vote upon payment of a nominal fee, was found to violate the equal protection clause.[11]

These new equal protection decisions were related in several significant ways: the legislation struck down by the Court had put a monetary condition upon the exercise of a right;[12] those adversely affected were too poor to be able to make the demanded payment, and thus were effectively foreclosed from exercising the right. Traditional constitutional analysis prevented the states from expressly discriminating against the poor by preventing them, for example, from entering the state;[13] the equal protection afforded in these cases went further, compelling the mitigation, if not the elimination, of the impact of poverty in certain contexts.

---

[8] Koremtsu v. United States, 323 U.S. 214 (1944). Where legislation, though fair on its face, has operated to discriminate against a racial or ethnic group, courts have not hesitated to strike down the legislation. Takahashi v. Fish & Game Comm'n., 334 U.S. 410 (1948); Yick Wo v. Hopkins, 118 U.S. 356 (1886). *Cf.,* Strauder v. West Virginia, 100 U.S. 303 (1880) at 307-8:

> What is this [Fourteenth Amendment] but declaring that the law in the States shall be the same for the black as for the white; that all persons, whether colored or white, shall stand equal before the laws of the States, and, in regard to the colored race, for whose protection the amendment was primarily designed, that no discrimination shall be made against them by law because of their color. . . . [that they shall be protected from] discriminations which are steps towards reducing them to the condition of a subject race.

[9] 351 U.S. 12 (1956).
[10] 372 U.S. 353 (1963).
[11] 383 U.S. 663 (1966).
[12] The use of the term "right" may appear question-begging; when one concludes that something is a right, entitlement to that right may follow. The paper discusses "right" following its examination of *Harper.*
[13] Edwards v. California, 314 U.S. 160 (1941).

Seen in this light, poverty was no longer "constitutionally an irrelevance."[14] The state was obliged to take affirmative action to overcome the effects of poverty.

The four opinions in the landmark *Griffin* case all treat poverty as the dominant motif. The Court focuses not on "rational legislative purpose," but on whether an individual is absolutely entitled to exercise the right to an effective appeal regardless of his financial capacity; on whether, conversely put, the state may condition the exercise of the right on an individual's ability to assume the bill incurred in that exercise. The Court finds that "the public aspects of criminal procedure must be the same" for rich and poor.[15]

To Justice Harlan, the vocal dissenter in this series of cases, equal protection has a "more limited scope"; it does not require the "anomalous result" that the state must make unequal efforts to compensate for differences in economic circumstances; it does not permit overturning a rational state policy which happens to treat some more harshly than others.[16]

Harlan's discussion of a "duty to discriminate"[17] evades serious encounter with what is an essentially moral concern, stated simply if sweepingly by Justice Black: "there can be no equal justice where the kind of trial a man has depends on the amount of money he has."[18] The Court's opinion in *Douglas* gave some substance to the scope of the state's affirmative duty. Merely affording effective review (which Illinois admitted was lacking in *Griffin*) was not sufficient, the Court found. The state was obliged to extend the same procedural courtesy to all defendants, regardless of their financial circumstances.

Griffin, Douglas, and related cases[19] have been praised by commentators as preserving the "essence of citizenship . . . We cannot conceive of a man as truly a citizen if he is too poor to have access to the courts."[20] Insofar as it is limited to criminal process, that praise seems too narrowly directed. As Justice Fortas has said:

The significance of these [criminal process] cases in terms of our national philosophy, goes beyond the criminal law. Apart from their specific meaning . . . they stand for the proposition that *the state may be obligated in some situations to bridge the gaps which in-*

---

[14] *Ibid.,* 184.

[15] Griffin v. Illinois, 351 U.S. 12, 23 (1956) (Frankfurter, J., concurring).

[16] *Ibid.,* 34 (Harlan, J., dissenting).

[17] *Ibid.,* 35.

[18] *Ibid.,* 19.

[19] See, for example, Rinaldi v. Yaeger, 384 U.S. 305 (1966).

[20] Willcox and Bloustein, "The Griffin Case: Poverty and the Fourteenth Amendment," *Cornell Law Quarterly,* XLIII (1957), 16.

digency has created between a person and his constitutional rights. They represent a refusal to accept the fact of poverty as relieving the state from an affirmative duty to assure that all persons have access to constitutional rights. They request the state to do whatever is necessary, even if it means spending state funds, to make constitutional rights a living reality for everyone.[21]

The right to vote is a second fundamental right of which the Court is particularly solicitous. In striking down Virginia's poll tax requirement in *Harper v. Virginia Board of Elections,* the Court again focuses upon the impact of legislation on the poor. The Court's holding rests on the importance of the right of suffrage, and not on the irrationality of state policy; the fundamental nature of that right restricts the state's usual freedom to set standards.[22] The Court substitutes reliance on the fundamental nature of the electoral process for the "equal justice" rhetoric of the criminal process cases.

The Court in all of these cases is seeking some standard by which to identify the spheres of public involvement that are sufficiently crucial—to the individual and to the community—to merit rigorous judicial attention. In those areas, the Court is abandoning its typical attitude of deference to the legislature and engaging in a balancing of personal and public interest not usually associated with equal protection cases. "The Court has in fact found state action to violate the equal protection clause where, *upon balance,* the good or benefit reasonably to be accomplished for society by the state action fails to outweigh the harm or deprivation imposed upon those individuals unfavorably classified."[23]

In its examination of these measures, the Court may look for evidence of the conventional wisdom, of what the community regards as appropriate and proper.[24] That evidence is relevant; it does not, however, conclude the inquiry. The patterns of the past need not be imposed upon the future; as Justice Frankfurter noted, "local customs, though hardened by time, are not decreed in heaven."[25] Some effort at comprehending fundamental rights that moves beyond the status quo is required, both to allay the fears of those who predict that inflexible standards will cause the demise of creative legislating, and to rebut the

[21] Fortas, "Equal Rights—For Whom?" *New York University Law Review,* XLII (1967), 410. (Emphasis added.)

[22] Hyman and Newhouse, "Standards for Preferred Freedoms: Beyond the First," *Northwestern University Law Review,* LX (1965), 78-79.

[23] Note, "Equal Protection and the Indigent: Griffin and Its Progeny," *Stanford Law Review,* XVI (1964), 399. (Emphasis added.)

[24] Note, "Discrimination Against the Poor and the Fourteenth Amendment," *Harvard Law Review,* LXXXI (1967), 439.

[25] Cooper v. Aaron, 358 U.S. 1, 25 (1958).

contrary assertion that *Griffin* and *Harper* are wholly unrelated instances of the Warren Court's liberalism.

An examination of what have been termed "ultimate values" protected by the law provides one way of identifying areas suitable for careful judicial equal protection scrutiny:

First, is *the value of man himself,* of the individual as a creature of dignity and essential worth. Corollary to this are *values of liberty and equality* which are nonetheless significant because it is difficult to define them with precision or determine their specific scope. Also basic to this value structure is some degree of the *material requisites of a decent life.* Finally, but not last among these fundamental values in the Judeo-Christian tradition, is *the opportunity for people to participate significantly in the control of their government.*[26]

These values, just as the values conserved in *Griffin, Douglas,* and *Harper,* are personal rights which permit a man to function with at least minimal effectiveness in the society; further, they assume that a certain economic standard, sufficient to assure "the material requisites of a decent life," will be maintained.

The values which merit expansive equal protection treatment may be defined in another perhaps more precise way by a slightly different set of standards.[27] *First,* does the right bear directly on the individual's effective participation in the political process? The popular nature of that process gives legitimacy to the coerciveness of the decisions reached through the process. A citizen's capacity to participate in the political process at some future time ought not be contingent on past outcomes of that process. *Second,* is the preservation of the right essential to the maintenance of the values of the society? In the area of criminal procedure, for example, one reason that a person may be regarded as having a claim to whatever is essential to his functioning effectively as a criminal defendant is because it benefits *society* that the defendant is able to function effectively in that role. *Third,* is the right generally considered essential for the individual's satisfactory life prospects?

These three measures, taken together, do not describe a standard to be applied mechanically. Nor do they provide a static definition; what is fundamental will vary with the varying expectations of the society. As the Court in *Harper* states: "Notions of what constitutes equal treatment for purposes of the Equal Protection Clause *do* change . . . We have long been mindful that where

---

[26] Harvey, "The Challenge of the Rule of Law," *Michigan Law Review,* LIX (1961), 608-609. (Emphasis added.)

[27] The "fundamental rights" analysis owes much to Professor Frank Michelman of the Harvard Law School, who has raised similar points both in unpublished course materials and in discussions.

fundamental rights and liberties are asserted under the equal protection clause, classifications which might invade or restrain them must be closely scrutinized and carefully confined."[28] These measures are useful in suggesting a rule of reason that can be applied to determine what state services are in fact rights, equal access to which is assured to all.[29]

The recognition and identification of fundamental rights compels a different understanding of what equal protection entails, and what is to be regarded as discriminatory state action. The state "discriminates" in offering fundamental goods and services if the way in which they are offered leaves some people unable to afford them. Put another way: the pertinent question for the Court is whether everyone has an equal share of the goods, measured according to need.

This analysis is useful for several reasons. It gives fundamental goods, or rights, a more definite meaning, suggesting that at least criminal procedure and suffrage are included within this class of rights. Furthermore, it suggests a balancing test determination of "fundamental": how significant is the good or service to the individual? to the society? how costly is the good? Finally, the analysis identifies the favored class of persons as those who cannot afford the good or service.[30] This makes the poor a constitutionally preferred class whose claims for equal treatment are to be looked upon with sympathy by the courts; a class to which the state's duty of equal treatment is not satisfied by a public offering, at the going rate, of fundamental goods.

II

The right to an equal educational opportunity merits special judicial solicitude because education shares with criminal process and suffrage the attributes of a fundamental right. Education bears directly on the individual's effective participation in the political process; it is essential to the maintenance of the society's values; it is crucial for the individual's satisfactory life prospects.

The actual importance of education to the individual and to the society has not been extensively examined. It has long been assumed (almost as an article of faith) that education is, as Justice Holmes put it, "one of the first objects of public care."[31] It is presumed, for example, that education can provide the skills

[28] Harper v. Virginia Board of Elections, 383 U.S. 663, 670 (1966).

[29] Cf., Reich, "The New Property," *Yale Law Journal*, LXXIII (1964), 733.

[30] "Afford" is ambiguous. Is it to be tested by a mere declaration? by some indigency test? more broadly, by an inability to take advantage of a public good or service? The question is taken up in greater detail in Section II.

[31] Interstate Consol. St. Ry. v. Massachusetts, 207 U.S. 79, 87 (1907).

that enable citizens to make intelligent political choices and thus participate effectively in a government that exercises coercive powers. As Alexis de Tocqueville once stated, commenting on the relationship between education and politics in America: "it cannot be doubted that in the United States the instruction of the people powerfully contributes to the support of the democratic republic... politics are the end and aim of education."[32]

The quality of education provided to communities or social classes within the society necessarily affects the entire society. What happens in the schoolhouse in a poor rural community has a hand in determining the public contribution that its residents can make; it also influences the impact that this community has on the economy and on the life style of the larger society. Sidney Webb writes of this in describing the mythical and blighted hamlet of Little Pedlington:

We cannot afford to let the inhabitants of Little Pedlington suffer the penalties of their own ignorance or their own parsimony, because the consequences fall, not on them alone, but also upon the neighboring districts, upon everyone who passes through this benighted area, upon all those who have intercourse with them, even upon the community as a whole, whose future citizens they are producing . . . If they are permitted to bring up their children in ignorance . . . it is not the Little Pedlingtonites alone who will have to bear the inevitable cost of the destitution and criminality thus produced. Hence modern administrative science is forced to recognize that we are all, in the plainest sense, "members of one another."[33]

Education is highly esteemed because of what is regarded as its profound and measurable impact on an individual's life chances. *Brown v. Board of Education* asserts the point more positively: "Education is perhaps the most important function of state and local government... In these days, it is doubtful that any child may reasonably be expected to succeed in life if he is denied the opportunity of education."[34]

Any attempt to measure the relative importance to the individual and to the society of publicly-provided services confronts irreconcilable differences of personal preference and economic analysis. Education can, however, be distinguished from other public services in several ways: it has a long history of high public esteem

[32] A. de Tocqueville, *Democracy in America* (New York: Vintage, 1954), pp. 329-330. See also Note, "Discrimination Against the Poor and the Fourteenth Amendment," which refers to education as "the very foundation of good citizenship."

[33] S. Webb, *Grants-in-Aid: A Criticism and a Proposal (1920)*, in C. Benson, *The Economics of Public Education* (Boston, Houghton Mifflin, 1961), p. 218.

[34] Brown v. Board of Education, 347 U.S. 483, 493 (1954).

in this country, dating at least to the Northwest Ordinance of 1787, which provided that "schools and the means of education shall forever be encouraged";[35] it has so typically been regarded a vital public service as to be compulsory throughout the nation; it may have a direct impact on the effectiveness of participation in a political system which makes priority choices among *other* public services for the future; it is more feasible that courts will order measures designed to equalize educational opportunity than that they will respond to demands for, say, an income equalization subsidy.

Education is thought to be most crucial to the poor because, as the American dream would have it, education can operate as a social equalizer.[36] Success in education, the assumption continues, is the traditional and most readily accessible route for the underclass to break free of the culture and condition of poverty, to take a place in the broad middle class of the society. If this view is accepted, failure in education becomes a personal tragedy. "Much as disadvantaged children may try to hide their knowledge, they recognize full well that failure in education is terribly final and for them spells the end of the American dream of progress through education."[37]

Recent research forces qualification of certain critical premises of this view. The poor have typically been unable to utilize the schools as social equalizers. As a class, they have suffered the worst schooling, by whatever rational standard is employed. Extensive sociological surveys of public schools reveal a disturbingly consistent pattern: poor children go to the most outmoded schools with the least motivated fellow classmates; they use the shabbiest facilities and are taught by the least capable teachers; they do the worst and may be looked upon by the system as capable of doing no better.[38] As a member of the Boston School Committee indelicately stated: "We have no inferior education in our schools. What we have been getting is an inferior type of student."[39] Furthermore, the number of years that a child spends in school may well be irrelevant to success in the society, measured in terms of income. "It is *not* the number of years spent in school that con-

[35] Ordinance of 1787, §14, Art. 3.

[36] See, for example, p. 81 of the preceding article by Alan Wilson on "Social Class and Equal Educational Opportunity."

[37] D. Hunter, *The Slums* (New York: Free Press, Macmillan, 1964), p. 109.

[38] See generally United States Commission on Civil Rights, *Racial Isolation in the Public Schools* (Washington, D.C.: U.S. Government Printing Office, 1967), chap. 3 (Hereafter cited as *Racial Isolation*); J. Coleman, *et al.*, *Equality of Educational Opportunity*, U.S. Dept. of Health, Education and Welfare (Washington, D.C.: U.S. Government Printing Office, 1966), chap. 3 (Hereafter cited as *E. O. Survey*); P. Sexton, *Education and Income* (New York: Viking, 1961).

[39] J. Kozol, *Death at an Early Age* (Boston: Houghton Mifflin, 1967), p. 60.

tribute to earnings—rather it is *what he has learned in school* . . . if one merely spends additional years in school without learning much, then subsequent earnings will not be affected."[40]

In short, the society values education highly, both for its importance to the individual and its importance to the society itself. Yet society has acted in a way that particularly disadvantages the poor, by providing them with measurably less than an equal education. In *Griffin v. Prince Edward County,* the Supreme Court hints that the fundamental importance of public education may render such treatment unconstitutional.[41]

Griffin v. Prince Edward County overturned the decision of one Virginia county, acting pursuant to state statute, to close the county's public schools rather than integrate them, and to make tuition payments to students attending private schools.[42] The Court manifested its impatience with a decade-long history of

---

[40] Hansen, Weisbrod, and Scanlon, "Determinants of Earnings: Does Schooling Really Count?" (Unpublished study, University of Minnesota, 1967).

[41] In the past, courts determined what educational opportunity meant only when faced with a claim that racial classification made the education available to the minority inferior to that offered to the majority. This stress on the adverse impact of racial classification has sound historical and practical roots. From its first Supreme Court examination in the *Slaughterhouse Cases,* 83 U.S. 36 (1873), the Fourteenth Amendment's safeguards have been read to apply with special force to state actions which discriminate against the Negro. The history of state-imposed segregation indicates that, at least in the South, separate—by whatever guise maintained—always meant *un*equal. Slavery gave way to Black Codes shortly after the Civil War; when the South was barred from using these overt caste systems, it turned to segregation, and imposed that regime upon the Negro "to maintain and further 'white supremacy' " (Black, "The Lawfulness of the Segregation Decision," *Yale Law Journal,* LXIX (1959), 426).

Discriminations which adversely affect the Negro raise political and moral questions of crisis dimension. See *Report of the Advisory Commission on Civil Disorders* (New York: Dutton, 1968). The profound social, psychological, and material harm caused by such discrimination requires that courts continue to treat Negroes as a constitutionally favored group. See Black, "Foreward: 'State Action,' Equal Protection, and California's Proposition 14," *Harvard Law Review,* LXXXI (1967), 69. When examining public schools, for example, the impact of state-condoned racial isolation on the Negro merits close judicial scrutiny; in defending such a policy, school boards should be required to show not only that the policy being followed is rational, but that no other alternative is feasible. See Horowitz, "Unseparate but Unequal: The Emerging Fourteenth Amendment Issue in Public School Education," *U.C.L.A. Law Review,* XIII (1965), 1147. The related issue, whether *de facto* segregation is barred absolutely by the Equal Protection Clause, has been much discussed. See, for example, Fiss, "Racial Imbalance in the Public Schools: The Constitutional Concepts," *Harvard Law Review,* LXXVIII (1965), 564; Wright, "Public School Desegregation: Legal Remedies for *De Facto* Segregation," *Western Reserve Law Review,* XVI (1965), 478; Kaplan, "Segregation, Litigation, and the Schools," *Northwestern University Law Review,* LVIII (1963), 157; *Northwestern University Law Review,* LIX (1964), 121; Sedler, "School Segregation in the North and West: Legal Aspects," *St. Louis University Law Journal,* VII (1963), 228.

[42] 337 U.S. 218 (1964). *Accord,* Hall v. St. Helene Parish School Board, 197 F. Supp. 649 (E.D. La. 1961), *aff'd,* 287 F.2d 326 (5th Cir. 1961), *aff'd,* 368 U.S. 515 (1962).

Virginia's resistance to, and evasion of, the 1954 desegregation mandate. The decision, striking down Virginia's statute, appeared to rest on a finding of constitutionally forbidden discriminatory motivation.

Motive presents a slippery judicial test, one traditionally regarded as irrelevant to a consideration of an act's constitutionality: it is difficult to ascertain and susceptible to a range of interpretation.[43] In this case, bad motive is not altogether apparent. Virginia may have had a legitimate end in mind: to maximize local self-control by permitting each locality to choose the type of educational facility it wished to provide.

Such state motivation in perfectly acceptable in a host of other situations, including the licensing of liquor distributors and the operation of public recreation facilities.[44] The fundamental importance of public education compelled a distinction and led the Court to the extraordinary remedy of ordering the county to levy taxes sufficient to reopen the public schools.[45]

In *Griffin*, not all of the county's schoolchildren were injured in any meaningful way by the school closing. Students able to attend private schools, supported by state tuition payments, may have fared as well as their counterparts in other counties. Just as in the criminal process and poll tax cases, it was the poor—especially the Negroes—who were injured. No school served that class of children; the county's action effectively deprived them of any education for five years. Such a consequence, *Griffin* indicates, is not constitutionally permissible. Once the state undertakes to provide education, the right "must be available to all on equal terms."[46] That an ostensibly equal offering operates in fact to injure a particular class is sufficient to condemn the arrangement without any further showing. *Griffin* suggests a vastly expanded role for the courts in considering alleged deprivations of equal educational opportunity.

III

In this country, the concept of educational opportunity has had almost from the beginning a special meaning which implied equality of opportunity. The basic

---

[43] Cf., Fletcher v. Peck, 10 U.S. (6 Cranch) 87 (1810). For a discussion of the relevance of motive in school desegregation cases, see Note, "Racial Imbalance in the Public Schools—Legislative Motive and the Constitution," *Virginia Law Review*, L (1964), 465.

[44] Cf., Tonkins v. City of Greensboro, 162 F. Supp. 579 (M.D.N.C. 1958); Palmer v. Thompson, 36 U.S.L.W. 2158 (9/19/67).

[45] 377 U.S. 218, 232-233 (1964).

[46] Brown v. Board of Education, 347 U.S. 483, 493 (1954).

tenets of that concept included universal free education to a given age; a common curriculum; and a common school (except in the South) for children of diverse backgrounds.[47] The concept made two basic assumptions about equality. "First, it implicitly assumed that the existence of free schools eliminates economic sources of inequality of opportunity . . . A second assumption implied by this concept of equality of opportunity is that opportunity lies in *exposure* to a given curriculum.[48] The school, this notion suggests, is obliged to be available, to make an offering; it is for the child to take advantage of the offering.

That understanding of equality of opportunity is still popularly held, and for almost a century it was tacitly accepted by the courts. Judicial analysis focused on what went into a school, on school facilities. The state's duty to provide equal educational opportunity was deemed satisfied if it provided the same caliber of facilities—schools, texts, equipment, teachers—in all schools. Equality did not necessarily mean one and the same; separate facilities could be provided for a class or race of children, as long as they were "separate but equal."[49]

The "equal facilities" standard had the apparent virtue of ease of judicial administration. A mechanical test of absolute equality developed: if School A, invariably the white school, provided a particular facility, then School B, the Negro school, had to do likewise.[50] Sixty years of overseeing the "separte but equal" doctrine proved it to be ultimately unworkable, for two very different reasons.

First, the separate schools for whites and Negroes maintained by law in most Southern states were by no means equal even in their most obvious and measurable characteristics. Per pupil expenditure for Negro students was forty to seventy percent of per pupil expenditure for white students in the Deep South; teacher accreditation requirements were different; facilities were of unequal quality; even the length of the school year varied between the white and Negro schools in a given district.[51]

Second, the Supreme Court came gradually to realize that equality was not fairly measured by examining facilities alone. Subtler factors, including the prestige

---

[47] The historical analysis is drawn from p. 9 of the Coleman article.
[48] *Ibid.*
[49] Plessy v. Ferguson, 163 U.S. 37 (1896).
[50] See, for example, Constantine v. Southwest Louisiana Institute, 120 F. Supp. 412 (D.C. La. 1954); Carter v. School Board, 182 F.2d 531 (4th Cir. 1950); Wilson v. Board of Supervisors, 92 F. Supp. 986 (E.D. La. 1950), *aff'd* 341 U.S. 909 (1950); McCreary v. Byrd, 195 Md. 131, 73 A.2d 8 (1950).
[51] Kaplan, "Segregation Litigation and the Schools—Part II: The General Northern Problem," *Northwestern University Law Review*, LVIII (1963), 162-164.

David L. Kirp

of the institution, the composition of the student body, and the impact on those served by the school had to be taken into account in ascertaining whether attendance at School B really did assure equal educational opportunity.[52]

In *Brown v. Board of Education,* the Supreme Court rejected the "separate but equal" doctrine, and held segregated education unconstitutional.[53] Interpretations of the basis of the decision and its effect on the meaning of equal educational opportunity vary. *Brown* may be read as asserting that the use of race as a standard for determining who goes to what school violates the Fourteenth Amendment. Another reading of *Brown* sees the Court's decision as broadening the concept of equal facilities to include integration as one of those "facilities."[54] A third reading regards *Brown* as asserting that equality of educational opportunity depends not on facilities, but upon the effects of schooling, and that the harmful effects of state-imposed segregation on Negro schoolchildren's performance render that segregation unconstitutional.[55]

Efforts to extend *Brown* through judicial decision to schools in the North and West have generally fastened upon the first reading suggested, and on this ground they have sought to compel racial integration. These cases have not pressed for equalization of facilities even though the constitutional requirement of equal facilities would seem to survive *Brown*.[56] This relative lack of interest in equalizing facilities does not imply that inequalities no longer exist. On the contrary, differences in such readily measurable factors as per pupil expenditures within and among school districts remain substantial. "Nationally, Negro pupils have fewer of some of the facilities that seem most related to academic achievement. They have less access to physics, chemistry, and language laboratories; there are fewer books per pupil in their libraries; their textbooks are less often in sufficient supply . . . . So too they have less access to curricular and extracurricular programs that would seem to have such a relationship."[57]

---

[52] Sweatt v. Painter, 339 U.S. 629 (1950); McLaurin v. Oklahoma State Regents, 339 U.S. 637 (1950).

[53] 347 U.S. 483 (1954).

[54] D. Cohen, "Jurists and Educators in Urban Schools: The Wright Decision and the Passow Report," *The Record* (Forthcoming).

[55] See pp. 18-24 of the Coleman article.

[56] Rousselot, "Achieving Equal Educational Opportunity for Negroes in the Public Schools of the North and West: The Emerging Role for Private Constitutional Litigation," *George Washington Law Review,* XXXV (1967), 714. If, however, facilities bear little relation to the outcomes of education, differences in facilities may be overlooked by the courts if other and more significant tests of equality are met.

[57] *E.O. Survey,* p. 12. See also Burkhead, Fox, and Holland, *Input and Output in Large City High Schools* (Syracuse, New York: Syracuse University Press, 1967).

Several considerations account for the apparent lack of interest in pressing for equal facilities. First, the cost of such an equalization would be immense; at the time of *Brown* the nationwide estimate was two *billion* dollars, and the price tag has doubtless gone up since.[58] Second, it seems both practical and proper to assume that if Negro plaintiffs succeed in their stated objective of compelling more than token integration, the problem of resource equalization will resolve itself. When Negroes become a visible part of the public school constituency, with needs inseparable from those of the white children, the needs of both will be satisfied to the best of the school board's ability. Third, and most important, recent extensive studies, including *Equality of Educational Opportunity* (commonly referred to as the Coleman Report) and *Racial Isolation in the Public Schools,* indicate that equalizing facilities may not significantly improve the education of poor children, white and black, if those children are compelled to go to school in social isolation.

It appears that variations in the facilities and curricula of the schools account for relatively little variation in pupil achievement insofar as this is measured by standard tests . . . The quality of teachers shows a stronger relationship to pupil achievement . . . . *a pupil's achievement is strongly related to the educational backgrounds and aspirations of the other students in the school* . . . . Children from a given family background, when put in schools of different social composition, will achieve at quite different levels . . . . The principal way in which the school environments of Negroes and whites differ is in the composition of their student bodies, and it turns out that the composition of the student bodies has a strong relationship to the achievement of Negro and other minority pupils.[59]

The Coleman Report suggests that if equality of opportunity is to be defined by "those elements that are effective for learning,"[60] the Court's focus should not be primarily on school *facilities,* but rather on the equalization of *human* resources,[61] for these resources most critically determine the fate of the individual schoolchild. The Report indicates further that, although racial composition has some effect on school achievement, social class composition has the most significant effect, and is an essential measure of equality of human resources.

[58] See Estimate of the U.S. Office of Education as reported in Supplemental Brief for United States on Reargument, October Term, 1953, *Brown v. Board of Education,* 347 U.S. 483 (1954). A recent estimate places the cost of adequate compensatory education at "between $100 and $160 billion in the first ten years of such an effort," not substantially different "in the order of magnitude of the costs involved for school desegregation." See p. 112 of the preceding article by David Cohen, "Policy for the Public Schools: Compensation and Integration."

[59] *E.O. Survey,* p.22 (Emphasis added.)

[60] Coleman, p. 20.

[61] The second reading of *Brown* suggested at Note 54, above.

David L. Kirp

The higher achievement of all racial and ethnic groups in schools with greater proportions of white students is largely, perhaps wholly, related to effects associated with the student body's educational background and aspirations. This means that *the apparent beneficial effect of a student body with a high proportion of white students comes not from racial composition per se, but from the better educational background and higher educational aspirations that are, on the average, found among white students.* The effects of the student body environment upon a student's achievement appear to lie in the educational proficiency possessed by that student body, whatever its racial or ethnic composition.[62]

A subsequent study of schools in Richmond, California, confirms these findings:

Allowing for variation in primary-grade mental maturity, *the social-class composition of the primary school has the largest independent effect upon sixth grade reading level.* Among students who attended schools with similar social class backgrounds, neither the racial composition of the school nor the characteristics of the neighborhood made any difference . . . . The achievement of white students who attended predominantly white elementary schools has been strongly affected by the social class composition of the school. *But the degree of racial integration of a school has no effect upon the achievement of white students who attended modally middle-class schools.*[63]

This modification of the underpinnings of *Brown* is heartening, politically significant, and of importance to the judicial analysis. It heartens because it reveals that what will most benefit poor Negro children is not the opportunity to go to school with poor white children (matching "dumb black kids with dumb white kids," as one Negro leader succinctly put it) but the opportunity to attend school with children who are better off—financially, socialy, culturally—than they are. (The needs of poor white children, it should be pointed out, are much the same.) It is politically significant, because to require the mixing of rich and poor, or underachievers and achievers, whatever their race may be, sounds more palatable than busing Negro children into white schools. In those areas where a large number of poor whites live, the results of a Coleman Report-inspired decision will differ significantly from the results of a *Brown*-inspired decision.

[62] *E.O. Survey*, p. 310. (Emphasis added.)
[63] Wilson, "Educational Consequences of Segregation in a California Community," in *Racial Isolation* (Appendices) (1967), pp. 180, 183 (Hereafter cited as Wilson, "Educational Consequences"). (Emphasis added.) See also P. Sexton, *Education and Income.* Wilson does credit racial composition with some effect on school achievement. He points out that "while race, along with social class has a differentiating effect upon pre-school development, it has no continuing additive effect during the elementary school years. . . . it has a large renewed effect when students enter junior high school" (Wilson, "Educational Consequences," p. 182).

Most important, these findings confront the courts with the need to articulate in terms more precise than those used in *Brown* what equal educational opportunity requires. Coleman himself suggests five possible different measures: (1) facilities—school plant, per pupil expenditure, quality of teachers; (2) racial composition of the school; (3) intangible factors—morale, prestige, expectations in the school; (4) consequences of the school for individuals with equal backgrounds and abilities; (5) consequences of the school for individuals with unequal backgrounds and abilities.[64] Quite obviously, the different measures of equality stemming from the Coleman Report and *Brown* make different demands on the school system.

Equalization of the first three measures is the least that any court can demand, after *Brown*.[65] These may well represent a consensus view of what the schools should be doing. Yet the education studies discussed above reveal that these measures are inadequate if *effective* equal opportunity is sought. Measures (4) and (5) imply an *outcomes*-test of equality, and not an equal *facilities* test.[66] Measure (5) places a further burden on the school; in effect, it calls upon the school to create achievement, overcoming the effects of the external environment on its students. "The schools are successful only insofar as they reduce the dependence of a child's opportunities upon his social origins. . . . *Thus, equality of educational opportunity implies, not merely 'equal' schools, but equally effective schools,* whose influences will overcome the differences in starting point of children from different social groups."[67]

Measures (4) and (5) define equality of opportunity as an end toward which schools should be aiming; just as in the criminal process and suffrage cases, no clear and exact standard can be asserted:

In this perspective, complete equality of opportunity can be reached only if all the divergent out-of-school influences vanish, a condition that would arise only in the event of boarding schools; given the existing divergent influences, equality of opportunity can only be approached and never fully reached. The concept becomes one of degree of proximity to equality of opportunity. This proximity is determined, then, not merely by the *equality* of educational inputs, but by the *intensity* of the school's influences relative to the external divergent influences. That is, equality of output is not so much determined by equality of resource inputs, but by the power of those resources in bringing about achievement.[68]

[64] Coleman, pp. 18-19.
[65] Cf., Note 52 above.
[66] The third reading of *Brown* suggested at Note 55, above.
[67] Coleman, "Equal Schools or Equal Students?" *The Public Interest* (Summer, 1966) p. 72.
[68] Coleman, pp. 23-24.

To focus on "effective" equal opportunity does not of course imply that everyone has a "constitutional right" to perform at the same scholastic level, or to earn an equal share of *A* grades and teachers' commendations, or to be admitted to Harvard. Students are not all equally intelligent; they vary in aptitude and ability.[69] Stressing the effectiveness of equal educational opportunity does however suggest that the school is obliged to exert its energies in overcoming initial differences that stem from variations in background, in home life (or lack of home life) and community.

In the past, schools have not been required to bring about achievement; they have long been thought of as "relatively passive...expected to provide a set of free public resources."[70] Yet when discussing other fundamental rights, criminal process and suffrage, the Court has recognized that the state does not satisfy its constitutional responsibility if it merely takes people as it finds them, setting equal standards of access. The state must assure each citizen effective utilization of the fundamental right, regardless of the disparity of effort that must be made to assure that utilization. This "effective utilization" standard varies with the different rights: the state is obliged to provide effective access to the criminal process; to assure the right to vote; to secure an equal chance for an equal educational outcome.

The word "opportunity" has ordinarily meant in the past that a facility was available, but that it was up to the individual to take advantage of the opportunity. The notion is that of a banquet offered, but the individual must serve himself. Our current concern with "equality of opportunity" seems to be introducing a higher type of morality that says that when soup is being served, those initially equipped with forks [or with no utensil at all] should be provided with spoons.[71]

---

[69] Stodolsky and Lesser suggest that "there may be patterns of attributes (cognitive, personality, motivational, and so forth) which are related in some regular way to ethnic group membership." (S. Stodolsky and G. Lesser, "Learning Patterns in the Disadvantaged," *Harvard Educational Review*, XXXVII (1967), 587).

[70] Coleman, pp. 23-24.

[71] Mosteller, "Design of Experimental, Field or Additional Survey Studies," in *Questions Raised and Excerpts from the Analysis*, Harvard Faculty Seminar on the Coleman Report (Unpublished progress report, 1966-67), p. 4.

In his provocative article, Professor Bowles suggests that even equivalent achievement scores will only begin to approximate equality of opportunity in the society. He suggests a sixth standard: equal economic results of education. See p. 115 of the preceding article, "Towards Equality of Educational Opportunity?"

IV

Almost without exception, lawsuits seeking to apply the rationale of *Brown v. Board of Education* outside the South have challenged the pupil placement policies followed in a school district. The suits have alleged that pupil placement policy has had the effect of isolating Negroes within the public school system; that this isolation has denied to the Negroes an equal educational opportunity; that some remedy, typically school boundary redrawing, was necessary to prevent further inequities. The suits have stressed the fact of separation within the system and have not focused primarily on the wretchedness—the physical disrepair, the less tangible but more significant atmosphere of despair—that prevails in the ghetto schools. In cases of *de jure* segregation, where purposeful school segregation by school authorities has been shown, the challenge to the existing order has invariably been accepted.[72] The judicial reaction has, however, been generally negative where racial separation has been *de facto*, brought about not by provable design but adventitiously, by adherence to an arguably rational policy, most typically the neighborhood school policy.[73]

In at least two cases, alleged inequality of educational opportunity has been successfully employed by parents as a shield, justifying keeping their children out of school. In *Dobbins v. Virginia,* the state court found that "the physical facilities and educational opportunities [of the all-white school] are far superior to those offered at [the all-Negro school, eighteen miles away]"[74] and upheld the parents' decision to keep their children at home. In *In re Skipwith,*[75] an action brought by the New York City Board of Education to compel parents to send their children to school, the New York City Domestic Relations Court ruled that the substantially smaller proportion of licensed teachers in certain ghetto schools

---

[72] See, for example, Taylor v. Board of Education, 195 F. Supp. 231 (S.D.N.Y. 1961), *aff'd* 294 F.2d 36 (2d Cir. 1961), *cert. denied* 368 U.S. 940 (1961); Jackson v. Pasadena City School District, 59 Cal. 2d 876, 382 P.2d 878 (1963).

[73] See, for example, Deal v. Cincinnati, 369 F.2d 55 (6th Cir. 1966), *cert. denied,* 36 U.S.L.W. 3138 (10/10/67); Gilliam v. School Board, 345 F.2d 325 (4th Cir. 1965), *vacated and remanded on other grounds,* 372 U.S. 103 (1965); Downs v. Board of Education, 336 F.2d 988 (10th Cir. 1964), *cert. denied,* 380 U.S. 914 (1965); Bell v. Gary, 324 F.2d 209 (7th Cir. 1963), *cert. denied,* 377 U.S. 924 (1964). But see Barksdale v. Springfield School Committee, 237 F. Supp. 543, (1965), *vacated on other grounds,* 348 F.2d 261 (1st Cir. 1965); Blocker v. Board of Education, 226 F. Supp. 208 (E.D.N.Y. 1962).

[74] 198 Va. 697, 699, 96 S.E.2d 154, 156 (1957).

[75] 14 Misc.2d 325, 180 N.Y.S.2d 852 (Dom. Rel. Ct. 1958).

rendered them inferior to predominantly white schools and upheld the parents' right not to send their children to the assigned ghetto school. While the Court heard educators and psychologists testify to the harmful impact of segregation, the opinion relies almost entirely on a single statistic showing that the school in question had unlicensed teachers filling 43 of 85 positions, a proportion substantially greater than the city-wide average. The Court based its decision on that finding alone; it explicitly rejected the argument that *de facto* segregation is unconstitutional.[76] The board of education's contentions—that it bore no responsibility for voluntary teacher choices; that it could not coerce teacher placement and still compete with neighboring suburban systems for teacher talent—were summarily dismissed.[77]

For a host of reasons, the *Skipwith* technique of asserting a denial of equal educational opportunity is unsatisfactory. First, it encourages parental action fundamentally inconsistent with the educational goals sought; keeping a child home may have dramatic impact, but it diminishes the child's chances for *some* kind of an education.[78] Second, the approach leaves to the Domestic Relations Court, whose competence is usually thought to be more limited, the necessity of making decisions which will have city-wide impact. Some more appropriate tribunal should be sought out. Third, it requires costly and wasteful relitigation of the same questions; the board of education, which brings the suit, can presumably limit any action to a single school, if not to a single child. Fourth, to keep a child home from school is a dubious sanction for the school system, which could conceivably decide not to force the child to return to school, thus evading any judicial confrontation.

The major objection to the *Skipwith* technique is that it bases a decision of potentially far-reaching impact on a showing of inequality of a single measure of a single resource. That measure might well not be a meaningful one. The board of education might have argued (but for obvious reasons did not argue) that unlicensed teachers tend to be better teachers because they are younger, more responsive, less given to a hardening of the categories. The board of education might also have shown that it was compensating for the teacher disparities by other expenditures for, say, compensatory educational programs or computer-aided in-

[76] *Ibid.* at 336, 180 N.Y.S.2d at 864.
[77] *Ibid.* at 344, 180 N.Y.S.2d at 871.
[78] "For those children whose family and neighborhood are educationally disadvantaged, it is important to replace this family environment as much as possible with an educational environment —by starting school at an earlier age, and by having a school which begins very early in the day and ends very late" (Coleman, "Equal Schools or Equal Students?," p. 74).

struction. The single factor approach of *Skipwith* appears to foreclose this option, and with it flexible educational planning.

Hobson v. Hansen[79] represents a very different approach to equal educational opportunity litigation. In an exhaustive opinion[80] touching on numerous practices and policies of the Washington, D.C. school system, the District Court upheld the claim of the Negro and poor white plaintiffs to a wide variety of remedies. These remedies include revisions in pupil and teacher assignment practices; changes in the current building program; abolition of the existing tracking system, a technique for grouping students according to a tested measure of their ability; requiring compensatory education "at least to overcome the detriment of segregation and thus provide, as nearly as possible, equal educational opportunity to all school-children." The Court also ordered the school system to undertake metropolitan planning, in hopes of inducing cooperation from the neighboring Maryland and Virginia suburbs.[81]

While the fact that segregation had been mandated by law in the District prior to 1954[82] makes the Court more willing to apply broad remedies,[83] reliance on the prior *de jure* segregation as justification for the new opinion is expressly disclaimed. The Court is willing to hunt out inequalities of opportunity even where a showing of rational school policy-making can be offered.[84] While the Court shows greater caution in mandating remedies to overcome the adverse effects of *de facto* segregation,[85] the rationale of the opinion is not limited to instances of *de jure* segregation.

Skipwith stresses a single factor (the proportion of permanently licensed teachers) in a single school. *Hobson* painstakingly examines those several aspects of the school system that seem significant, either because the factor has traditionally warranted judicial attention, or because it is deemed to have an impact on the effectiveness of the education offered. These factors include racial and social class imbalance among students and professionals in the schools, and the system's efforts to deal with that imbalance; equality of facilities; differences in per pupil expenditure within the system; the relative quality of the faculty in the predomi-

[79] 269 F. Supp. 401 (D.C.D.C. 1967) (hereafter cited as *Hobson*).
[80] The findings of fact and opinion of law occupy 118 pages in the reporter.
[81] *Hobson* 514-518.
[82] Bolling v. Sharpe, 347 U.S. 497 (1954).
[83] Cf., U.S. v. Jefferson County Board of Education, 372 F.2d 836 (5th Cir. 1966), *aff'd en banc*, 380 F.2d 385 (1967).
[84] *Hobson* 503-511.
[85] *Ibid.*, 515.

nantly white and predominantly Negro schools (quality being measured by the amount of advanced education and numbers of temporary teachers, for example); quality and adequacy of the curricula offered; the impact of the tracking system. In its fact findings, the Court borrows heavily both from the traditional "equal facilities" analysis and from the Coleman Report's stress on the importance of human resources.[86]

The Court finds a common thread running through both sets of factors: children in the poor and Negro schools fare less well in all respects than do their neighbors in the middle class and white schools. The one hundred dollar per pupil expenditure difference between students in the predominantly Negro schools and students in the predominantly white schools accurately reflects a difference in the quality of resources available, and in the results attained.[87]

Equally noteworthy is the recognition in *Hobson* that the right of Negroes *and the poor* to a decent education merits special judicial attention. The Court is clear that the disgruntled suburbanites' claim of unequal treatment could more easily be dismissed than could the claim of the Negro or the poor. The Court also asserts that the government has a greater constitutional obligation when public schools, and not some other public facility, are under scrutiny.

If the situation were one involving racial imbalance but in some facility other than the public schools, or unequal educational opportunity but without any Negro or poverty aspects . . . it might be pardonable to uphold the practice on a minimal showing of rational basis. But the fusion of these two elements in *de facto* segregation in public schools irresistibly calls for additional justification. What supports this call is our horror at inflicting any further injury on the Negro, the degree to which the poor and the Negro must rely on the public schools in rescuing themselves from their depressed cultural and economic condition, and also our common need for the schools to serve as the public agency for neutralizing and normalizing race relations in this country.[88]

The Court recognizes only with some hesitancy the right of the poor to make a claim traditionally made by Negroes. Note the difference between passages (1) and (2):

---

[86] The Court finds as fact:
1. Racially and socially homogeneous schools damage the mind and spirit of all children who attend them—the Negro, the white, the poor and the affluent. . . . whether the segregation occurs by law or by fact.
2. The scholastic achievement of the disadvantaged child, Negro and white, is strongly related to the racial and socioeconomic composition of the student body of the school (*Hobson* 406).
[87] *Ibid.*, 437.
[88] *Ibid.*, 508.

(1) Theoretically, therefore, purely irrational inequalities even between two schools in a culturally homogeneous, uniformly white suburb would raise a real constitutional question. But in cases not involving *Negroes or the poor*, courts will hesitate to enforce the separate but equal rule rigorously.[89]

(2) But the law is too deeply committed to the real, not merely theoretical (and present, not deferred) equality of the *Negro's* educational experience to compromise its diligence when cases raise the rights of *the Negro poor*.[90]

In Washington, D.C., the *Hobson* setting, the passages are reconcilable. The Court is not called upon to distinguish the demands of the poor from the demands of the Negro; in Washington, the poor are almost entirely Negro. In such a situation, "effective *social class* integration requires racial integration."[91] The opinion's references to the special problems of the poor may be read as an effort to propose broader judicial policy.

When the rights of a disadvantaged minority, however defined, are adversely affected, *Hobson* places on the school system the duty of justifying its policies, showing that the justification outweighs the harm. "Given the high standards which pertain when racial minorities and the poor are denied equal educational opportunity ... justification must be in terms not of excusing reasons of this stripe but of positive social interests protected or advanced."[92] Placing such a burden on the school system characterizes the new equal protection analysis.

Public school boards must provide equal educational opportunity for all students. Neither administrative convenience, desire to expend funds for other purposes, limited demand, higher costs, nor similar considerations would necessarily make consequent inequalities in educational services the product of constitutionally permissible classifications. In each case, assuming a 'rational basis' for a specific inequality [the usual equal protection test] were shown, the controlling issue would be whether the school board can demonstrate that there are not other 'rationally based' means of carrying out its programs which would have less adverse impact on the children who are provided the lower quality educational services.[93]

The *Hobson* opinion expresses dismay at the familiar story of the adverse effect of racial and class isolation;[94] among the remedies it ordered are meas-

---

[89] *Ibid.*, 497. (Emphasis added.)

[90] *Ibid.*, 497. (Emphasis added.)

[91] Schwartz, Pettigrew, and Smith, "Is Desegregation Impractical?," *The New Republic* (Jan. 6, 1968), p. 27.

[92] *Hobson* 498.

[93] Horowitz, "Unseparate but Unequal," p. 1165.

[94] *Hobson* 498.

ures designed to undo the effects of segregation. In Washington, D.C., however, a court order limited in scope to integrating the city's schools would be most unsatisfactory. At the time of the trial, the city's school system was 90.2 percent Negro, and the percentage of Negro students was increasing.[95]

In Washington, D.C., constitutional theory (segregation is unlawful) and educational theory (the indigent schoolchild's chances are most significantly improved by placing him in a school where most of the students are from a higher social class) confronted and were stymied by a political boundary as fixed as a wall. No tinkering with school district boundaries *within* the city could produce meaningful class or racial integration. The Court sought to overcome this special handicap by ordering the diversity of remedies already recited, thus operating within the bounds of the feasible. There is little discussion of the nature of the equality that the decision secures; the Court recognizes that no single feasible remedy could yield "equality," and that intervention at many points is in order.

The Court's dilemma is apparent in the findings of an extensive survey of the District's schools commissioned by the system.[96] The survey expresses the belief that "the fundamental task of the District Schools is the same as that for every other American school system: to provide for every child, whatever his race, education of a quality that will enable him to make the most of himself and to take his place as a free person in an open society."[97] While it urges that each child "have the help he needs to reach maturity prepared to compete on fair terms in an open society," and that "the schools must furnish unequal education . . . to provide equal opportunity,"[98] the study also asserts, realistically, that "it would be absurd to deny or ignore the special problems that a racially isolated school faces in preparing its pupils for life in an open society."[99] Racial isolation cannot be overcome by exhortations, or by judicial hand-wringing. The pattern will not be altered "until enough Marylanders, Virginians, Washingtonians, and Americans are convinced that their interests will be better served by making the national capital area a well-integrated metropolitan community than by keeping it the white-encircled black ghetto that it is now."[100]

[95] *Ibid.*, 410.
[96] H. Passow, *et al.*, *A Study of the Washington, D.C., Public Schools* (New York: 1967). (Mimeographed.)
[97] *Ibid.*, p. 18.
[98] *Ibid.*, p. 191.
[99] *Ibid.*, p. 185.
[100] *Ibid.*, p. 186. The Passow Report does find one saving feature in the social composition of the District. It notes that "the presence of many Negro middle-class families of superior educational background offers opportunities available in few if any other large cities" (Passow, "Washington, D.C., Public Schools," p. 190).

For the present, Washington, D. C., is an atypical case: a city lacking the mix of human resources that the Coleman study suggests is crucial to effective educational opportunity. In other jurisdictions, courts have ordered redistricting of existing school districts, and careful planning of new school districts, to assure a somewhat greater social mix in the schools.[101] These measures, however, only begin to remove the inequalities.

Suits against a muncipality can have only limited success, if the end sought is *effective* equalization of opportunity. The city may be compelled to reshuffle its internal priorities—to build new schools in places it had not intended to; to assign teachers and students to schools it had not planned to—but the jurisdiction of the city administration, and of the court reviewing the actions of that administration, stops at the municipal boundary. Only a mapmaker's line separates Great Neck, Long Island, from New York City; Brookline from Boston. But the parent in Poor City who chooses to sue the school administrator is restricted to the administrator of his municipality. He has no legal basis for complaining that the administrator in the neighboring suburb of Richville is spending too much money on Richville's students. The Poor City parent pays no taxes in Richville; he casts no vote in the elections in which Richville chooses its school board. While he can appeal to Richville to accept its just share of the social burden of Poor City's downtrodden, he can expect to encounter the same unresponsive attitude that the Maryland and Virginia suburbs display to Washington, D.C.[102] Should the Richville School Board be so rash as to think that it had a moral obligation to salvage Poor City's children, a taxpayer of Richville might be able to go to court and prevent Richville from making a "gift" of its public assets.

[101] Barksdale v. Springfield School Committee, 237 F. Supp. 543 (1965), *vacated on other grounds*, 348 F.2d 261 (1st Cir. 1965); Blocker v. Board of Education, 226 F. Supp. 208 (E.D.N.Y. 1964).

[102] In a few cities—Boston, Hartford, Rochester—programs which bus poor children (usually Negro children) out of the city's slums to suburban schools have been initiated. These programs, however, invoke only a minute percentage of the Poor City schoolchildren; the suburbs have been willing to make only that token effort which does not "dilute" the quality of a suburban education. In Rochester . . . those being bused to the suburbs number only 220, out of a total Negro grade school population in Rochester that is close to 10,000. The children being bused have been carefully chosen for good past performance and high future potential. Even so, the majority of Rochester's suburbs are now resisting a plan to bus out a few beggarly hundreds of additional children . . . And in Hartford, Boston, and all other cases known to me of center-city-suburban busing, it is again the same story of a few hundreds, usually specially selected, out of the many thousands of children who constitute the true problem (Alsop, "Ghetto Education," *The New Republic* (Nov. 18, 1967) p. 20).

One possible, much-discussed approach to city-suburban cooperation is the creation of educational parks. Each park would include several schools, primary and/or secondary, offering a wider range of facilities and courses than any single school could offer. The park would draw on a metropolitan area student body. See *Racial Isolation*, pp. 167-183.

David L. Kirp

The usual judicial action brought by parents against Poor City or Poorville, seeking congeries of remedies called equal educational opportunity, will at best result in a more equal dispersal of insufficient resources. This "equal but insufficient" resolution is unlikely to appease the citizens of Poor City who began the action, nor will it greatly benefit their children.[103]

The state, and not the municipality, has the capacity to provide meaningful relief for inequalities of educational opportunity, and thus is the more logical governmental unit to turn to for relief. Constitutional and statutory provisions, judicial decisions, and long-standing custom all bear witness to the state's responsibility for public education. "Education is not a subject pertaining alone, or pertaining essentially, to a municipal corporation. Whilst public education in this country is now deemed a public duty in every State. . . . it has never been looked upon as being at all a matter of local concern only. . . . In this State, the subject of public education has always been regarded and treated as a matter of State concern."[104]

The state may, under a constitutional home rule provision, be free to delegate certain powers to its subdivisions. It cannot, however, free itself of the underlying responsibility for the success of the educational enterprise by "pointing to the distribution of power between itself and its subdivisions—a distribution which the state itself has created."[105] In *Reynolds v. Sims,* the Supreme Court rejected a justification for state apportionment based on factors other than population that likened political subdivisions within the state to states within the Union. "Political subdivisions of States—counties, cities, or whatever—never were and never have been considered as sovereign entities. Rather, they have been traditionally regarded as subordinate governmental instrumentalities created by

---

[103] The point has been made with reference to Boston's public schools:
There must be change. There must be change in school districts and academic practice. There must be change everywhere in this historic and now decaying system. But almost all the changes discussed are fragmentary, or symbolic or, in some instances, self-defeating. It is hard to reform a system in which most of the staff, most of the electorate, and much of tradition are against you. It is hard to revolutionize an ancient city, hard even to know what you want ideally to achieve (P. Schrag, *Village School Downtown* [Boston: Beacon, 1967], p. 131).

[104] City of Louisville v. Commonwealth, 134 Ky. 488, 492, 493; 121 S.W. 411, 412 (1909).
"Every state has included provisions for free public education in its constitution and general statutes" (*Racial Isolation,* p. 260). For representative cases, see People *ex rel.* Nelson v. Jackson Highland Building Corp., 400 Ill. 533, 81 N.E.2d 528 (1948); Malone v. Hayden, 329 Pa. 213, 197 Atl. 344 (1938); Grant v. Michaels, 94 Mont. 452, 23 P.2d 266 (1933); Piper v. Big Pine School Dist., 193 Cal. 664, 226 Pac. 926 (1924).

[105] *Racial Isolation,* p. 261.

the State to assist in the carrying out of State governmental functions."[106] As Judge Wisdom declared, in striking down a local option statute which permitted a parish (the county unit) to close its public schools:

The equal protection clause speaks to the state. The United States Constitution recognizes no governing unit except the federal government and the state. A contrary position would allow a state to evade its constitutional responsibility by carve-outs of small units. At least in the area of constitutional rights, and *specifically with respect to education, the state can no more delegate a power to discriminate than it can itself directly establish inequalities.* When a parish wants to lock its school doors, the state must turn the key. If the rule were otherwise, the great guarantee of the equal protection clause would be meaningless.[107]

No single remedy will be equally appropriate for each of the many actions that might be brought against the state which has failed to provide the equal educational opportunity sought by Poor City and Poorville parents for their children. No single measure of equal opportunity can be insisted upon. "The constitutional command for a state to afford 'equal protection of the laws' sets a goal not attainable by the invention and application of a precise formula."[108] It is appropriate, however, in evaluating the possible remedies that might be sought, to consider how each would bear on *effective* equality; in other words, how useful each would be. The most likely potential remedies—an adjustment of school district boundaries and a reallocation of state financial support—will be taken up in turn.

By enlarging school districts, the state (or its creation the school board) could diversify the social class make-up of its public schools. Such a remedy, the Coleman Report implies, would do most to better the chances of the poor, presently locked into predominantly lower class schools. Conceivably, a Poor City parent (or the Poor City school board) could seek to have the state redraw the boundaries of its school districts by creating larger districts with more equal tax bases. Such a solution would alleviate the fiscal inequality between districts; more importantly it would alleviate the inequality of human resources between districts,

[106] 377 U.S. 533, 575 (1964).
[107] Hall v. St. Helene Parish School Board, 197 F. Supp. 649, 658 (1961).
[108] Kotch v. River Port Pilot Comm'rs., 330 U.S. 532, 556 (1947).
In assessing potential remedies, this essay does not consider the role—present and potential— of the federal government in supporting public education. That omission is due not to any lack of appreciation for what the federal government could accomplish, but rather to the determination, in limiting the scope of the paper, to focus on the state, presently the largest single source of funds for schools (forty per cent). National Education Association, *Estimates of School Statistics* (Washington: 1966).

by creating economically and socially diverse districts and enabling the Poor City schoolchildren to go to school in a heterogeneous environment.[109]

A requirement that the state take affirmative action to alleviate natural and inevitable differences (or so the state will argue) raises novel constitutional problems. Where the state's redrawing of political boundaries has resulted in discriminatory treatment of an indentifiable group, the Court has ordered the state to resurrect the former boundaries.[110] But the theory of the "equal opportunity" suit rests on a long-standing discrimination, not a newly created one; conceivably the Court might be more hesitant to upset established practice than to reject a discriminatory innovation.

The reapportionment cases provide a most tempting analogy. In the reapportionment cases, as in the hypothetical Poorville redistricting suit, affirmative relief—in both cases, the redrawing of a political boundary—is sought. Those cases like the "equal opportunity" case involve "civil rights," rights that the Court is particularly solicitous of. The reapportionment cases required redistricting so that "as nearly as is practicable one man's vote in a Congressional election is to be worth as much as another's;"[111] in the hypothetical action, a rough measure of equal outcomes would probably be the standard sought.

Yet the two instances are not identical. The reapportionment cases compelled redistricting because no other remedy could overcome the effect of disparities between districts or could overturn the rural dominance of the state legislature. In education, the availability of other, more traditional remedies, notably, increased financial support, may make the Court reluctant to insist upon school redistricting.

The Court concluded, in deciding the reapportionment cases, that the equal protection clause required apportionment of state and congressional voting districts on a population basis. That reading of equal protection was not the only way that equality could be understood.

In *Reynolds v. Sims,* for example, Mr. Justice Warren declared that "the right to vote" was "diluted," "debased," and "impaired" by unequal apportionment. But as Mr. Justice Frankfurter suggested in his dissent in *Baker v. Carr,* such a view assumes its conclusion: "one cannot speak of 'debasement' or 'dilution' of a value of the vote until there is first

[109] Professor Benson states that school districts should be no smaller than 250,000 if they are to provide adequate school services. C. Benson, *The Cheerful Prospect* (Boston: Houghton Mifflin, 1965) p. 45.

[110] Gomillion v. Lightfoot, 364 U.S. 339 (1960); cf., Wright v. Rockefeller, 376 U.S. 52 (1964).

[111] Wesbery v. Sanders, 376 U.S. 1, 7-8 (1964); *accord.* Schaefer v. Thomson, 240 F. Supp. 247 (D. Wyo. 1964).

defined a standard of reference as to what a vote should be worth. What is actually asked of the Court . . . is to choose among competing bases of representation—ultimately, really, among competing themes of political philosophy . . .[112]

The "political philosophy" that the Court chose to adopt views equal protection as requiring an equally effective vote: "Full and effective participation by all citizens in state government requires . . . that each citizen have an equally effective voice in the election of members of the state legislature."[113] The *equally effective* standard is also the theoretical underpinning of the hypothetical school redistricting action. Only if Poor City's schoolchildren can break free of their environment, will they have an equal chance to compete effectively—and to succeed in the competition. The importance of the right involved, and the necessity of the remedy sought, may well make a school redistricting order palatable to the courts. When political lines rather than school district lines shield the inequality, as shown in the reapportionment cases, courts are not helpless to act. "The political thicket, having been pierced to protect the vote, can likewise be pierced to protect the education of children."[114]

In a pending New York State suit the NAACP is seeking to have the Wyandanch, Long Island school district, a small, poor, almost all-Negro district, dissolved and parcelled out among the several adjacent districts, each of which is larger, richer, and predominantly white.[115] Wyandanch presents a case particularly favorable to the assertion that the creation of larger and more heterogeneous districts is a wise approach: the district is presently too small to be economically efficient;[116] it can be divided among the adjacent districts without overly burdensome impact on any one of those districts. The anticipated judicial resolution of the Wyandanch case should provide the first test of the appropriateness of seeking to redraw school district boundaries in order to remedy existing inequalities.

A challenge to the equity of state aid-to-education formulas is a second way that a Poorville resident could state his claim of unequal educational opportunity. In-

---

[112] Note, "Reapportionment," *Harvard Law Review*, LXXIX (1966), 1242.

[113] Reynolds v. Sims, 377 U.S. 533, 565 (1964).

[114] Wright, "Public School Desegregation," p. 498.

[115] The NAACP sought administrative relief; their claim has been rejected by the New York State Commissioner of Education. A suit in the state supreme court to challenge the Commissioner's ruling is anticipated. *New York Times*, Nov. 16, 1967; July 26, 1968.

[116] A survey of New York State's school districts concludes that "size has a negative effect upon very small districts and upon very large districts" (A.D. Swanson, *The Effect of School District Size Upon School Costs* (State University of New York at Buffalo, 1966), p. 41. See also Benson, *The Cheerful Prospect.*

deed, in rural areas where distances between communities render regional solutions infeasible, an increase in Poorville's share of state school aid may be the only remedy that the state is competent to give.

State grants account at present for approximately 40 percent of the local school district's budget.[117] These grants are meant to serve several purposes: to reduce extreme differences in tax burden among local districts, to afford relief for local taxation, and to stimulate local expenditures.[118] The most widely accepted state aid formula asserts that "equalization" is its primary objective. "There [should] be an adequate minimum offering everywhere, the expense of which should be considered a prior claim on the state's economic resources."[119]

The effect of state school aid has not in fact been to equalize resources or capabilities. Some state aid is offered to all districts, regardless of their need. Even when equalizing grants are included, "states in seven of twelve major metropolitan areas are contributing more per pupil to the suburban schools than to those in the cities. State aid programs designed decades ago to assist the then poorer suburban districts often support the now wealthier suburbs at levels comparable to or higher than the cities."[120] Thus state education grants, designed in part to equalize expenditures, may actually serve to widen the gap that divides rich districts and poor districts.

One conceivable grant reallocation remedy would require that *equal facilities* be available to each school district. Such a remedy would bring about a major reallocation of resources, benefiting financially those districts with a presently inadequate tax base. Yet compelling equalization of facilities seems an over-simple and unsatisfactory resolution of the problem. If a low-level equalization were set, the formula would impose unfortunate limitations on school districts willing to make a more than minimal effort; in all likelihood, no district would be significantly better off. On the other hand, to require that there be available in every school district the facilities provided by the state's richest and most education-conscious district would place an undue burden on the poorer districts and on the state.

[117] Benson, *The Cheerful Prospect*, p. 187.
[118] *Ibid.*, pp. 223-224.
[119] G. Strayer and R. Haig, *Financing of Education in the State of New York* (New York: Macmillan, 1923), p. 173. A. Wise, *Rich Schools, Poor Schools: The Promises of Equal Educational Opportunity*, (Chicago: The University of Chicago Press, 1968) discusses the constitutionality of unequal educational expenditures in greater detail.
[120] *Racial Isolation*, p. 28.

Nor would equalization of facilities serve any recognizable meritorious goal of public education. If equal protection compels *effective* equal opportunity, the Coleman Report indicates that merely equalizing school resources will not do the trick; equal treatment is not a sufficient state effort. "Were we merely to raise the quality of the teaching resources devoted [to Negroes] to the level of that currently devoted to whites, we would significantly improve Negro achievement. Nevertheless, we would reduce the gap in Negro and white verbal achievement at Grade 12 by only a little more than a quarter. . . . Equal school inputs will not produce equal school outputs."[121]

Focusing on effective equalization—an equal chance for equal achievement— stresses the obligation of the state to make a greater financial effort in those school districts whose needs are greater because their schoolchildren are less well-prepared for school. The state has a constitutional obligation to develop schools which will compensate as fully as possible for inequalities of prior training and background. The cost of such an effort, seriously undertaken, will be immense; the result well worth the cost.[122]

The theory of state responsibility for educational opportunity is currently being advanced in several suits, including an action brought by the Detroit School Board against the State of Michigan, which alleges that the state's school aid apportionment formulas unconstitutionally deny Detroit schoolchildren an equal educational opportunity.[123] The basic formulas in the School Aid Act utilize only two variables in apportioning aid: number of pupils and state equalized valuation of property in the school district. The school board asserts that these formulas have resulted in "substantial disparities in the financing of public education, and, therefore, in the quality and extent of availability of educational services and facilities among the several school districts."[124]

The state aid formulas are in no way related to the needs of the different districts; they fail to take into account differences among the districts. The state aid

---

[121] Bowles, p. 121.

[122] The Passow Report estimated the cost of compensatory education at "three or four times the cost of meeting the educational needs of the child whose home environment has already done a good portion of the job even before the child enters school" (Passow, "Washington, D.C., Public Schools," p. 259).

The magnitude of the necessary effort may seem to some to represent an overreliance on schooling as a tool for social amelioration. While a court will not be able to choose among alternative social policies (better schools *or* better housing *or* more jobs, etc.) it may, by denying plaintiff's claim, tacitly express its reluctance to order a major readjustment of fiscal and social priorities.

[123] *New York Times*, Jan. 24, 1968. A similar action has been brought by Chicago parents against the state of Illinois. McInnis *et al.* v. Shapiro, No. 68-C-673 (N.D. Ill. 1968).

[124] Complaint, Board of Education v. Michigan ¶11 (1968).

equation considers neither differences in the quality of facilities presently available, nor differences in the cost of providing the same facilities in different parts of the state, nor the added costs of adequately educating disadvantaged children. The theory of the suit is that even equal expenditures in all districts would not be sufficient; that equally effective education should be the end sought; the burden of financing an adequate public education system should ultimately rest with the state.

V

The ever-increasing involvement of the courts in reviewing administrative decisions concerning educational policy has disturbed some commentators, who point out that judicially-declared constitutional doctrine tends to be relatively inflexible, imposing a uniform standard where such a standard may be plainly inappropriate. Furthermore, it is suggested that removing discriminations against the poor usually requires governmental expenditures; the courts are not equipped to undertake an examination of alternative approaches, to determine how public moneys can best be spent to maximize public benefit. A third concern is that courts will be reluctant to undertake the commitment of judicial energy necessary to oversee the implementation of a judicial decision; failure to supervise this process effectively may reduce the prestige of the courts.[125]

These doubts are not easily put to rest. Judicial success in desegregation cases has not been spectacular. More Negro children are in segregated schools today than fourteen years ago, at the time of *Brown*.[126] The reapportionment cases have been extremely costly in terms of judicial time, and the decisions have on occasion been threatened by congressional counterattacks.[127] Were one somehow free to select the branch of government best suited to resolve the problems of equality of educational opportunity, the judiciary would not be the branch picked. Massive inaction of the other two branches, however, makes the judiciary the instrument of last resort for the assertion of fundamental constitutional rights.

The courts should be aware of their limitations in reaching their decisions, and in framing appropriate decrees. Rigid formulas, such as *Skipwith* imposes, are

---

[125] Fiss, "Racial Imbalance in the Public Schools," pp. 564, 612-617; Note, "Discriminations Against the Poor and the Fourteenth Amendment," pp. 435, 442-443.

[126] *Racial Isolation*, p. 8.

[127] See Note, "Reapportionment," pp. 1228, 1231-1238.

not in order; what is needed is a careful, *Hobson*-type case-by-case determination of the needs, the constitutional requirements, and the practicalities. For all of its massiveness, the Coleman Report does not pretend to offer an answer, or even a set of alternative answers, to our schools' problems. The Report reveals how little is actually understood of the ways that children learn, and how overwhelming is the schools' failure to structure patterns of learning and mastery effectively. Thus, guidelines to govern school policy, patterned after the school desegregation guidelines,[128] cannot and should not be imposed on the public schools. However, proposals intended to make over (and make better) whole school systems, such as the Bundy Report's plan to decentralize the New York City system,[129] should be critically evaluated by the courts in light of the contribution to an understanding of "equal educational opportunity" made by the Coleman Report. It may well be impossible to create school districts which strengthen the "natural communities" of a city,[130] promoting a "sense of community among residents of (school) districts"[131]—the core of the Bundy proposal—and maintain at the same time the heterogeneous school environments that the Coleman Report indicates are the vital determinants of school achievement. In short, community control and social class integration may well be incompatible goals. This incompatibility—and the effect upon schoolchildren's chances for an equally effective education—requires careful assessment before the rush to make major changes in the structure and operation of a school system receives judicial blessing.

Courts cannot and should not attempt the task of running the schools. Should the judiciary intervene unduly in the operation of the schools, the very able people who ought to be finding imaginative ways of making practicable the equal protection standard will be driven from school administration. Yet school administrators cannot be permitted to erect pedagogical expertise as a barrier to *any* judicial action. The very problems that the courts are called upon to resolve result from lack of administrative attention and competence in the face of basic educational demands. If the administrator refuses to countenance any relinquishment of policy-making authority, another, more politically responsive person will succeed him. To achieve a viable working relationship between the courts and the school administrators is yet another reason for suggesting the need for judicial flexibility

---

[128] 45 C.F.R. Part 181.

[129] *Reconnection for Learning*, Report of the Mayor's Advisory Panel on Decentralization of the New York City Schools, 477 Madison Ave., New York, New York (1967) (referred to popularly, and in the text, as the Bundy Report).

[130] *Ibid.*, p. 17.

[131] *Ibid.*, p. 77.

in framing decrees, and for urging that school administrators have a hand in framing those decrees.

At the conclusion of his opinion in *Hobson v. Hansen,* Judge Wright speaks to this problem:

> It is regrettable, of course, that in deciding this case this Court must act in an area so alien to its expertise. It would be far better indeed for these great social and political problems to be resolved in the political arena by other branches of government. But these are social and political problems which seem at times to defy such resolution. In such situations, under our system, the judiciary must bear a hand and accept its responsibility to assist in the solution where constitutional rights hang in the balance.[132]

If the judiciary accepts its responsibility, and acts with imagination and sensitivity, it may be able to show the way to the beginnings of solution, to make good the American promise of an equal chance for all through public education.

[132] *Hobson* 517. See Wright, "Public School Desegregation"; Freund, "Civil Rights and the Limits of Law," *Buffalo Law Review,* XIV (1964), 199.

Alternative Public School Systems*

KENNETH B. CLARK

Metropolitan Applied Research Center

The author asserts that American public education suffers from "pervasive and persistent" inefficiency, particularly in the schools provided for Negro and other underprivileged children. After discussing the obstacles to "effective, nonracially constrained" education, the author proposes a strategy for providing excellent education in ghetto schools in conjunction with efforts to bring about effective school desegregation. Because the present patterns of public school organization are themselves a principal factor in inhibiting efforts to improve the quality of education, it will be necessary, he contends, to find "realistic, aggressive, and viable competitors" to the present public schools. The paper concludes with a discussion of alternatives to existing urban public school systems, including such possibilities as industrial demonstration schools and schools operated by the Department of Defense.

It is now clear that American public education is organized and functions along social and economic class lines. A bi-racial public school system wherein approximately 90 per cent of American children are required to attend segregated schools is one of the clearest manifestations of this basic fact. The difficulties encountered in attempting to desegregate public schools in the South as well as in the North point to the tenacity of the forces seeking to prevent any basic change in the system.

The class and social organization of American public schools is consistently associated with a lower level of educational efficiency in the less privileged schools.

* This article appeared originally in the Winter 1968 issue of the *Harvard Educational Review*. It was first presented as a paper at the National Conference on Equal Educational Opportunity in America's Cities, sponsored by the U.S. Commission on Civil Rights, November 16-18, 1967.

Kenneth B. Clark

This lower efficiency is expressed in terms of the fact that the schools attended by Negro and poor children have less adequate educational facilities than those attended by more privileged children. Teachers tend to resist assignments in Negro and other underprivileged schools and generally function less adequately in these schools. Their morale is generally lower; they are not adequately supervised; they tend to see their students as less capable of learning. The parents of the children in these schools are usually unable to bring about any positive changes in the conditions of these schools.

The pervasive and persistent educational inefficiency which characterizes these schools results in:

(1) marked and cumulative academic retardation in a disproportionately high percentage of these children, beginning in the third or fourth grade and increasing through the eighth grade;

(2) a high percentage of dropouts in the junior and senior high schools of students unequipped academically and occupationally for a constructive role in society;

(3) a pattern of rejection and despair and hopelessness resulting in massive human wastage.

Given these conditions, American public schools have become significant instruments in the blocking of economic mobility and in the intensification of class distinctions rather than fulfilling their historic function of facilitating such mobility. In effect, the public schools have become captives of a middle class who have failed to use them to aid others to move into the middle class. It might even be possible to interpret the role of the controlling middle class as that of using the public schools to block further mobility.

What are the implications of this existing educational inefficiency? In the national interest, it is a serious question whether the United States Government can afford the continuation of the wastage of human resources at this period of world history. Although we cannot conclusively demonstrate a relation between educational inefficiency and other symptoms of personal and social pathology such as crime, delinquency, and pervasive urban decay, there is strong evidence that these are correlates.

Increasing industrialization and automation of our economy will demand larger numbers of skilled and educated and fewer uneducated workers. The manpower needs of contemporary America require business and industry to pay for the added burden of re-educating the mis-educated. This is a double taxation. The burdens of the present inefficient public education include this double taxation in addition to the high cost of crime and family stability and the artificial constriction of the labor and consumer market.

Beyond these material disadvantages are the human costs inherent in the failure to achieve equality of educational opportunity. This dehumanization contributes significantly to the cycle of pathology—poor education, menial jobs or unemployment, family instability, group and personal powerlessness. This passive pathology weakens the fabric of the entire society.

Obstacles to the Attainment of Efficient Education

The obstacles which interfere with the attainment of efficient public education fall into many categories. Among them are those obstacles which reflect historical premises and dogmas about education, administrative realities, and psychological assumptions and prejudices.

The historical premises and dogmas include such fetishes as the inviolability of the "neighborhood school" concept which might include the belief that schools should be economically and racially homogeneous. The administrative barriers involve such problems as those incurred in the transportation of children from residential neighborhoods to other areas of the city. Here again the issue is one of relative advantages of the *status quo* versus the imperatives for change.

The residual psychological prejudices take many forms and probably underlie the apparent inability of society to resolve the historical and administrative problems. Initially the academic retardation of Negro children was explained in terms of their inherent racial inferiority. The existence of segregated schools was supported either by law or explained in terms of the existence of segregated neighborhoods. More recently the racial inferiority or legal and custom interpretations have given way to more subtle explanations and support for continued inefficient education. Examples are theories of "cultural deprivation" and related beliefs that the culturally determined educational inferiority of Negro children will impair the ability of white children to learn if they are taught in the same classes. It is assumed that because of their background, Negro children and their parents are poorly motivated for academic achievement and will not only be unable to compete with white children but will also retard the white children. The implicit and at times explicit assumption of these cultural deprivation theories is that the environmental deficits which Negro children bring with them to school make it difficult, if not impossible, for them to be educated either in racially homogeneous or heterogeneous schools.

This point of view, intentionally or not, tends to support the pervasive rejection of Negro children and obscures and intensifies the basic problem.

There are more flagrant sources of opposition to any effective desegregation of American public schools. White Citizens' Councils in the South, parents' and taxpayers' groups in the North, and the control of boards of education by whites who identify either overtly or covertly with the more vehement opposition to change are examples of effective resistance. School officials and professional educators have defaulted in their responsibility for providing educational leadership. They have tended, for the most part, to go along with the level of community readiness and the "political realities." They have been accessories to the development and use of various subterfuges and devices for giving the appearance of change without its substance and, in doing so, have failed to present the problem of the necessary school reorganization in educational terms. This seems equally true of teachers and teachers' organizations. In some cases, teachers, textbooks, and other teaching materials have either contributed to or failed to counteract racism.

Within the past two years another formidable and insidious barrier in the way of the movement towards effective, desegregated public schools has emerged in the form of the black power movement and its demands for racial separatism. Some of the more vocal of the black power advocates who have addressed themselves to the problems of education have explicitly and implicitly argued for Negroes' control of "Negro Schools." Some have asserted that there should be separate school districts organized to control the schools in all-Negro residential areas; that there should be Negro Boards of Education, Negro superintendents of schools, Negro faculty, and Negro curricula and materials. These demands are clearly a rejection of the goals of integrated education and a return to the pursuit of the myth of an efficient "separate but equal"—or the pathetic wish for a separate and superior —racially-organized system of education. One may view this current trend whereby some Negroes themselves seem to be asking for a racially segregated system of education as a reflection of the frustration resulting from white resistance to genuine desegregation of the public schools since the *Brown* decision and as a reaction to the reality that the quality of education in the *de facto* segregated Negro schools in the North and the Negro schools in the South has steadily deteriorated under the present system of white control.

In spite of these explanations, the demands for segregated schools can be no more acceptable coming from Negroes than they are coming from white segregationists. There is no reason to believe and certainly there is no evidence to support

the contention that all-Negro schools, controlled by Negroes, will be any more efficient in preparing American children to contribute constructively to the realities of
the present and future world. The damage inherent in racially isolated schools was
persuasively documented by the comprehensive study conducted by the United
States Commission on Civil Rights.[1]

Furthermore, the more subtle and insidious educational deprivation for white
children who are required to attend all-white schools is furthered by both the
black and the white advocates of racially homogeneous schools.

Attempts at Remedies

In spite of these obstacles in the path of genuine desegregation of American public schools and the attainment of effective, nonracially constrained education for
all American children, there have been persistent attempts to compensate for the
deficits of racial isolation in the American public schools. A tremendous amount
of energy and money has been expended in the attempt to develop special programs designed to improve the academic achievement of Negro children, who are
the most obvious victims of inferior, racially segregated public schools.

The United States Commission on Civil Rights report, *Racial Isolation in the
Public Schools,* has presented facts which raise questions concerning the long-
range effectiveness of these programs. There is some evidence that these special
programs do some good and help some children; but they clearly underline the
inadequacy of the regular education these children receive. In addition to the
fact that they obscure the overriding reality that underprivileged children are
being systematically short-changed in their regular segregated and inferior schools,
these programs may also be seen as a type of commitment to the continuation of
segregated education.

If one accepts the premise which seems supported by all available evidence, and
above all by the reasoning of the *Brown* decision, that racially segregated schools
are inherently inferior, it would seem to follow that all attempts to improve the
quality of education in all-Negro and all-white schools would have necessarily
limited positive effects. All programs designed to raise the quality of education in
racially homogeneous schools would therefore have to be seen as essentially eva-
sive programs or as the first stage in an inferior approach to a serious plan for ef-

---

[1] U.S. Commission on Civil Rights, *Racial Isolation in the Public Schools* (Washington: U.S.
Government Printing Office, 1967).

fective desegregation of public schools. Given the resistance to an immediate reorganization of the present system of racially organized schools so as to create a more effective system of racially heterogeneous schools, however, one may be required to attempt to increase the efficiency of education in all-Negro schools as a necessary battle in the larger struggle for racially desegregated schools.

The problem of the extent to which it is possible to provide excellent education in a predominantly Negro school should be re-examined thoroughly in spite of the basic premise of the *Brown* decision that racially segregated schools are inherently inferior. Some questions which we must now dare to ask and seek to answer as the basis for a new strategy in the assault against the inhumanity of the American system of racial segregation are:

(1) Is the present pattern of massive educational inferiority and inefficiency which is found in predominantly Negro schools inherent and inevitable in racially segregated schools?

(2) Is there anything which can be done within the Negro schools to raise them to a tolerable level of educational efficiency—or to raise them to a level of educational excellence?

If the answer to the first question is *yes* and to the second question is *no,* then the strategy of continued and intensified assault on the system of segregated schools is justified and should continue unabated since there is no hope of raising the quality of education for Negro children as long as they are condemned to segregated schools—there is no hope of salvaging them. If, on the other hand, the answers to the above questions are reversed, it would suggest that a shift in strategy and tactics, without giving up the ultimate goals of eliminating the dehumanizing force of racial segregation from American life, would be indicated. This shift would suggest that given the present strong and persistent resistance to any serious and effective desegregation of our public schools, that the bulk of the available organizational, human, and financial resources and specialized skills be mobilized and directed toward obtaining the highest quality of education for Negro students without regard to the racial composition of the schools which they attend. This attempt would demand a massive, system-wide educational enrichment program designed to obtain educational excellence in the schools attended by Negro children.

Recent experiences in New York City, Boston, Chicago, Philadelphia and other northern cities reveal that this temporary shift in the battleground will not in itself lead to any easier victory. School boards and public school officials seem as resistant to developing or implementing programs designed to improve the quality and efficiency of education provided for Negro children in segregated schools as they are deaf to all requests for effective desegregation plans and programs. The interests and desires of white middle-class parents, and the interests of the increasingly powerful teachers' federations and professional supervisory associations are invariably given priority over the desire of Negro parents for nonsegregated quality education for their children. The interests of the white parents, teachers, and supervisors are often perceived by them as inimical to the desires of the Negro parents. Furthermore, the capture and control of the public schools by the white middle-class parents and teachers provided the climate within which the system of racially segregated and inferior schools could be developed, expanded and reinforced and within which the public schools became instruments for blocking rather than facilitating the upward mobility of Negroes and other lower-status groups. One, therefore, could not expect these individuals and groups to be sympathetic and responsive to the pleas of Negro parents for higher quality education for their children. Negro parents and organizations must accept and plan their strategy in terms of the fact that adversaries in the battle for higher quality education for Negro children will be as numerous and as formidable as the adversaries in the battle for nonsegregated schools. Indeed they will be the same individuals, officials, and groups in different disguises and with different excuses for inaction but with the same powerful weapons of evasion, equivocation, inaction, or tokenism.

An effective strategy for the present and the future requires rigorous and honest appraisal of all of the realities, a tough-minded diagnosis of the strengths and weaknesses of the Negro and his allies. We cannot now permit ourselves to be deluded by wishful thinking, sentimental optimism, or rigid and oversimplified ideological postures. We must be tough-mindedly pragmatic and flexible as we seek to free our children from the cruel and dehumanizing, inferior and segregated education inflicted upon them by the insensitive, indifferent, affable, and at times callously rigid custodians of American public education.

In developing an appropriate strategy and the related flexible tactics, it must be clearly understood that the objective of improving the quality of education provided for Negro children is not a substitute for or a retreat from the fundamental goal of removing the anachronism of racially segregated schools from American life. The objective of excellent education for Negro and other lower-status children is inextricably linked with the continuing struggle to desegregate public education. All of the public school, college, and professional school civil-rights litigation instituted by the legal staff of the NAACP arose from recognition of the obvious fact that the segregated schools which Negroes were forced by law to attend were inferior and therefore damaging and violative of the equal protection clause in the 14th amendment of the United States Constitution.

The suggested shift in emphasis from desegregation to quality of education is not a retreat into the blind alley of accepting racial separation as advocated by the Negro nationalist groups, nor is it the acceptance of defeat in the battle for desegregation. It is rather a regrouping of forces, a shift in battle plans and an attempt to determine the most vulnerable flanks of the opposition as the basis for major attack. The resisting educational bureaucracies, their professional staffs, and the segment of the white public which has not yet been infected fatally by the American racist disease are most vulnerable to attack on the issue of the inferior quality of education found in Negro schools and the need to institute a plan immediately to raise the educational level of these schools. The economic, political, military, social-stability, international democratic, humane, and self-interest arguments in favor of an immediate massive program for educational excellence in predominantly Negro schools are so persuasive as to be irrefutable. The expected resistance should be overcome with intelligently planned and sustained efforts.

The first phase of an all-out attack on the inferior education now found in racially segregated schools should be coordinated with a strategy and program for massive and realistic desegregation of entire school systems. This more complicated phase of the over-all struggle will continue to meet the resistances of the past with increased intensity. It will be necessary, therefore, to break this task down into its significant components and determine the timing and phasing of the attack on each or combinations of the components. For example:

The evidence and arguments demonstrating the detrimental effects of segregated schools on the personality and effectiveness of white children should be gathered, evaluated, and widely disseminated in ways understandable to the mases of whites.

The need to reorganize large public school systems away from the presently inefficient and uneconomic neighborhood schools to more modern and viable systems of organization such as educational parks, campuses, or clusters must be sold to the general public in terms of hard dollars and cents and educational efficiency benefiting all children rather than in terms of public-school desegregation.

The need to consolidate small, uneconomic, and relatively ineffective school districts into larger educational and fiscal systems in order to obtain more efficient education for suburban and exurban children must also be sold in direct practical terms rather than in terms of desegregation of schools.

The need to involve large metropolitan regional planning in the mobilization, utilization, and distribution of limited educational resources on a more efficient level must also be explored and discussed publicly.

The movement toward decentralization of large urban school systems must be carefully monitored in order to see that decentralization does not reinforce or concretize urban public school segregation—and to assure that decentralization is consistent with the more economically determined trend toward consolidation and regional planning allocation of resources and cooperation.

A final indication that phase one, the struggle for excellent education for Negro children in ghetto schools, is not inconsistent with phase two, the struggle for nonsegregated education for all children, is to be seen in the fact that if it were possible to raise the quality of education provided for Negro children who attend the urban schools to a level of unquestioned excellence, the flight of middle-class whites to the suburbs might be stemmed and some who have left might be attracted back to the city. Hence, phase one activity would increase the chances of obtaining nonsegregated education in our cities. Similarly, some of the program suggestions of phase two such as educational parks and campuses and the possibilities of regional planning and educational cooperation across present municipal boundaries could lead to substantial improvements in the quality of education offered to inner-city children.

The goal of high quality education for Negro and lower-status children and the goal of public school desegregation are inextricable; the attainment of the one will lead to the attainment of the other. It is not likely that there could be effective desegregation of the schools without a marked increase in the academic achievement and personal and social effectiveness of Negro and white children. Neither is it possible to have a marked increase in the educational efficiency of Negro schools and the resulting dramatic increase in the academic performance of Negro children without directly and indirectly facilitating the process of public school desegregation.

Problems of Educational Monopoly

It is possible that all attempts to improve the quality of education in our present racially segregated public schools and all attempts to desegregate these schools will have minimal positive results. The rigidity of present patterns of public school organization and the concomitant stagnation in quality of education and academic performance of children may not be amenable to any attempts at change working through and within the present system.

Kenneth B. Clark

Until the influx of Negro and Puerto Rican youngsters into urban public schools, the American public school system was justifiably credited with being the chief instrument for making the American dream of upward social, economic, and political mobility a reality. The depressed immigrants from southern and eastern Europe could use American public schools as the ladder toward the goals of assimilation and success. The past successes of American public education seem undebatable. The fact that American public schools were effective mobility vehicles for white American immigrants makes even more stark and intolerable their present ineffectiveness for Negro and Puerto Rican children. Now it appears that the present system of organization and functioning of urban public schools is a chief blockage in the mobility of the masses of Negro and other lower-status minority group children. The inefficiency of their schools and the persistence and acceptance of the explanations for this generalized inefficiency are clear threats to the viability of our cities and national stability. The relationship between long-standing urban problems of poverty, crime and delinquency, broken homes—the total cycle of pathology, powerlessness, and personal and social destructiveness which haunts our urban ghettos—and the breakdown in the efficiency of our public schools is now unavoidably clear. It is not enough that those responsible for our public schools should assert passively that the schools merely reflect the pathologies and injustices of our society. Public schools and their administrators must assert boldly that education must dare to challenge and change society toward social justice as the basis for democratic stability.

There remains the disturbing question—a most relevant question probably too painful for educators themselves to ask—whether the selection process involved in training and promoting educators and administrators for our public schools emphasizes qualities of passivity, conformity, caution, smoothness, and superficial affability rather than boldness, creativity, substance, and the ability to demand and obtain those things which are essential for solid and effective public education for all children. If the former is true and if we are dependent upon the present educational establishment, then all hopes for the imperative reforms which must be made so that city public schools can return to a level of innovation and excellence are reduced to a minimum, if not totally eliminated.

The racial components of the present crisis in urban public education clearly make the possibilities of solution more difficult and may contribute to the passivity and pervading sense of hopelessness of school administrators. Aside from any latent or subtle racism which might infect school personnel themselves, they are hampered by the gnawing awareness that with the continuing flight of middle-class whites from urban public schools and with the increasing competition which education must engage in for a fair share of the tax dollar, it is quite possible that Americans will decide deliberately or by default to sacrifice urban public schools on the altars of its historic and contemporary forms of racism. If this can be done without any real threat to the important segments of economic and political power in the society and with only Negro children as the victims, then there is no realistic basis for hope that our urban public schools will be saved.

The hope for a realistic approach to saving public education in American cities seems to this observer to be found in a formula whereby it can be demonstrated to the public at large that the present level of public school inefficiency has reached an intolerable stage of public calamity. It must be demonstrated that minority group children are not the only victims of the monopolistic inefficiency of the present pattern of organization and functioning of our public schools.

It must be demonstrated that white children—privileged white children whose parents understandably seek to protect them by moving to suburbs or by sending them to private and parochial schools—also suffer both potentially and immediately.

It must be demonstrated that business and industry suffer intolerable financial burdens of double and triple taxation in seeking to maintain a stable economy in the face of the public school inefficiency which produces human casualties rather than constructive human beings.

It must be demonstrated that the cost in correctional, welfare, and health services are intolerably high in seeking to cope with consequences of educational inefficiency—that it would be more economical, even for an affluent society, to pay the price and meet the demands of efficient public education.

It must be demonstrated that a nation which presents itself to the world as the guardian of democracy and the protector of human values throughout the world cannot itself make a mockery of these significant ethical principles by dooming one-tenth of its own population to a lifetime of inhumane futility because of remediable educational deficiencies in its public schools.

These must be understood and there must be the commitment to make the average American understand them if our public schools and our cities are to be effective. But it does not seem likely that the changes necessary for increased efficiency of our urban public schools will come about because they should. Our urban public school systems seem muscle-bound with tradition. They seem to represent the most rigid forms of bureaucracies which, paradoxically, are most resilient in their ability and use of devices to resist rational or irrational demands for change. What is most important in understanding the ability of the educational establishment to resist change is the fact that public school systems are protected public monopolies with only minimal competition from private and parochial schools. Few critics of the American urban public schools—even severe ones such as myself—dare to question the givens of the present organization of public education in terms of local control of public schools, in terms of existing municipal or political boundaries, or in terms of the rights and prerogatives of boards of education to establish policy and select professional staff—at least nominally or titularly if not actually. Nor dare the critics question the relevance of the criteria and standards for selecting superintendents, principals, and teachers, or the relevance of all of these to the objectives of public education—producing a literate and informed public to carry on the business of democracy—and to the goal of producing human beings with social sensitivity and dignity and creativity and a respect for the humanity of others.

A monopoly need not genuinely concern itself with these matters. As long as local school systems can be assured of state aid and increasing federal aid without the accountability which inevitably comes with aggressive competition, it would be sentimental, wishful thinking to expect any significant increase in the efficiency of our public schools. If there are no alternatives to the present system—short of present private and parochial schools which are approaching their limit of expansion—then the possibilities of improvement in public education are limited.

Alternative Forms of Public Education

Alternatives—realistic, aggressive, and viable competitors—to the present public school systems must be found. The development of such competitive public school systems will be attacked by the defenders of the present system as attempts to weaken the present system and thereby weaken, if not destroy, public education. This type of expected self-serving argument can be briefly and accurately disposed of by asserting and demonstrating that truly effective competition strengthens rather than weakens that which deserves to survive. I would argue further that public education need not be identified with the present system of organization of public schools. Public education can be more broadly and pragmatically defined in terms of that form of organization and functioning of an educational system which is in the public interest. Given this definition, it becomes clear that an inefficient system of public systems is not in the public interest:

—a system of public schools which destroys rather than develops positive human potentialities is not in the public interest;

—a system which consumes funds without demonstrating effective returns is not in the public interest;

—a system which insists that its standards of performance should not or cannot be judged by those who must pay the cost is not in the public interest;

—a system which says that the public has no competence to assert that a patently defective product is a sign of the system's inefficiency and demands radical reforms is not in the public interest;

—a system which blames its human resources and its society while it quietly acquiesces in, and inadvertently perpetuates, the very injustices which it claims limit its efficiency is not in the public interest.

Given these assumptions, therefore, it follows that alternative forms of public education must be developed if the children of our cities are to be educated and made constructive members of our society. In the development of alternatives, all attempts must at the same time be made to strengthen our present urban public schools. Such attempts would involve re-examination, revision, and strengthening of curricula, methods, personnel selection, and evaluation; the development of more rigorous procedures of supervision, reward of superior performance, and the institution of a realistic and tough system of accountability, and the provision of meaningful ways of involving the parents and the community in the activities of the school.

The above measures, however, will not suffice. The following are suggested as possible, realistic, and practical competitors to the present form of urban public school systems:

Regional State Schools. These schools would be financed by the states and would cut across present urban-suburban boundaries.

Federal Regional Schools. These schools would be financed by the Federal Government out of present state aid funds or with additional federal funds. These schools would be able to cut through state boundaries and could make provisions for residential students.

College- and University-Related Open Schools. These schools would be financed by colleges and universities as part of their laboratories in education. They would be open to the public and not restricted to children of faculty and students. Obviously, students would be selected in terms of constitutional criteria and their percentage determined by realistic considerations.

Industrial Demonstration Schools. These schools would be financed by industrial, business, and commercial firms for their employees and selected members of the public. These would not be vocational schools—but elementary and comprehensive high schools of quality. They would be sponsored by combinations of business and industrial firms in much the same way as churches and denominations sponsor and support parochial or sectarian schools.

Labor Union Sponsored Schools. These schools would be financed and sponsored by labor unions largely, but not exclusively, for the children of their members.

Army Schools. The Defense Department has been quietly effective in educating some of the casualties of our present public schools. It is hereby suggested that they now go into the business of repairing hundreds of thousands of these human casualties with affirmation rather than apology. Schools for adolescent drop-outs or educational rejects could be set up by the Defense Department adjacent to camps—but not necessarily as an integral part of the military. If this is necessary, it should not block the attainment of the goal of rescuing as many of these young people as possible. They are not expendable on the altar of anti-militarism rhetoric.

With strong, efficient, and demonstrably excellent parallel systems of public schools, organized and operated on a quasi-private level, and with quality control and professional accountability maintained and determined by Federal and State educational standards and supervision, it would be possible to bring back into public education a vitality and dynamism which are now clearly missing. Even the public discussion of these possibilities might clear away some of the dank stagnation which seems to be suffocating urban education today. American industrial and material wealth was made possible through industrial competition. American educational health may be made possible through educational competition.

If we succeed, we will have returned to the dynamic, affirmative goal of education; namely, to free man of irrational fears, superstitions, and hatreds. Specifically, in America the goal of democratic education must be to free Americans of the blinding and atrophying shackles of racism. A fearful, passive, apologetic, and inefficient educational system cannot help in the attainment of these goals.

If we succeed in finding and developing these and better alternatives to the present educational inefficiency, we will not only save countless Negro children from lives of despair and hopelessness; and thousands and thousands of white children from cynicism, moral emptiness, and social ineptness—but we will also demonstrate the validity of our democratic promises. We also will have saved our civilization through saving our cities.

Race and Education:
A Search for Legitimacy*

CHARLES V. HAMILTON

Roosevelt University

The author asserts that the educational questions and issues being raised by many black parents, students, and teachers today are substantially different from the traditional concerns of experts. The black spokesmen are questioning the legitimacy *of the educational institutions; they no longer believe that it is sufficient to try to increase the* effectiveness *of those institutions. This difference has caused a tension between those who have been victims of indifferent and inefficient policies and practices and those who believe it is still possible to make the existing institutions operable. Black people are calling for community control, not for integration. They are focusing as much on Afro-American culture and awareness as they are on verbal and arithmetic skills. Some black people are thinking of entirely new, comprehensive forms of education, based on substantially different normative values.*

An article on public policy, race, and education in the United States in the late 1960's cannot overlook the clear existence of tremendous ferment taking place in the various black communities in this country. The nature of that ferment is such that, if we would devise relevant policy for educating vast numbers of black people today, we cannot focus merely, or even primarily, on achievement

* This article appeared originally in the Fall 1968 issue of the *Harvard Educational Review*.

in verbal and mathematical skills as criteria for educational improvement. At one time, possibly to the mid-1960's, it was possible to talk about educational policy largely in terms of "integration" (or at least, desegregation) and assume that plans to implement integration would be dealing with the core of the problem of educational deficiency. This is no longer the case.

Today, one hears wholly different demands being raised in the black community. These demands are better represented by the kinds of resolutions coming out of the workshops of the newly formed (June, 1968) National Association of Afro-American Educators than by the conclusions reached by the report on *Equality of Educational Opportunity* (Coleman Report). These demands are reflected more clearly in the demonstrations of black high school students in many cities for more emphasis on Afro-American history and culture and for better science lab facilities than by the findings of the United States Commission on Civil Rights (*Racial Isolation in the Public Schools*). These demands are more clearly illustrated in the positions taken by the Harlem chapter of the Congress of Racial Equality (CORE), calling for an independent school system for Harlem, and by many of the Concerned Black Parents groups than in policy recommendations found in the statement issued by the Board of Education of Chicago, Illinois in August, 1967 (Redmond Report).

First, I would like to indicate why it is more important at this time, from a socio-political point of view, to put more credence in the wishes of the black community than in the statements and findings of the experts. Second, I would like to give examples of the kinds of things on the minds of some of those black people taking an active interest in new directions for education in the black community. Third, I want to present a sketch of a proposal for dealing with some of the problems in some of the large, urban areas. I am not sanguine that the proposal will be applicable in all places (I assume it will not be), but neither do I believe it possible or necessary to develop one model to fit all occasions. My proposal attempts to combine some of the fervent wishes of a growing number of black people with the clear need to think in wholly new institutional terms. I am fully aware that public policy in this area has been influenced by such dichotomies as "integration vs. segregation" (*de jure* and *de facto*) and "integrated education vs. quality (compensatory) education." My presentation will not use these terms as primary focal points, but it is clear that the main thrust of my proposal will support the involvement of more parents in the school system and the improvement of educational opportunities within the black community. Some critics will view this as an "enrichment" proposal, or as an effort at "compensatory" education, or even as a black power move to maintain and further divisiveness in the society. I simply acknowledge these criticisms at the outset and intend to let my proposal stand on its own merits.

A Crisis of Educational Legitimacy

It is absolutely crucial to understand that the society cannot continue to write reports accurately describing the failure of the educational institutions *vis-à-vis* black people without ultimately taking into account the impact those truths will have on black Americans. There comes a point when it is no longer possible to recognize institutional failure and then merely propose more stepped-up measures to overcome those failures—especially when the proposals come from the same kinds of people who administered for so long the present unacceptable and dysfunctional policies and systems. Professor Seymour Martin Lipset once wrote:

Legitimacy involves the capacity of the system to engender and maintain the belief that the existing political institutions are the most appropriate ones for the society. The extent to which contemporary democratic political systems are legitimate depends in large measure upon the ways in which the key issues which have historically divided the society have been resolved.

While effectiveness is primarily instrumental, legitimacy is evaluative. Groups regard a political system as legitimate or illegitimate according to the way in which its values fit with theirs.[1]

And in another place, he has written:

All claims to a legitimate title to rule in new states must ultimately win acceptance through demonstrating effectiveness. The loyalty of the different groups to the system must be won through developing *in them* the conviction that this system is the best—or at least an excellent—way to accomplish their objectives. And even claims to legitimacy of a supernatural sort, such as "the gift of grace," are subjected on the part of the populace to a highly pragmatic test—that is, what is the payoff?[2]

The United States gradually acquired legitimacy as a result of being *effective*.[3]

---

[1] Seymour Martin Lipset, *Political Man: The Social Bases of Politics* (New York: Doubleday, 1963), p. 64.

[2] Seymour Martin Lipset, *The First New Nation: The United States in Historical and Comparative Perspective* (New York: Basic Books, 1963), pp. 45-46. (Emphasis added.)

[3] *Ibid.*, p. 59. (Emphasis in original.)

189

The important point here is that loyalty, allegiance, is predicated on performance. What decision-makers *say* is not of primary importance, but it is important what black people *believe*. Do they *believe* that the school systems are operating in their behalf? Do they *believe* that the schools are *legitimate* in terms of educating their children and inculcating in them a proper sense of values? With the end product (i.e., their children graduating from high school as functional illiterates) clearly before their eyes at home and with volumes of reports documenting lack of payoff, it is not difficult to conclude that black people have good reason to question the legitimacy of the educational systems.

They begin to question the entire process, because they are aware that the schools, while not educating their children, are at the same time supporting a particularly unacceptable situation. They know that the schools are one of the major institutions for socializing their children into the dominant value structure of the society. Professor V. O. Key, Jr. concluded in his book, *Politics, Parties and Pressure Groups:*

In modern societies the school system, in particular, functions as a formidable instrument of political power in its role as a transmitter of the goals, values, and attitudes of the polity. In the selection of values and attitudes to be inculcated, it chooses those cherished by the dominant elements in the political order. By and large the impact of widely accepted goals, mores, and social values fixes the programs of American schools. When schools diverge from this vaguely defined directive and collide with potent groups in the political system, they feel a pressure to conform.[4]

The relevance of all this is that makers of policy and their advisers must recognize that there is a point beyond which vast numbers of black people *will* become alienated and will no longer view efforts on their behalf, however well-intentioned, as legitimate. When this happens, it behooves decision-makers, if they would search for ways of restoring faith, trust, and confidence, to listen to the demands of the alienated. The "experts" might see integration as socially and educationally sound and desirable, but *their* vision and empirical data might well be, at this juncture, irrelevant. Unless this is understood, I am suggesting that public policy might well find itself in the position of attempting to force its programs on a reluctant black community. And this is hardly a formula for the development of a viable body politic.

---

[4] V. O. Key, Jr., *Politics, Parties and Pressure Groups* (New York: Thomas Y. Crowell Company, 1964), pp. 12-13.

A clear example of a paternalistic, objectionable policy is contained in the report of the Chicago Board of Education, *Increasing Desegregation of Faculties, Students, and Vocational Education Programs,* issued August 23, 1967. The Report called for busing black children into all- or predominantly white schools. It contains the very revealing paragraph:

The assignment of students outside their neighborhood may be objected to by Negro parents who prefer that their children attend the segregated neighborhood school. This viewpoint cannot be ignored. Prior to implementation of such a transfer policy the administration must take steps to reassure apprehensive sending area parents that transfer will be beneficial not only in terms of integration but of improved education for their children. The generation of a favorable consensus in the designated sending area is important. *If such a consensus is unobtainable, the transfer program would have to proceed without a popular base.* In the light of the dismal alternatives such a program perhaps should proceed even without consensus, but every effort should be made to attain it.[5]

This is a perpetuation of the pattern of telling the black community what is best for it. My point is that this position will only increase alienation, not alleviate it. At the present time, when the educational systems are perceived as illegitimate, it is highly unlikely that such a policy could lead to success. In order for the program to work, support *must* be obtained from the black community. This means that educational achievement must be conceived more broadly than as the mere acquisition of verbal and mathematical skills. Very many black parents are (for good reason) quite concerned about what happens to the self-image of their black children in predominantly white schools—schools which reflect dominant white values and mores. Are these schools prepared to deal with their own white racism? Probably not, and a few summer institutes for white, middle-class teachers cannot prepare them. Are these schools prepared to come to terms with a young black child's search for identity? Will the black child indeed acquire certain skills which show up favorably on standardized tests, but at the same time avoid coming to grips with the fact that he or she should not attempt to be a carbon copy of the culture and ethos of another racial and ethnic group? Virtually all the social scientists, education experts, and public policy-makers who emphasize integration overlook this crucial, intangible, psychological factor. Many concerned black parents and teachers do not overlook it, however. And their viewpoint has nothing to do with black people

[5] *Increasing Desegregation of Faculties, Students, and Vocational Education Programs* (Board of Education, City of Chicago, August 23, 1967), p. B-20. (Emphasis added.)

wanting to perpetuate "separate but unequal" facilities, or with attitudes of "hate whitey." This concern is simply a necessary reaction to the fact that many white (and black) liberal, integration-oriented spokesmen are tuned in to a particular result and overlook other phenomena. They fail to understand that their criteria for "educational achievement" simply might not be relevant anymore.

What I am stating (in as kind a way as possible) is that setting criteria for measuring equal educational opportunity can no longer be the province of the established "experts." The policy-makers must now listen to those for whom they say they are operating; which means of course that they must be willing to share the powers of policy-making. The experts must understand that what is high on the liberal social scientist's agenda does not coincide with the agenda of many black people. The experts are still focusing on the effectiveness of existing educational institutions. Many black people have moved to the evaluation of the legitimacy of these institutions.

American social scientists generally are unable to grasp the meaning of alienation when applied to certain groups in this country. (Most of the recent perceptive literature on alienation and modernization deals with new nations of Africa and Asia.)[6]

Consequently, Grant McConnell, in an important book, *Private Power and American Democracy,* could write:

In general the use of government has depended on a particular group's capacity to isolate the relevant governmental agency from influences other than its own and to establish itself as the agency's constituency—at once giving an air of validity to its own ends and endowing it with the added disciplinary power of public authority over its own members.[7]

---

[6] See: Myron Weiner, ed., *Modernization, The Dynamics of Growth* (New York: Basic Books, 1966);

David Apter, *The Politics of Modernization* (Chicago: University of Chicago Press, 1965);

S. N. Eisenstadt, *Modernization: Protest and Change* (Englewood Cliffs, N. J.: Prentice-Hall, Inc., 1966);

Edward Shils, *Political Development in the New States* (New York: Humanities Press, 1964);

Thomas Hodgkin, *Nationalism in Colonial Africa* (New York: New York University Press, 1957);

K. H. Silvert, *Expectant Peoples: Nationalism and Development* (New York: Random House, 1964);

Lucian W. Pye, *Politics, Personality and Nation Building: Burma's Search for Identity* (New Haven: Yale University Press, 1962).

[7] Grant McConnell, *Private Power and American Democracy* (New York: Random House, 1965), pp. 346-347.

And later:

... farm migrant workers, Negroes, and the urban poor have not been included in the system of "pluralist" representation so celebrated in recent years.[8]

Then finally:

It can be readily agreed that if explosive mass movements are a genuine threat to America, a politics of narrow constituencies might be desirable to counter the danger. Small associations probably do provide order and stability for any society. In the United States some associations may serve in this manner to a greater degree than others. The American Civil Liberties Union and the League of Woman Voters have given notable service to American democracy. Trade unions and farm organizations have undoubtedly also been similarly useful at various times. Nevertheless, it should be clear that a substantial price is paid for any guarantee against mass movements provided by a pattern of small constituencies. That price is paid in freedom and equality. Although the price would be worth paying if the danger were grave, it can hardly be argued that such an extremity is present.[9]

There are voices in the black community (accompanied, as we well know, by acts of expressive violence) saying precisely that the danger *is* grave and that the extremity *is* present. The educational systems are particularly vulnerable, because of their very conspicuous inability to "pay-off."

An Alternative Agenda

It is instructive, then, to examine some of the major items presented by certain voices in the black community. Clearly, one source of constructive ideas would be black teachers, those persons who not only teach in ghetto schools, but whose children attend those schools (in most instances), who, themselves, grew up in the black community, and who, for the most part, still live in black communities.[10] Approximately 800 such teachers met in Chicago, June 6-9, 1968, in a national conference and formed the National Association of Afro-American Educators. They did not spend the four days discussing the Coleman Report or

---

[8] *Ibid.*, p. 349.

[9] *Ibid.*, pp. 355-356.

[10] In a column entitled "Quality Teaching in Decentralized Slum Schools," Fred M. Hechinger, education editor of *The New York Times*, wrote: "It seems more realistic and, for the long pull, more constructive to face the fact that part of the answer to the crisis must come through the efforts of Negro teachers. If young Negro college graduates can be channeled into these schools and if their greater identification with the children's and the parents' own background can more easily gain the pupils' confidence and attention, then to sacrifice some of the present licensing requirements may be a small price to pay" (*The New York Times*, April 29, 1968).

the report of the U.S. Civil Rights Commission. One could identify four particular areas of concern at that conference, and these areas coincide to a great extent with the issues raised by associations of Concerned Black Parents as well as various Afro-American History clubs in the high schools around the country.

(1) Control

It was generally concluded that the existing educational systems were not responsive to the wishes of the black community. Therefore, those structural arrangements now operating should be changed substantially. The decision-making process in most ghetto school systems was challenged. The workshop on the black school and the black community issued the following statement:

—Whereas, the educational systems of this nation have criminally failed the Black youth of this country,

—Whereas, Black parents have not had a voice in determining the educational destiny of their youth,

—Whereas, the Black youth and Black parents are demanding relevant education to meet their needs,

—Therefore, be it resolved that we encourage, support and work to organize local communities to control their own schools through local or neighborhood school boards and further that this organization go on record to immediately implement such plans.

—The goal of the National Association of Afro-American Educators should be Black control of the Black Community schools.[11]

One hears these kinds of statements increasingly among newly politicized people in the black communities. The focus has shifted; emphasis is now on viable ways to gain enough leverage to drastically revise a system. Black people, having moved to the stage of questioning the system's very legitimacy, are seeking ways to create a new system. This is difficult for most Americans to understand precisely because they have assumed the continuing legitimacy of the present educational system.

(2) Parent Involvement and Alliance with Black Teachers

It is becoming clearer and clearer that the major agents of control should be black parents in the community working closely with the teachers in the school.

---

[11] Excerpt from notes of discussion and reports of workshops of National Association of Afro-American Educators (Chicago, Illinois, 1968). (Mimeographed).

For this reason, if no other, many black spokesmen do not favor various compulsory plans for busing black children out of their commmunities into white schools, in some instances, miles away from home. Are we to assume that black parents, likewise, will travel miles across town in the evenings to attend PTA meetings—frequently to be surrounded by a sea of white faces, more articulate and with more organized voting strength? The principle of busing overlooks the very important factor of facilitating black parent participation in the child's schooling. If in fact the home has a critical role to play in the educational process, then we would be well advised not to pursue policies which would make that role more difficult.

The participation of black parents in the child's schooling is one of the points high on the agenda of some black people. And it is clearly at odds with one of the stated objectives of the Redmond Report: to bus black children into white schools, but to maintain a quota (no white elementary school would be over 15 percent black; no high school over 25 percent black), in order to guard against the possibility of a white exodus. James Redmond, Superintendent of Schools in Chicago, said: "Chicago will become a predominantly Negro city unless dramatic action is taken soon . . . School authorities (must) quickly achieve and maintain stable racial proportions in changing fringe areas."[12] Trying to placate whites simply is not a matter of top (or high) priority to many black people, especially if it must be done by manipulating black children.

Discussion of parental involvement and control has serious implications for the standards of professionalism we adopt. Black parents might well have different notions about what is methodologically sound, what is substantively valuable. They might well be impatient with some of the theories about teaching reading and writing. And at this stage who is to say that their doubts are not valid? The present approaches have hardly proved efficacious. Therefore, when we get sizeable black parental participation, we are opening up the profession to question and challenge about what constitutes educational legitimacy. No profession welcomes such intrusion from laymen. This is quite understandable; professionals have a vested self-interest. All those years of college courses and

---

[12] Quoted in an editorial in *Chicago Sun-Times*, January 12, 1968, p. 27. The editorial, which favored the Redmond Plan, further stated: "That part of the Redmond Plan that has excited opposition calls for fixing immediately a balanced racial enrollment in those all-white schools that are in the way of the Negro expansion. It would be roughly 90 per cent white, 10 per cent Negro. The Negro pupils (who are from middle-class families) would be acceptable to white families and keep them anchored in the neighborhood, whereas they would flee to the suburbs if the Negro proportion became greater than 25 per cent. The plan may not work. If it does it is at best only a holding action until the entire metropolitan area faces up to the demographic realities of our time. But it should be tried."

practice teaching and certifying exams, all those credentials of legitimacy may be going by the board. But that is precisely what happens in societies which are modernizing, in societies where new groupings—alienated from traditional norms—rise to make new normative demands. It is disturbing, disruptive, painful. It is change. And this is the phenomenon American social science has been unable to come to terms with in the latter half of the twentieth century—especially with reference to the issue of race relations.

(3) Psychological Impact

A third matter of concern to these new black voices is the psychological impact of educational institutions on the black children. Many black people are demanding more black principals in predominantly black schools, if only because they serve as positive role models for the children. Children should be able to see black people in positions of day-to-day power and authority. There is a demand to have the schools recognize *black* heroes with national holidays. There is concern for emphasizing group solidarity and pride, which is crucial for the development of black Americans. And there is very serious question whether a predominantly white, middle-class ethos can perform this function. Again, the Coleman data measure verbal skills and mathematical abilities, but there are other areas of equal importance. One should not assume that symbols of cultural pride are unimportant. Professor Lipset was correct when he described the impact of these symbols, but he was incomplete when he applied them to the United States—when the growing awareness of black Americans is taken into account. He wrote:

A major test of legitimacy is the extent to which given nations have developed a common "secular political culture," mainly national rituals and holidays. The United States has developed a common homogeneous culture in the veneration accorded the Founding Fathers, Abraham Lincoln, Theodore Roosevelt, and their principles.[13]

The schools serve as a major instrument to transmit such a common homogeneous culture. And yet, we are beginning to see black Americans call for the recognition of other heroes: Frederick Douglass, Martin Luther King, Jr., Malcolm X, and so forth. Students are demanding that the traditional Awards Day programs at their schools include such awards as a Malcolm X Manliness Award, a Marcus Garvey Citizenship Award, and Frederick Douglass and Martin Luther King, Jr. Human Rights Awards. We see black writers challenging the idea of a common secular political culture. John Oliver Killens and Lerone

[13] Lipset, *Political Man*, p. 68.

Bennett, Jr. are two prominent examples. Killens captured the mood when he wrote:

We (black Americans) even have a different historical perspective. Most white Americans, even today, look upon the Reconstruction period as a horrible time of "carpet-bagging," and "black politicians," and "black corruption," the absolutely lowest ebb in the Great American Story . . .

We black folk, however, look upon Reconstruction as the most democratic period in the history of this nation; a time when the dream the founders dreamed was almost within reach and right there for the taking; a time of democratic fervor the like of which was never seen before and never since . . .

For us, Reconstruction was the time when two black men were Senators in the Congress of the United States from the State of Mississippi; when black men served in the legislatures of all the states in Dixie; and when those "corrupt" legislatures gave to the South its first public-school education . . .[14]

Even our white hero symbols are different from yours. You give us moody Abe Lincoln, but many of us prefer John Brown, whom most of you hold in contempt as a fanatic; meaning, of course, that the firm dedication of any white man to the freedom of the black man is *prima-facie* evidence of perversion or insanity.[15]

And Lerone Bennett, Jr. challenged much of American historical scholarship when he challenged the role and image of Abraham Lincoln:

Abraham Lincoln was *not* the Great Emancipator. As we shall see, there is abundant evidence to indicate that the Emancipation Proclamation was not what people think it is and that Lincoln issued it with extreme misgivings and reservations.[16]

A growing number of black Americans are insisting that the schools begin to reflect this new concern, this new tension. We simply cannot assume a common secular political culture. If we continue to operate on such false assumptions, we will continue to misunderstand the very deep feeling of alienation in the black community. And misunderstanding cannot be a viable basis for enlightened public policy. Likewise, it is not only important that Afro-American history be taught in the black schools, but that it also be incorporated into the curriculum of white schools throughout this country. It is not sufficient that only black children be given an accurate historical picture of the race; all

[14] John Oliver Killens, *Black Man's Burden* (New York: Trident Press, 1965), pp. 14-15.
[15] *Ibid.*, p. 17.
[16] Lerone Bennett, Jr., "Was Abe Lincoln a White Supremacist?" *Ebony*, 23, No. 4 (February, 1968), p. 35.

Americans must have this exposure—in the inner city, the suburbs, the rural schools.

Who can predict what the "tests" will show when we begin to expose black children to these kinds of innovations? What sort of impact will this have on the motivation of those "slow learners," those "high risks," those (and here is the misnomer of them all) "culturally deprived?" The legitimacy of the "standardized tests" must be questioned as long as they overlook these very essential components.

(4) Curricula and Instructional Materials

Closely related to the third point is a concern with the kinds and content of materials used, especially in black schools. How are black people portrayed? Do the textbooks reflect the real experience of black Americans in history and in contemporary society? The workshop on instructional materials at the Afro-American Educators Conference concluded:

> In each local community black educators must develop a criteria for selection of materials which will be presented to the Board of Education, to local textbook committees, and to the major publishing houses which provide text and supplemental materials to that community. It is incumbent upon us, if we are to serve this society, that instructional material which we select be both educationally sound and incorporate a strong black orientation.

> Black classroom teachers must help black students to speak the language of the market place and assist them as they move back and forth between "their own thing and a white American thing." Since all groups usually speak two languages, one at home and within their group and another in the economic world; by nurturing and respecting our own language and effectively manipulating the other we will become a truly bilingual people. This is necessary to achieve a viable economic base . . .

> Black teachers must become connected with major textbook publishing firms as authors, editors and consultants to create the materials available on the market. We must pressure major publishers to reflect the needs of black children in schools. We will work for a factual inclusion of the scientific contribution of black scientists to medical and scientific advancement. For example, Dr. Daniel Hale Williams (open heart surgery) and Dr. Charles Drew (developer of blood plasma) must receive their rightful place in elementary and secondary science texts.[17]

These are some of the things on the agenda of many black people as they consider possible solutions of our vast educational problems. It is far too soon to

[17] Excerpt from notes and discussion and reports of workshops of National Association of Afro-American Educators. (Chicago, Illinois, 1968). (Mimeographed.)

evaluate the results of most of these proposals—in some instances they have not even been implemented. And in most cases they are in the embryonic stage. We are without precedent in these matters, and it would be presumptuous of American social scientists to attempt to prejudge results, or even to suppose that they could. Black people are searching for new forms of educational legitimacy, and in that kind of modernizing atmosphere the traditional criteria for measuring effectiveness might well be irrelevant and anachronistic.

An Alternative Model

The rhetoric of race and education, as stated earlier, is prolific with dichotomies of segregation vs. integration, quality education vs. integrated education, compensatory programs vs. busing, and so forth. Too much is assumed by these simplistic terms, and a superficial use of these labels frequently restricts and predetermines discussion at the outset. While this is unfortunate, it is probably unavoidable, given the historical context and the highly emotional atmosphere. Those persons favoring "neighborhood" schools and opposing busing have traditionally been, in the North, white parents and taxpayer groups, usually identified as anti-Negro in their basic racial views. These groups would normally be found opposing open housing laws as well. Therefore their motivations are questioned when they argue that they are essentially concerned about "educational standards" and property values. When it is pointed out to them that white students do not suffer academically and (if panic selling is avoided) property values do not go down, they do not listen. And their intransigence leads their opponents to label them as racial bigots and segregationists.

Proponents of busing and integration see a positive academic and social value in racially heterogeneous classrooms. Integration to these people is virtually synonymous with quality. And black people who once worked for desegregated schools but who no longer do so are viewed as having given up the fight, as having joined the white racists, and, indeed, as having become black racists and advocates of "Black Power separatism."[18]

---

[18] An example of this attitude was contained in the report of the President's civil disorders commission (Kerner Commission). "The Black Power advocates of today consciously feel that they are the most militant group in the Negro protest movement. Yet they have retreated from a direct confrontation with American society on the issue of integration and, by preaching separatism, unconsciously function as an accommodation to white racism" (*Report of the National Advisory Commission on Civil Disorders* [New York: E. P. Dutton & Company, 1968], p. 235).

Charles V. Hamilton

I state this simply to acknowledge an awareness of some of the positions taken before I proceed to suggest an alternative educational plan. The fact that my ideas would appear more closely akin to the views of some white segregationists whose ultimate goal is to deny educational opportunity to black people is an *appearance* I cannot avoid. It is important however to point out that a close examination of the ultimate goals of my suggestions will indicate a clear divergence from views held by the segregationists. In other words I am motivated by an attempt to find an educational approach which is relevant to black people, not one that perpetuates racism. The plan I am suggesting is not a universal panacea; it is not applicable in all black ghettos. Where it is feasible—particularly in the large urban communities—I strongly propose it for consideration.

This is a model which views the ghetto school as the focal point of community life. The educational system should be concerned with the entire family, not simply with the children. We should think in terms of a Comprehensive Family-Community-School Plan with black parents attending classes, taking an active, day-to-day part in the operation of the school. Parents could be students, teachers, and legitimate members of the local school governing board. A similar plan is already in operation in Chicago: the Family Education Center. There are two centers, the Westinghouse and Doolittle Centers, which provide basic adult education, prevocational and vocational training, and work experience programs.

Mr. William H. Robinson, Director of the Cook County Department of Public Aid, has stated:

The Center's most unique feature is the Child Development Program for the students' (parents') pre-school children, who come to school with their mothers and spend the day in a well-equipped, professionally staffed nursery school. Mothers can attend classes with the assurance that their children are receiving proper care and mental stimulation. Thus, the program makes participation in an educational program possible for many recipients who were prevented previously because they could not obtain adequate child care services.[19]

Since the inception of the program two years ago, 1,300 adults and 500 children have been involved in the centers.

This concept should be expanded to include fathers as well, those unemployed and willing to obtain skills. Many of these parents could serve as teachers,

[19] Cook County Department of Public Aid, *The Challenge of Change* (Annual report, Chicago, 1967), p. 11.

200

along with a professional staff. They could teach courses in a number of areas (child care, auto mechanics, art, music, home economics, sewing, etc.) for which they are obviously now trained. The Comprehensive Plan would extend the school program to grades through high school—for adults and children—and it would eliminate the traditional calendar year of September to June. (There is no reason why the educational system could not be revised to take vacations for one month, say in December of post-Christmas, and another month in August. The community educational program would be a year-round function, day and evening.)

The school would belong to the community. It would be a union of children, parents, teachers (specially trained to teach in such communities), social workers, psychologists, doctors, lawyers, and community planners. Parent and community participation and control would be crucial in the hiring and firing of personnel, the selection of instructional materials, and the determination of curriculum content. Absolutely everything must be done to make the system a functioning, relevant part of the lives of the local people. Given the present situation of existing and growing alienation, such involvement is essential.

If it can be demonstrated that such a comprehensive educational institution can gain the basic trust and participation of the black community, it should become the center of additional vital community functions. Welfare, credit unions, health services, law enforcement, and recreational programs—all working under the control of the community—could be built around it. Enlightened private industry would find it a place from which to recruit trained, qualified people and could donate equipment and technical assistance. The several advantages of such a plan are obvious. It deals with the important agencies which are in daily, intimate contact with black people; it reduces a vast, fragmented service bureaucracy which now descends on the black community from many different directions, with cumbersome rules and regulations, uncontrolled by and unaccountable to the community. It provides the black people with a meaningful chance for participation in the very important day-to-day processes affecting their lives; it gives them educational and vocational tools for the future. All these things reflect the yearnings and aspirations of masses of black people today.

The Comprehensive Plan envisions the local school as a central meeting place to discuss and organize around community issues, political and economic. All of the establishments functioning under the plan would provide relevant intermediary groups to which the people could relate. The size of the community involved would vary, with several factors to be considered: geography, number of participating agencies, available funds (from federal, state, and local governmental sources), and manageability. At all times, the primary concern would be about the active involvement of people and about their possession of real power to make decisions affecting the Comprehensive Plan. They would hire consultants and experts whose legitimacy would be determined by their relevance to the community, not by a predetermined set of criteria superimposed from outside.

The proposed Comprehensive Plan attempts to come to grips with the understandable alienation discussed in the first section and with the appropriateness of the agenda items described in the second section of the paper. This plan is better understood when one keeps in mind the premise presented earlier: black people are questioning, evaluating the *legitimacy* of existing educational institutions, not simply searching for ways to make those institutions more *effective*. I am suggesting that we are at a point in the process of modernization and social transformation when we must begin to think and act in wholly new normative and structural terms.

Discussion: Implementing Equal Educational Opportunity

The recent controversy over equality of educational opportunity has focused large-ly on the findings and pronouncements of social scientists. In this discussion, five educational practitioners—each of whom is involved in attempts to implement equal educational opportunity—have been asked to comment on the best means to achieve this equality. Some make reference to the findings of social scientists, but they speak basically from their own varied experiences and perspectives within the educational enterprise.

The Case for All-Black Schools*

NOEL A. DAY

Organization for Social and Technical Innovation

It is now generally accepted that northern urban areas will become increasingly segregated in the years ahead unless major new and radically different policy decisions are forthcoming which will generate simultaneously both forceful and massive interventions and extensive reorganization of traditional political, economic, and social concepts. Current demographic trends indicate that those white families who remain in the city will be older; they will have fewer children; and they will be even more insulated than they are now from the life of that expanding part of the urban core that is the "black man's land." At the same time, the Negro population, particularly that part which continues to migrate from rural to urban America, will be younger and of childbearing age. And of course they will be poorer.

These trends mean that, although it is true that in terms of absolute numbers more Negro children will attend integrated schools in the next few years, the overwhelming majority of Negro children will be locked into schools in the ghetto areas of the core city. That is, the problem of urban education will become even more identified with the problems of educating Negro children than it is now.

What is that problem? It is usually defined as a problem of differential performance, and it is usually measured in terms of differences in mathematical

* This article is an expansion of the ideas originally presented in the Winter 1968 issue of the *Harvard Educational Review*.

and verbal-skill achievement levels, differences in drop-out rates, and in the rates of college attendance for Negro and white students. In the past—the not-too-distant past—these differences were attributed to inherent differences between the races. More recently, and as a result of more nearly scientific assaults on the theories of innate racial distinctions that upheld this view, differences in performance between white and nonwhite children have been blamed on inequality of educational opportunity or ascribed more generally to educational "disadvantagedness."

The distinction is crucial. The notion of "disadvantagedness" tends to locate the responsibility with the Negro child, his family, or his community, while the idea of inequality of opportunity, of differentiated access to the means of education, assigns the responsibility more clearly to the society and to those within it who control access to opportunity. However, this distinction commonly goes unrecognized. Most of the programs that have been designed to address the problem of unequal performance reflect this confusion; as a result they fail to define the problem properly or to confront the underlying political issues.

For years after the theory of inherent inferiority was discredited, Negroes continued to suffer from unequal access to educational opportunity, and white America—including most social scientists and educators—evinced not the least flicker of concern. In fact it has only been since dissatisfaction on the part of Negroes, expressed through militant action, had led to dislocations of the accepted order that there has been any significant evidence of willingness to consider institutional modifications. Therefore, the problems involved in implementing equal educational opportunity seem to be at least as much political as they are educational. It is indeed possible to support the view that those institutional commitments that have been made as political responses were aimed at containing Negro aspirations and challenges within boundaries set by the white majority's demands that its comfort and convenience—much less its ability to survive—not be unduly imposed upon. In this view, attempts to compensate Negroes for past deprivations—including educational programs—have been designed to be as painless to the majority as possible and have been based on a set of ethnocentric assumptions about the ultimate desirability of the existing social order.

Of course, if these programs had been effective and had offered adequate compensation, there would be little justification for penance or for requiring conscious disaccommodation on the part of the majority. Most programs, however, have been neither effective nor adequate. And in large part their failure seems to stem from the larger society's inability either to question the validity of its own attitudes and behavior or to involve the Negro meaningfully in the search for an operative definition of what constitutes adequate compensation.

If we can conceive of programs aimed at increasing integration in schools as being basically compensatory in nature, they appear to offer the most effective form of compensation we have found to date. Negro children do seem to perform better in racially and socially integrated settings. As the Coleman Report points out, however, significant disparities in the achievement levels of Negro and white children persist even in integrated schools. One explanation of these disparities may be rooted in the fact that programs to integrate schools have been oriented toward movement—both physical and cultural—in one direction only, away from the Negro community. What does this movement say to the children who are involved? Does it make an implicit statement to the children about themselves, their families, and their community? Do they get a message that reinforces the lesson society has already taught so many Negroes so well: that what is black is intrinsically less worthwhile and less desirable? What does this mean in terms of their achievement and their emotional growth?

The Coleman Report clearly implies, and is supported in its implications by the body of educational experience, that children are affected by what they unconsciously "tune into" around them. That is, children absorb and learn a tremendous amount informally and implicitly. If this is true, then a program that moves children out of a black community into a white community without reciprocal action may be little more than a clear object lesson that denies the worth of the black community.

One approach currently being developed addresses the difficulties that may be created by one-way integration programs: the league-of-metropolitan-schools concept. This concept differs radically from all the other metropolitan schemes that have been put forward. First of all, it would enroll children (on a voluntary basis, of course) in the metropolitan setting from the earliest grades. It would not waste the learning potential of the early grades in encapsulated settings. Second, it differs from the educational part in that it does not seek "neutral ground" for the school. It assumes that the school should become engaged with the community around it and use that community—whether it be inner-city or suburb, white or black, rich or poor—as one of the school's educational resources. Finally, it assumes that in the course of their school careers children should be exposed to and involved in a number of different communities. Therefore, as children proceed through school, they will attend league schools located in several types of communities. Thus, in addition to insuring that the Negro child will perceive his community as being of value, the league-of-schools concept also addresses the "racial isolation" of the white child.

But what of the children—the majority of Negro children in this generation—who will not get out of the ghetto? There have been two general approaches to making equal educational opportunity available to those pupils whose only educational experience will be segregated. One is compensatory education, usually in the form of remedial and enrichment programs. The other is the development of so-called community control over the schools.

The major problem with compensatory education programs is that they do not compensate for the right things, in the right proportion, and in the right way. Operation Counterpoise, a pilot compensatory education program operated by the Boston School Department offers a perfect, although by no means unique illustration.

In the words of its major architect, the purpose of Operation Counterpoise was to "compensate for the parental lack of values." To accomplish this end, the program decreased the pupil-teacher ratio, provided new textbooks (including some integrated texts), brought in several remedial specialists, instituted team-teaching and a master-teacher system, and introduced special cultural programs (including an elaborate Negro History Week). However, the teachers assigned to the program were, for the most part, the same teachers who failed "to turn the kinds on" in the first place. The in-service training program for Counterpoise teachers did nothing to challenge these teachers' attitudes about their students. For example, the ethnic background of the students and the implications of ethnicity were not considered suitable subjects for discussion in training sessions.

Other compensatory programs begin by assuming an inadequate child rather than an inadequate parent. Such programs speak of the disadvantaged, the hard-to-reach, the unmotivated, or the uneducable child. Although in educational usage these terms have become almost synonymous with the Negro child, the programs attempt to compensate for lack of advantages, lack of services, or lack of motivation rather than for being a Negro in a society that is racist to its bones. Until these programs can confront the issue of what it means to be black in this society, they will fail really to reach or really to motivate the Negro child. A few pictures of black folk heroes and Negro History Week once a year will not do the job. The teachers may need to learn about George Washington Carver and Booker T. Washington and Crispus Attucks, but the Negro child may gain more from learning about Nat Turner, Malcolm X, Martin Luther King, and Stokely Carmichael.

Nor is it sufficient to call for community control of the schools unless the community controls the decisions that are educationally critical—what the school does, who teaches, and what and how they teach.

The idea of community control is, of course, deeply imbedded in the American educational tradition and presumably it is still possible in some settings for parents and other citizens to have a direct and substantial impact on the local school system. In the nation's expanding urban areas, however, that has become less and less possible, and "community" control has become a responsibility delegated to elected officials or to good and civic-minded appointees. In either case, the notion of accountability has been largely lost or has proven to be impractical—given the highly bureaucratized character of the modern educational system. Even those institutional forms that have been developed to represent "community" and parental opinion—home and school associations or parent-teacher associations—have tended to become almost as aloof from the community as the school system and almost as isolated from the school system as the average parent. They have, in most cases, either been relegated to making meaningless decisions (who will chaperone the senior dance or how the proceeds of the cake sale will be spent), or they have (as in Boston where the Home and School Association's by-laws forbid criticism of the School Department) become instruments of school policy rather than active participants in the formulation of school policy.

What seems to be even more distressing to educational policy makers and implementers than the idea of giving over, or at least sharing, the power to make decisions is the identity of those in the inner city with whom power will have to be shared if community control is to be substantive and not merely symbolic. Recent experience has shown that community control will not be expressed only—or even primarily—through an articulate, relatively secure, well-educated elite that shares a common language and many common values with the professional educators and the good and civic-minded men on the school board. Indeed, many of those most truly representative of the ambitions and concerns of the black enclave will also be those who harbor the greatest anger and hostility toward the school system; who have had the least prior experience with effective power; who have suffered the most discourtesy and condescension at the hands of the school's representatives in the past; and who bring with them a language and symbolic and logical systems indigenous to the ghetto but quite foreign to middle-class America.

It will not be easy for the professional to learn to listen to community leaders or to talk with them; it will be even more difficult to build new programs, approaches, and methods that are creatively responsive to their expressed and felt needs. But despite the difficulty, it may be precisely these abilities that are required of professionals if schools and other aloof social institutions are to become relevant to black communities.

However, even community control may not be a sufficient answer to the educational needs of black children, even though the Coleman Report also suggests a positive correlation between feelings of control and participation and improved performance. There are other hard issues that community control will not necessarily address. Do Negro children have educational needs that are distinctive, for example? Are new methods and materials required? And is it possible and desirable to develop a "black" curriculum—one that is responsive to the reality of the Negro child's existence? Until such questions are answered, we will run the risk of perpetuating a new set of myths that ignore differences among individuals and that lead us to continue to design and carry out programs that are ameliorative rather than fundamental in character. I believe that to find the answers to these questions, to learn how better to provide quality education in segregated schools, the establishment of several "all-black" laboratory schools in selected ghetto communities will be required.

Resistance to this idea will be high, and it will come from a variety of sources. Several moderate Negro leaders have already expressed fear that an emphasis on black culture might lead to a lack of emphasis on the development of mathematical and verbal skills. Others will oppose the idea on the basis of an *a priori* assumption that there are no significant differences between Negro children and white children. Those who subscribe to compensatory education theories based on the assumption that the programs compensate children for a "parental lack of values" are most certain to resist a school based on those values that the parents share with other Negroes. So too will those who will be offended by a curriculum that is seen as abrasive or as an encouragement of "inverse racism." Still others will fear that the "all-black" school will offer aid and succor to the kinds of separate development theories that have assisted the systematic suppression of the Negro in the past.

For the most part, these are real dangers. But it is also dangerous to the well-being of the Negro child to be stripped of selfhood or to be exposed to bigoted teachers who are assigned to after-school remedial and enrichment programs even though they have failed the same children all day.

The laboratory school under all-black control might assume a number of forms depending upon the objectives which various groups of blacks decide the educational process is meant to develop.

In a recent article in *Liberation* magazine, Herman Ferguson (a teacher in the New York City public schools) strongly implied that the Negro child must be trained to assume the role of a revolutionary, prepared either to participate in the overthrow of the current order—through violence if necessary—or to defend his community against genocidal assaults by the white majority. The assumptions about the character of the society that underlie Mr. Ferguson's objectives are clear. He believes that the society is incapable of orderly change within the extremely limited period of time still permitted by the accelerating pace of rising expectations on the part of Negroes, and he also believes that the society is capable of waging open warfare on the black community.

The educational program suggested by Mr. Ferguson reflects his beliefs. He calls for the development of a core curriculum built around mandatory courses and practicums in the military arts. He suggests, for example, not only training in the handling and use of firearms, but a closely related mathematics curriculum where problems in trajectory and muzzle velocity present opportunities of immediate relevance, and a homemaking program including intensive units on first aid and survival. And although Mr. Ferguson's approach may easily be characterized as extreme, he is not a completely lonely voice crying in the wilderness; his assumptions and sentiments are shared particularly by those elements in the black community who are most disenfranchised and who have seen little in their experience that is contradictory to Mr. Ferguson's view.

Other objectives, generally more commonly expressed, include the development of self-acceptance and group consciousness on the part of Negro youth or the development of black people capable of and skillful in competing within the mainstream society. An all-black school designed to accomplish the first of these objectives might build its curriculum around the immediate experiences of the students, and the history and present mores and values of non-western cultures.

The second set of objectives might lead to more conventionally designed and operated educational programs but emphasize quality and improved performance in those skill areas most useful in successful competition with white Americans.

The "all-black" school concerned with self-acceptance and group consciousness has therapeutic connotations although it remains somewhat ambiguous about the acceptability of the social order. It, in a sense, defers judgment on the character of the society while it seeks to develop a "black psyche" and a "black consciousness" that will offer support to the individual when he has to finally make a decision to opt into or to oppose the society. On the other hand, the school designed to promote and support effective competition implicitly accepts the cultural values and assumptions of the society. Even here, however, an all-black faculty and new methods of delivering educational content may be required to reach the alienated black child as well as to distinguish this type of school from the increasing number of inner-city schools where racially mixed or all-white faculties teach all, or almost all, black children.

To establish and fund such schools, even on a pilot basis, will require delicate political negotiations as well as a fair amount of political and social courage. There will also be a staffing problem since black teachers who are personally secure enough to share the philosophy and orientation of the program are still in short supply. Finally, there are the potential dangers of distortions of the program by various vested interests.

Yet, the information to be gained from experimental all-black schools and the desperate need to learn quickly how to provide equality of educational opportunity suggests that potential dangers and difficulties cannot be allowed to stand in the way of the establishment of such schools. For if all-black experimental schools are not established, we run the much greater risk of bringing to adulthood another generation of children who have found school irrelevant and who are more disaffected, more alienated than the current generation of very angry black men.

Kelyn and Carolyn*

BILL AYERS

The Children's Community

> When I ride the train and sit next to a person
>   of the opposite race
> I feel like a crow in a robin's nest
> And I feel dirty.
>
>   Carolyn Jackson, age 11†

Carolyn Jackson knows what it means to be black in America. She knows that white and black aren't just different races, but that they are "opposites." She knows that blackness isn't good; that being black is something close to being "dirty." And she knows that to be here and to be black is to be a stranger; it is to be ugly and unwanted—truly a "crow in a robin's nest."

Carolyn's poem accuses and frightens us. Can it be that this eleven-year-old black girl, merely seeing us on a train, feels this depth of anguish? Can our whiteness be that repulsive to this brown-skinned child? Did we have something to do with the slaughter of this innocent girl? Is this, blown up twenty million times, what the system of segregation means? Has this, in human terms, been the cost of racism and discrimination?

There is another story to be told by another child, a five-year-old boy named Kelyn—also brown-skinned, poor, American. Late last year, Kelyn, with me and a half-dozen other kids, was on a spontaneous trip from school to visit the county jail. As we drove, we played the game "I Spy." "I spy something red and white with the letters S-T-O-P on it," I said. (My choices are often the easiest and, espe-

---

† From "I Don't Mind" in Richard Lewis (ed.), *Miracles* (New York: Simon & Schuster, 1966).
* This discussion appeared originally in the Winter 1968 issue of the *Harvard Educational Review*.

cially when too consciously geared toward "learning experiences," the most boring.) "Stop sign!" cried seven voices in unison.

A big, brown truck pulled up to the stop sign opposite us. A four-year-old girl eagerly offered the next challenge. "I spy something brown," she said. Kelyn's eyes lit up and a broad smile crossed his face. He sat up as tall as he could and with his right hand spread-fingered and flat upon his chest and his left hand pulling excitedly on his cheek, he shouted, "Hey! That's me! That's me!"

Kelyn's response was excited and uncontrolled. It was obvious that he was unashamed—a bit proud. Somehow he had escaped the imposed self-hatred that Carolyn felt with such intensity. The other kids in the car didn't sense anything peculiar or taboo or funny in Kelyn's response. After all, the girl had asked for something brown, and Kelyn *is* brown.

Kelyn and I and the others are all members of The Children's Community, an experimental school in Ann Arbor, Michigan, attended by twenty-seven kids, and founded by parents in 1965. The school was originally a nursery and kindergarten, but has been able to add the equivalent of a grade each year and is currently accredited through second grade.

The Children's Community is an integrated school, but special care is taken to avoid the destructive side-effects of schools where integration means simply placing black children in a white environment. In The Children's Community, integration is based primarily on an acceptance of all kids and all cultures as they are; each individual is allowed to be himself and to exchange with others as he sees fit.

Certainly the fact that Kelyn has positive feelings about his color and about himself is not solely attributable to The Children's Community. We, too, have seen the inevitable scar of discrimination and racism in our students: the self-denigrating "swear-words" like "nappy" and "nigger," the occasionally expressed desire to have lighter skin, the partially wish-induced confusion about color ("When I grow up, I'll be white"), the characterization of unpleasant or negative things as "black." But The Children's Community has offered Kelyn (as well as the others) the chance to grow and to build upon what he already is.

Tony, six years old, is another Negro boy in The Children's Community. A few weeks ago, he dictated a story to one of the staff: "We went to look for hoboes today. I was the onliest one who knew where they was. They ain't mean and scary, though. And Dougie dressed like a hobo for Halloween, but he didn't look like them. Bill gave one some money, and Duke gave them a penny. The End."

Tony was proud of his story. He took it around with him for three days, reading it to staff and other kids, when they would listen. He took it home and colored a picture to go along with it, then brought it back and taped it to the wall. He entitled it "Tony's Story" and wrote "By Tony" at the bottom. The story was important to him; it expressed his thoughts and observations exactly.

To tell Tony that "onliest" isn't a word would have been meaningless and absurd at best, since onliest *is* a word—widely used and acceptable in Tony's world. Tony doesn't care that "only" cannot be compared and therefore cannot have a superlative. Tony isn't asking for help in grammar or word usage. He is merely expressing himself proudly and openly. To impose my form rather than to deal with his content is to imply that what he said makes no difference, as long as he said it correctly. It is to have a narrow, constricted view of the importance of language and communication.

Most judgments made about a child's language or culture, performance or behavior, are at best redundant, and at worst absolutely destructive. Certainly, to say, "It's not nice to hit," is to say the obvious. No one hits to be nice; one hits to hurt someone else, and to express one's feelings to him.

When a child's behavior is placed and measured on a moral level, debilitating fears and conflicts are necessarily built up. Most parents and teachers today recognize the harmful effects of such not-too-archaic techniques as corporal punishment and threats of hell-fire in dealing with children. But all moral judgments have those destructive qualities about them, partly because such judgments are at a level of criticism which is at odds with the child's level of understanding. If it's "wrong" to hit or "bad" to steal, and a child, for whatever reasons, feels like taking something or hitting someone, how does he come to terms with himself? The judgment has nothing to do with his own feelings or needs or desires. In fact, his reality is completely ignored; judgments are made "up there," where he can neither see, nor understand, nor hope to challenge them. They have a power and importance greater and more convincing than any of his experiences.

Finally, moral judgments and preachments, no matter how subtle or seemingly benevolent, never teach what they're supposed to; they merely create misunderstanding and conflict between expressed and experienced truths. A year ago, I went with a group of kids to the airport, and an assistant bought them each a piece of candy. Later, as we were walking through the terminal, a fight broke out between two of the kids. When it was broken up and everyone was in tears, one of the protagonists explained to me through sobs that he had asked for a piece of the other's candy and had been refused. He decided to take the candy because, as he said, "Kids gotta share." This was obviously a moral principle which he grudgingly acted out when he was forced to but which he championed whenever it favored his own interests. It had nothing whatever to do with his own feelings or experiences and offered little toward explaining concepts of tolerance or understanding or cooperation. These concepts must be felt as the natural outcome of a certain amount of experience, failure, and success. Love will never be taught by preachment.

If moralizing achieves anything, it is repression and fear. A child will learn better without these. Tony, who is acknowledged and respected in The Children's Community for his knowledge and experiences, will grow and develop through new experiences and contacts. The Children's Community will spare him the ordeal of learning to hate his language, his customs, his parents, and eventually himself as preparation for learning "proper" English and "acceptable" behavior. As Tony learns the power of language and the importance of communication through manipulating words, reading, and writing his own thoughts, he will find out how others use words, and for what reasons. And he will discover how he communicates best. "Dick and Jane" could conceivably teach Tony the skill of reading, but it would also teach him that reading is dull, imposed stuff, learned to please others. The fact that language has power cannot be memorized.

Moral judgments, implicit and explicit, are in constant use in most classrooms. It is, of course, easier for adults to cope with children's behavior when there is a higher judgment, an official dogma, to fall back on. One abdicates all responsibility for understanding or dealing with situations for what they are; some things are defined as "right," others "wrong." One can then avoid the difficult task of rationally and humanely reconciling conflicts among the students, and between the students and the teachers. One can hide his own fears and ignorance concerning his feelings and desires and behavior, as well as the feelings, desires, behavior of others.

Integration tends to bring with it a whole new set of moral judgments. The judgments usually follow a pattern something like this: there are a number of ways of acting in a given situation; white and black kids tend to act differently; the white kids are, in general, right; the black kids are wrong. This holds true explicitly in areas like speaking and writing, and implicitly in most other areas, like reading and music and history.

How does a child feel when everything he tries to express is considered stupid or meaningless or wrong? What happens to his natural enthusiasm and curiosity? And what conclusions will he draw when he sees that the only available

books are flat and sterile, presenting only one extremely limited, socially acceptable attitude toward life (some of the characters in these classics have recently
become one shade darker, but they are just as flat and sterile and limited as their
lighter-skinned brothers); or that the only music in the school is something he
doesn't quite understand or enjoy, and that the music he has known all his life
has no place here? Negro kids are made to think of themselves as stupid and
worthless, and to spend most of their time trying desperately to live up to the
pressures of the dominant society. And for every instance of a black child's
self-concept suffering, there is a corresponding white child who will suffer. The
master-mentality is also hollow and debilitating.

At The Children's Community, there is an open acceptance of differences.
Seen without value judgments, these differences are merely new things to learn
about, new experiences to be had. This does not mean that people pretend that
there are no differences or are reluctant to discuss them. When we avoid commenting on racial and cultural differences, we tell a child that there is something so horribly wrong with his condition that even to mention it would be
somehow cruel and unkind. Once last year, Duke, a seven-year-old black child,
asked me to sit with him while he did a portrait of the two of us. As he drew, we
talked about what he saw and how he would draw it. "You have yellow curly
hair," he said, "and mine's black and curlier." He didn't draw noses and used
only two straight lines for our mouths. This year as I was driving to the lumber
yard with a number of kids, Duke suddenly broke out laughing and, pointing
at my nose, said, "Your nose is so pointy and straight." Everyone joined in
laughing. I said, feeling my nose, "It really is, isn't it? Hey, your nose is flat and
short." There was general laughter as everyone started describing his own or
someone else's nose: Renée's was straight, Darlene's short, Cory's like a button.
No one was embarrassed or self-conscious about his nose; different noses were
suddenly exciting new discoveries.

There is no pre-planned or structured way in which exchange is expected to
take place in The Children's Community. The environment is full of different
people and diverse activities. Kids are allowed to accept or reject, to pick up
or put down whatever they want to.

The white children who came to The Children's Community the first year
were for the most part more quiet, less active, more academically-oriented than
the Negro children. On trips, they stayed close to adults and didn't do nearly
as much independent exploring as their black classmates. As the year progressed,
they became more and more confident and were increasingly able to go off on

their own, to ask questions about what interested them, to relate to strangers. A number of Negro kids began to ask for stories, to sit quietly for longer periods of time, to make thoughtful choices about which activities they would become involved in. The group, which had earlier been divided primarily along racial lines, was beginning to divide itself along activity-oriented lines. Each group had given something which was felt to be of value to the other; and every child gained from the process.

Exchanges are taking place constantly. Mona teaches a number of people to make grilled-cheese sandwiches in cooking class one day; later, Doug brings his mother's recipe for corn-bread and pig's-feet. Or Duke teaches Mike a phrase and learns one from Mike. "Hey, Cool Jerk" comes to replace "Good morning. How are you?" and for these kids expresses something more.

The Children's Community is a small model of what integrated schools could be. Kids seem to thrive and develop in the school environment. Each child is given the opportunity to move at his own speed in the direction he feels is most important; teaching is part of an active process which begins with the child, not with an objective body of subject matter to be covered. The Children's Community is a good school which is integrated; it is not a good school because it is integrated.

Fourteen years after that most celebrated and monumental Supreme Court decision ending segregation in the schools, it is apparent that segregation will be the reality for countless years ahead. The Coleman Report indicated a number of reasons why meaningful integration is so far away; this paper has indicated others. Even if there were a radical shift in the political boundaries and population patterns of this country, integration would be a long way off. For integration, as defined by the educational system, is a one-way process. It involves the "uplifting" or "headstarting" of black kids into a white world. It centers on terms like "culturally deprived," which means simply that the identified culture is not acceptable to white, middle-class standards, although it is clear that Negroes have a very distinct and rich culture of their own. Integration of this kind can more accurately be called assimilation, for it has nothing whatever to do with mutual exchange and growth.

As the dust begins to settle from those fourteen years of civil rights activity, one begins to realize that mere physical integration of the schools was the wrong issue. Certainly the Negro youngster suffers in his ghetto school. But his poor-white counterpart in his inner-city ghetto school, and his middle-class counterpart in his suburban ghetto school also suffer. The schools are generally constricting and destructive; they are simply using different methods and forcing people into different levels of slavery. Integrating the schools in itself does nothing to affect this.

White Americans must begin to face up to the real problems. Our society is racist and oppressive. Its schools are destructive to all children. We must find ways to deal with that. So far we have failed. If the recent reaction of black Americans to our failure frightens us, let us remember Carolyn Jackson's poem. In the poem, Carolyn remains the victim; she finds fault for her situation only in herself. When she identifies and strikes out at her oppressor, remember the violence that was done to her.

Compensation and Integration: The Berkeley Experience*

NEIL V. SULLIVAN

Massachusetts Board of Education (formerly Berkeley Unified School District)

As have most other school districts in the nation, Berkeley has sought to "pull ghetto children up by the bootstraps" through compensatory education, Headstart, Follow Through—the full complement of enrichment, remedy, and experiment, including individual tutoring, perceptive counseling, team-teaching, and nongraded programs. Berkeley has been zeroing in on reading for the past four years. So far the results have been disappointing.

A second direction has been an increasing commitment to the desegregation of all schools in the Berkeley system. The system has been partially desegregated since the fall of 1964, when each secondary school was racially balanced. Four elementary schools in "the foothills" are desegregated. An elementary-school busing program under Title I of the Elementary and Secondary Education Act has been in operation for a year and a half. Approximately two hundred and fifty Negro elementary-school children have been transported from the overcrowded poverty-area schools in south and west Berkeley to previously white hill schools and, in smaller numbers, to some underused foothill schools. On April 18, 1967, under pressure from many segments of the Negro community joined by the teachers' association and the union, the Berkeley Board of Education committed itself to the complete desegregation of all Berkeley schools by September, 1968.

This is the direction which Berkeley and other school systems must take, for our experience shows that there cannot be quality education for all children

* This discussion appeared originally in the Winter 1968 issue of the *Harvard Educational Review*.

without desegregation. But desegregation is only the first step. To achieve mean-ingful integration, we must move toward the educational park, which will enable full use of the modern technology of education, specialized teaching and auxiliary personnel, and cafeteria, recreational, and cultural facilities. This is the Berkeley direction, one in which at least eighty-five city school districts are actively inter-ested.[1]

What we thought four years ago we know now, for evidence is piling up which overwhelmingly damns segregated education, both racial and social. The Cole-man Report and studies carried out by the U.S. Commission on Civil Rights in-dicate the picture nationwide, pointing up that ghetto education is inferior in all aspects, that the factor of separation is most damaging to the achievement of the minority child, and that such damage increases with each succeeding grade. The Coleman Report shows that the progress in achievement made by the lower-class Negro child attending the "upper-class advantaged white school" far exceeds the progress of the Negro child receiving crash compensatory education in the sep-arate-but-enriched ghetto classroom, and is also significantly better than those lower-class Negro children who have been brought together in classrooms with lower-class white children.[2] Alan Wilson's investigations have buttressed the Cole-man findings; these studies show that the social-class composition of the school is decisive in improving student achievement through desegregation, and that race cuts across and correlates closely with social class.[3] Coleman's findings are further strengthened by reports from White Plains, New York, where children from a closed-down Negro elementary school were transported to schools in upper-middle-class, white residential areas. Negro students attending these schools are achieving far better than those who attended the segregated center-city school. Those who have been in integrated schools since the first grade are doing better than those who started in a segregated school. White youngsters in desegregated schools are doing as well and sometimes better than the students in the all-white schools before 1964. There has been no white exodus from White Plains.[4]

What these studies have shown for other school districts, we in Berkeley are

[1] Max Wolff, *Educational Park Development in the United States, 1967* (New York: Center for Urban Education, 1967). (Mimeographed.)

[2] James S. Coleman *et al.*, *Equality of Educational Opportunity* (Washington: U.S. Government Printing Office, 1966), pp. 67-73; U.S. Commission on Civil Rights, *Racial Isolation in the Public Schools* (Washington: U.S. Government Printing Office, 1967), pp. 2-10.

[3] Alan B. Wilson, *Educational Consequences of Segregation in a California Community* (Berke-ley, Calif.: Univ. of California, Survey Research Center, 1966), pp. 66-9.

[4] *New York Times*, October 22, 1967, p. E9; *San Francisco Chronicle*, October 16, 1967, p. 1. De-tailed results of this six-year study will be published shortly.

discovering ourselves through our own experience and evaluations. First, partial evaluation of the secondary-school reorganization has yielded the following results:

(1) Both students and faculty who experienced the reorganization have generally accepted it easily. Attitudes toward teachers, counselors, school programs, and fellow students of other races are generally increasingly positive as time goes on and the "trauma of change" recedes.[5]

(2) Average grades achieved by the tenth-grade students who experienced the new desegregated seventh-and-eighth-grade school and the desegregated separate ninth-grade campus of the high school were generally better than the average of those who did not. Tenth-grade marks of students from the desegregated secondary schools continue to improve over the marks achieved by tenth-graders who received their seventh-, eighth-, and ninth-grade education in the segregated Negro or the segregated white junior high school.[6]

(3) Attendance did suffer temporarily, but since has continued to improve. This is most notable at the new desegregated ninth-grade campus of the high school.[7]

More significantly, the evaluation of the program wherein two hundred and fifty Negro students were transported from overcrowded, segregated schools to underused, predominantly white, foothill and hill schools showed, within the limits of available comparable test data, that:[8]

(1) Although all target-area children continued to score under national norms in achievement, the bused children made higher average gains than those who were not bused and higher gains than the bused children had averaged in the

[5] Leonard A. Marascuilo, *A Second Report to the Board of Education, Berkeley Unified School District, on Students' Attitudes toward the Secondary School Reorganization* (Berkeley, Calif.: Berkeley Unified School District, 1967). (Mimeographed.); and *Report to the Board of Education, Berkeley Unified School District, on Students' Attitudes toward the Secondary School Reorganization* (Berkeley, Calif.: Berkeley Unified School District, 1965), 25 pp. plus Appendix. (Mimeographed.)

[6] Daniel K. Freudenthal, *Memorandum to Dr. Neil V. Sullivan on the Marascuilo Report and Supplementary Investigations* (Berkeley, Calif.: Berkeley Unified School District, 1967). (Mimeographed.); and *Analysis of Teacher Marks for the Berkeley High School Tenth Grades, 1963-64 and 1965-66. By School of Origin* (Berkeley, Calif.: Berkeley Unified School District, 1967). (Mimeographed.)

[7] *Report on Effects of the Secondary Reorganization on Attendance in Grades 7 and 8 Combined and in Grade 9* (Berkeley, Calif.: Berkeley Unified School District). (Mimeographed.)

[8] Harold J. Jonsson, *Report of Evaluation of ESEA Title I Compensatory Education Activities for 1966-67* (San Francisco, Calif.: Berkeley Unified School District, 1967). (Mimeographed.); and *Statement of ESEA Title I Evaluation Summary to the Board of Education* (San Francisco, Calif.: San Francisco State College, 1967). (Mimeographed.)

previous years. These gains were better than would have been predicted on the basis of average measured intelligence.

(2) Receiving-class students, predominantly white, who were in the same classes as the bused children, continued to score high in achievement and to make large gains in their achievement.

(3) Attitudes of staff, parents, and students toward the project remained largely favorable.

In the spring of 1967, reading test scores for students in Berkeley's predominantly Negro target schools, which have compensatory programs supported by Title I, ESEA funds, showed very slight gains from the previous year. All scores were significantly below the district average; all scores were up to six months under the gains made in the racially-mixed foothill schools and from six months to almost a year under the gains made in the predominantly-white hill schools. These disappointing data came after three years of continuing compensatory education, four years of strong emphasis on reading (both developmental and remedial), three years of Headstart, and three years of special small-class instruction in the ghetto schools. Generally, achievement has continued in the traditional pattern. The children from south and west Berkeley are approximately a year behind those in the hill schools as they begin school. By the time they reach the sixth grade, they have lost an additional year's ground, the full complement of compensatory education to the contrary notwithstanding. For example, the Stanford-Binet grade-six scores in word-meaning indicated that sixth-graders in one of the target schools achieved a grade 4.3 in word-meaning and 4.2 in paragraph-meaning. That same school, a nongraded school with a unique experimental emphasis on reading, received recognition as a "National Demonstration School." Sixth-graders in one of the racially-mixed schools achieved at the 8.1 grade level in word-meaning and the 8.8 grade level in paragraph-meaning. This racially-mixed school was among the top four sixth grades in the district in word-meaning, and the leading sixth grade in paragraph-meaning. There was no compensatory education there and less priority given to small class-size than in target schools. In general, target-school students continue to achieve below district averages and national averages in the various subjects tested under the state testing program.[9] This is the story of the slum-ghetto school even in a small city where the slums

---

[9] Berkeley Unified School District, *Report of Group Test Results of Intelligence and Academic Achievement: School Year—Fall, 1966; Spring, 1967* (Berkeley, Calif.: Berkeley Unified School District, 1967).

don't look like slums and where the slum schools receive a wealth of compensatory educational opportunities.

Entirely consistent with these findings is Berkeley's own "Baby Coleman Report." Spring, 1967 student performance, grades 1 through 6, in the paragraph-meaning section of the Stanford Achievement Test was compared by type of school and race. (See Tables 1-4.) Paragraph-meaning achievement correlates closely with achievement in general, and, therefore, was used in the Berkeley study. The district norm, which is higher than national or state norms, was the base.[10] In accordance with the Tryon pattern, achievement was grouped into low, middle, and high thirds as was socio-economic level. Key findings were as follows:

(1) Over 50 per cent of Berkeley's grades 1 through 6 Negro students were in the low-achievement group, or about four times the percentage of whites and other non-Negro groups. By contrast, about seven times the proportion of whites plus other non-Negro groups achieved in the highest third compared to the Negro students. However, almost as high a percentage of Negro students achieved in the middle third as did the other group. (See Table 1.)

(2) Tables 2, 3, and 4 can be used to compare the achievement of Negroes and whites in the predominantly Negro, foothill, and hill schools. An over-all pattern of much higher achievement for both whites and Negroes in the integrated foothill and hill schools is again apparent from these tables.

While 66.2 per cent of Negro students achieve in the lower third in the predominantly Negro schools with compensatory education, only 33.4 per cent in the hill schools, and 43.3 per cent in the foothill schools are in this lowest category.

In the predominantly Negro schools, we find only 4.5 per cent of Negro students in the highest achievement category, while in the integrated schools the figures are 21.4 per cent and 12.6 per cent. Likewise, in the middle-achievement group, we find only 29.2 per cent of Negroes from the predominantly Negro schools while the integrated schools have, respectively, 45.2 per cent and 44.1 per cent.

In the comparison of the predominantly Negro schools with the foothill schools, it is impossible to separate the effects of integration from the effects of the student's own social class. Exact social-class data are not available on individuals,

[10] A. D. Dambacher, *Proportional Distribution of Achievement Scores by Race and by Grade* (Berkeley, Calif.: Berkeley Unified School District, 1967); *Socio-Economic Achievement Scores by Race and Grade for Grades K-8, by School* (Berkeley, Calif.: Berkeley Unified School District, 1967). For the basic method used by A. D. Dambacher in identifying social class, see Robert C. Tryon, *Identification of Social Areas by Cluster Analysis—A General Method with an Application to the San Francisco Bay Area* (Berkeley and Los Angeles, Calif.: Univ. of California Press, 1955).

but one can assume that there is some social-class difference between Negro
dents attending the predominantly Negro schools and those in the foothill schoo,

However, this difficulty does not present itself in the comparison between th
predominantly Negro schools and the hill schools, since the hill schools were integrated by busing students from the predominantly Negro lower-class area of
Berkeley. Differences in achievement can be attributed to integration.

It is important to emphasize also that white students achieve significantly better in the integrated schools of the hills and foothills than in predominantly-Negro
schools. We find the best achievement for both whites and Negroes in these integrated situations.

PERCENTAGES OF STUDENTS' READING SCORES FALLING INTO LOW, MEDIUM, AND
HIGH TERTILES IN THE BERKELEY GRADE SCHOOLS. (Percentages are broken down by
race. Read percentages across.)

TABLE 1
All District Grade Schools

	Low	Medium	High	Total
Negro	58.7	33.8	7.5	100 (N = 2809)
Other	13.1	36.2	50.7	100 (N = 4238)
Total	31.3	35.2	33.4	100 (N = 7047)

TABLE 2
Predominantly Negro Schools with Compensatory Education

	Low	Medium	High	Total
Negro	66.2	29.2	4.5	100 (N = 2028)
Other	43.8	40.5	15.7	100 (N = 395)
Total	62.4	31.1	6.5	100 (N = 2423)

TABLE 3
*Predominantly White Schools (Hill Schools) Integrated by Negro Students
Bused from Lower-Social-Class Areas*

	Low	Medium	High	Total
Negro	33.4	45.2	21.4	100 (N = 234)
Other	8.2	34.3	57.5	100 (N = 2660)
Total	9.9	35.5	54.6	100 (N = 2899)

TABLE 4

Integrated Schools (Foothill Schools) in Racially-Mixed Residential Areas

	Low	*Medium*	*High*	*Total*
Negro	43.3	44.1	12.6	100 (N = 562)
Other	14.6	39.4	46.0	100 (N = 1207)
Total	23.6	40.9	35.5	100 (N = 1769)

Students in the slum-ghetto schools came out worst of all in paragraph-meaning achievement on the Stanford-Binet test despite all of the compensation, experimentation, and enrichment at those schools. There was significant improvement for those who attended racially-mixed, middle-class schools. They came out best, all around, and most of these children had been transported to the hill schools which had been predominantly white and upper-class. What better verification could there be of Coleman's findings and of Wilson's findings? What better validation of the White Plains six-year study? What better basis for recommending that Berkeley desegregate completely by September, 1968—both racially and socioeconomically?

Nevertheless, there remains a considerable achievement gap between Negro and other students even at the hill schools. Generations of enforced deprivation on top of a heritage of slavery cannot be rubbed out easily or quickly. Moreover, what is lacking in the hill schools is that essential revolution in teaching programs, styles, and technology which has only just begun. Certainly there can be no equal educational opportunity in Berkeley or any other place without racial integration of the schools *and* massive educational revolution for which community educational centers offer the most promise.

Now that national and local returns are in from Coleman, the Civil Rights Commission, Berkeley, and White Plains, how can educators and communities of good faith and good will procrastinate further? Desegregate now!

After desegregation has been completed, and even after the potential of the educational park has been realized, the ghetto will still remain. Educational reform itself is not sufficient—a total attack must be mounted on the larger social and economic problems. Massive amounts of federal, state, local, and private money must be poured into ghetto improvements that would:

(1) Guarantee a minimum economic level for all ghetto residents.

(2) Give ghetto residents political power and control over institutions that affect their lives.

(3) Develop centers of education, culture, and human services tied into comprehensive community and regional plans that cut across archaic local lines.

(4) Prepare all wage-earners for meaningful work through massive job-training and re-training programs.

Our financial commitment to these necessary changes must be at least as extensive as our present commitment to the Vietnam war. These necessary changes may require a new relationship between education and community, new regional problem-solving units, a new tax structure, and perhaps new political forms centered in the community. Only if we take such basic steps, however, can we move toward an interracial, interclass democracy, fitted to the twenty-first century.

Some Modest Proposals*

HERBERT KOHL

Teachers and Writers Collaborative

Children go through a year of Headstart classes. The next year there is no kinder-garten available for them. They have a good year in a sixth grade, then are sent to an understaffed junior high school. Before going to high school, they are told that they can pass only general or vocational courses. During senior high school, the guidance counselor fails to inform them of the possibility of entering pre-college and Upward Bound programs. These are not rare occurrences; rather they are the general rule in ghetto schools. There is no continuity in the child's school career, and there is no way that his parents, alienated and intimidated by the school system and its middle-class personnel, can submit a grievance and be as-sured that it will be considered seriously.

The lack of continuity shows up particularly as a child passes from elementary to junior high school (or intermediate school). The two schools have completely unrelated staffs, and the junior high with its departmentalized program allows no one adult in the school to be close to the individual child.

The guidance counselor is supposed to know the children as individuals and help them with their school problems. However, since he has some two hundred children to worry about, reality makes a mockery of the job. Worse, the guidance counselor is usually a former teacher who is delighted to be out of the classroom and who doesn't have knowledge of how children in the slums are forced to live

* This discussion appeared originally in the Winter 1968 issue of the *Harvard Educational Review*.

228

or of the problems that are significant to them. The children sense this and most commonly lie to their guidance counselors, refuse to bring problems to them, and are content to act dumb and inarticulate in interviews.

Many talented children are lost in this indifferent system, and many minor problems grow to major human tragedies. This fault cannot be blamed entirely upon the school system. After all, the system (*qua* system, not with respect to personnel and supplies) is quite the same as the middle-class school system where discontinuity and disorder do not exist. One difference is obvious, however. Middle-class children have their parents as advocates and guardians of continuity and order in the school. There are adults who know what their children are entitled to and insure that they get it. Not so with the poor and especially with the black poor. The parents do not usually know what their children are entitled to and, in addition, are neither respected by the school authorities nor kept informed by them. They are poor advocates for their children and worse guardians of order in a system that manifests lack of respect for their children.

This situation must be remedied; and there may be a way, though it is not without political dangers. Many young men in ghetto communities between the ages of twenty and thirty-five, fatherless themselves, have taken it upon themselves to be the guardians and protectors of youngsters in their neighborhoods. They take upon themselves the responsibilities for the child's safety in the street and his education in the ways of men and the Man. In a sense, they are individual ombudsmen for several children. They intercede for children with the police, with neighbors, with merchants, and with employers. They help the children to learn how to get jobs, hustle money, buy clothes—all but what is most essential to youth in our society: how to make it in school. There they have no power. Often they are dropouts themselves and don't know how to be the children's advocates with respect to the school system. Yet they could learn easily and their advocacy could be legitimized in the following way.

These young men could be trained and paid to be ombudsmen for, say, fifteen children from their own neighborhoods. Their jobs would be to see those fifteen children through school and make sure (1) of the receipt by the child of the education legally and morally due him, (2) of the conduct and progress of the child in school, (3) of the acquisition of remedial help for the child, and (4) of the continuing education of each child's parents in their child's actual progress in school and of his future possibilities.

These men would perform this function after a training period during which they would learn about the system and, if they desired, take college courses in sociology, psychology, and other relevant subjects. Moreover, these men would consider their pay for this particular role as supplemental to their income and would be allowed to maintain full-time jobs as well.

To make this plan work, such ombudsmen would have the power to enter the schools and scrutinize what goes on there. Such an organization may indeed be one productive way to give local school boards or parents' associations in ghetto areas of large cities the effective power they need to ensure the development of quality education in their schools.

Teacher-training as it presently is carried on fails to prepare teachers to work successfully in ghetto areas. But perhaps this is not so much the fault of teacher-training as of the fact that in a difficult, strange situation one is bound to come close to failing the first time through. I became a "good" teacher in an impossibly "bad" school, but not the first time I taught, despite six months of student-teaching and a full MA program at Teachers College, Columbia. My student-teaching was academic. The real problems arose when I had my own class and there was no one there to support me in any way. For new teachers, it is essential that their teacher-training programs extend at least two years into their careers and that they include at least six months of supervised internship. Even this will be worthless if the supervisors have never taught in ghetto schools themselves and are too impatient for the teacher's success. This means acknowledging that many children will continue to be poorly taught while a generation of teachers is being trained. But at least such a process will hold out more hope than exists in the schools presently.

These teachers-in-training would benefit immensely by direct contact with the community. They should work closely with the proposed corps of ombudsmen which was discussed above, both before entering the classroom and during the first few years of training. Teachers and ombudsmen should take classes together and participate in seminars on an equal basis. Teachers should also work with their students in their neighborhoods to experience the differences between the child's behavior in the classroom and in a nonthreatening, individual situation. In this way, the teacher may become better able to understand the pathology of the ghetto classroom and less likely to locate the problem in himslf or the children.

To teach honestly and not anger or alienate the children, one must be honest about failure and hypocrisy in American life. One cannot talk of equal chance and freedom of choice to people who have no opportunity or freedom, or at best very little. One cannot avoid the depths of prejudice in this society nor the misunderstandings of cultural differences. It is necessary to avoid subjective judgments about, say, the superiority of western civilization, judgments that are the very life of texts used in our schools. This is true not only for the poor—it is true for all children. There is no more thorough way to keep alienating the young in our society than by continuing to feed them myths and lies about who we are when the children know perfectly well that we don't believe it ourselves.

A social studies curriculum which is devoted to man and his successes and failures, the problems he has faced, and the range and ingenuity of his *solutions* must be developed. We must allow children to recognize how subjective the notions of "strange," "savage," and "primitive" are, and how self-justifying and misleading so much of the propaganda they receive is. Not that the children, especially black children, don't know these things. On the contrary, their acute awareness demands that an adult admit these sad truths before the child can begin to feel that the adult has something to teach that may be worth learning.

The study of literature should also reflect the realities and complexities of life. The teacher has to be willing to admit conflict, violence, the unpleasant into the classroom. The children must think about these realities before they are forced to live them without preparation. It is a pathetic comment on our schools that so many young people find themselves unprepared for life even with the "finest" of educations we offer.

To promote this radical revision of educational practices, new ways of attracting and using talented teachers are the key consideration. This country does not lack potential talent, as the Peace Corps, Vista, the civil rights and Vietnam protest movements have shown. The question is how to utilize this talent and draw these people into careers that may affect the lives of our children in significant ways. I can only make several suggestions:

(1) Entice as many men as possible into the elementary schools; give them the freedom to experiment with new curricula and the salaries to make teaching a possible career. Make it possible for them to take every third year off to study at a university or to travel. Encourage them to develop intellectually and provide opportunities for them to communicate with other teachers about the issues that are crucial and controversial in contemporary education. Insure that these meetings are not bogged down in the tasks of developing self-respect for the profession and respectable salaries.

(2) Create two administrations for elementary and secondary schools—one for academic matters and one for business. Let the business administrator be drawn from the business community, and choose the academic administrator on the basis of his prior experience and success in the kind of school that he is being

asked to lead. In other words, don't choose as principal of a ghetto elementary school a man who has been a successful mathematics teacher in a middle-class high school and an inefficient and indifferent accountant.

(3) The greatest obstacle to true experimentation in education has been the U.S. Office of Education and the pseudo-scientific models it applies in defining educational research. The USOE has a false paradigm of hypothesis-test-confirmation in mind when it judges proposals for educational research. What is really needed, however, is the chance for good people to spend their time discovering what is good. After sufficient time to experiment freely, they can formulate hypotheses, test, and replicate their work. But they must be allowed time to entertain many possibilities and fail many times before they can be expected to "produce" results. A scientist may be supported to develop an intuitive line of investigation. Why is it that in education, where this type of investigation is so essential, a more rigid model of "scientific" correctness is indiscriminately employed?

(4) Make it possible for people in the intellectual, artistic, industrial, political, and business communities to enter schools temporarily. Make it possible for people to be visiting-teachers or visiting-administrators just as they can be visiting-professors at universities. Many people who cannot devote their lives to the education of children would willingly devote a year or two. They are needed; the schools just don't connect up with the society at large. Perhaps the poets, playwrights, actors, newspapermen, community organizers, business executives who would be invited into the elementary and secondary schools should be supported by federal funds. We must learn to make a public and legitimate place in education for these people whose time and commitment is presently lost.

As a final and wildly impractical suggestion, I would like to present a counterproposal to Christopher Jenck's proposal for making schools private and competitive.[1] I submit that the only way to a solution of the problems of our public schools is the opposite—the abolition of all private schools. This is unfortunately tantamount to saying that there are no solutions to our problems, and that may be. Last April, I attended a meeting at a Harlem junior high school. It was a prelude to the IS 201 crisis. Mayor Lindsay, Superintendent of Schools Donovan, and several other officials were present to listen to the complaints of the community. They heard plenty. They were told that if the Board of Education did not live

---

[1] Christopher Jencks, "Is the Public School Obsolete?," *The Public Interest*, No. 2 (Winter, 1966), 18-27.

up to its promise of integration, 201 would be closed down in the fall. Lindsay and Donovan expressed concern and let it be known that the community had made an impression on them. It could not have been a lasting one, however, for the next fall the Board of Education opened up a segregated IS 201. But why should Lindsay and Donovan care more than their jobs demanded—their children weren't involved, and couldn't be since they were nicely protected from the problems of public education by being in private schools. It is also ironic to note that the children of two of the most articulate critics of the Board of Education—Milton Galamison and Thelma Johnson—are also in private schools. It is not enough to fight for other people's children's schools; the fight for superior public education must be the fight for superior education for our own children. That is the only way in which equality of educational opportunity can be even approximated in this country.

Intervention Alternatives
for Urban Education*

MARIO D. FANTINI

The Ford Foundation

A vision that arouses both fears and hope is emerging from the crisis in public education, especially in our cities. That prospect is that public education will return to the direct control of the public—but not just a traditionally "prepared" public; not simply the civic leaders who serve on city-wide school boards, or parent-association leaders who are endowed with verbal and organizational skills and college degrees; not just the enlightened business leaders who recognize good schools as a drawing card to local economic development (or a dampener on racial unrest). The murmurs now being heard in two or three large cities are coming from the "garden variety" of parent and community resident—including ghetto parents with little formal education—calling for a say in the operation of public schools.

The prospect is frightening to many because it rises from the soil of civil strife and growing racial hostility, assertiveness, and even hatred. But even without these factors, the prospect would alarm the majority of professional educators (and many sympathetic laymen) who fear the dismemberment of complex systems of education by the hand of people said to be incompetent. For, after all, we are not talking about a plaything. We are discussing a vaunted American institution, which is credited with advancing democratic practices and with opening the doors

* This discussion appeared originally in the Winter 1968 issue of the *Harvard Educational Review*.

of opportunity to millions of immigrants for more than a century. Moreover, it is an institution with an enormous and growing capital plant and annual operating budget.

The positive aspects of this kind of public control are more difficult to perceive. One possibility is that under the right conditions, real public control of public education could provide more effective education. It could also foster the revitalization of one of the most revered canons of American society, citizen participation in democratic processes. And, on the most profound level, perhaps intimate public engagement in public education could lead to realization of one of the most fundamental goals of education: to make better citizens, all along the age spectrum. Merely to suggest these prospects is to invite accusations of romanticism or naïve idealism. But an examination of more hard-headed approaches to modern public education suggests that this idealistic path may turn out to be the most practical and efficient.

Some Premises

Before examining past and future approaches to the solution of the educational crisis, it would be well to make explicit the premises of my argument:

(1) That public education is failing generally. The most visible failure is in the urban, low-income, racial-minority ghettoes. But if one holds education responsible in part for shortcomings throughout American society, education has failed more widely. The shortcomings include such features of contemporary life as the alienation and withdrawal of many economically and culturally advantaged college-age youth and the impotence of social consciousness in mobilizing an adequate response to the nation's domestic crises. Public education's precise share of the blame for these shortcomings need not be calculated in order to assert that it bears *some* share, even a substantial one.

(2) That public education is a governmental function. It is supported by the public at large, not simply by the immediate users, and it is subject at least to review, if not to close accountability, by elected public representatives somewhere along the line.

(3) That while the goals of American public education are not confined to skill development, the present operational definition of quality education is performance in basic skills at or above grade-level as measured by standardized tests.

(4) That the growing complexity of the education process is no cause for attrition of the concept of public control of public education.

(5) That public education is a universal right. Therefore it cannot, even *de facto*, be limited to those who are responsive and congenial to whatever the prevailing mode of public education happens to be. Public education has an affirmative obligation to meet the needs not only of the "normal" but also of the physically and otherwise handicapped, and of those who are unresponsive or hostile to the prevailing process.

(6) That the public has a right to determine educational policy and to hold professionals accountable for implementing policy. Thus, when 70 per cent of ghetto children are not reading at grade-level their parents have a right to question professional performance since the schools are supposed to educate everyone.

(7) That urban education is synonymous with the education of low-income racial minorities whose growing despair is both a threat and a challenge to America's great cities. The general urban crisis is inextricably linked to the crisis of urban education.

The Nature of the Crisis

In the last twenty years, the nation has overcome with reasonable success what were regarded as "crises" in public education. The first was a deficit in facilities and personnel, due mainly to deferred spending during World War II and to a rise in the birth rate. We still have not caught up, but the capital investment has been truly impressive, and progress on the number and salaries of personnel has been almost as significant.

The second "crisis," escalated to a national emergency by Sputnik, was the inadequacy of training in science and mathematics. Sputnik led to additional offerings in these fields, and large-scale curriculum experimentation has resulted in more and better-prepared students in these fields.

But all these improvements in public education have left the basic system unchanged. They have strengthened the status quo, enabling the system to serve better those it has always served best. The heart of the present crisis in public education is the realization that the system has failed a major segment of the population. This failure was the most intractable crisis all along, but it did not come to full public awareness until the nation took official cognizance of poverty amidst affluence and until the nonwhite fourth of society's economic underclass began to assert its civil rights and demand a full share in political and economic opportunity.

Our present preoccupation with the disadvantaged, however, has not diverted critics from concluding that the total system of education is incapable of addressing the challenge of providing excellent education for a diverse student population. Consequently, the mission of fundamental educational reform is not for the poor alone, but for all.

There is little agreement regarding the locus of the problem of school failure. At one extreme is the assumption that the failure of any child to learn lies primarily with the learner—in his physical, economic, cultural, or environmental deficits. At the other pole is the notion that if pupils are failing the school system itself needs basic rehabilitation. Under this assumption, the school's obligation is to diagnose the learner's needs, concerns, and cognitive and affective style, and adjust its program accordingly. In the early stages of concern about the learning problems of the disadvantaged, the searchlight played almost entirely on the shortcomings of the learners. A salutory shift toward a more comprehensive diagnosis of the teaching and learning system as well as the problems of the learner himself seems now to be developing. Emerging with the shift is a set of prescriptions—alternatives for intervention designed to reform the process and practice of public education.

Intervention Alternatives

A continuum of five basic approaches to intervention may be identified: compensatory education, desegregation, model subsystems, parallel systems, and total system reform. With the exception of compensatory education, these are largely untried concepts, but in some cases—model subsystems, for example—the few existing examples are sufficient to provide a basis for examining the likelihood of success or failure.

Compensatory Intervention

Compensatory education—attempts to overcome shortcomings in the learner—is the most prevalent form of intervention designed to raise pupils' academic achievement. It characterizes such efforts as the Ford Foundation-supported Great Cities School Improvement Programs, Title I of the Elementary and Secondary Education Act and New York City's early Higher Horizons Program and recent More Effective Schools Program. Compensatory education seeks to attack a spectrum of defects in the learner—verbal retardation, lack of motivation, and experiential and sensory deprivation—that presumably prevent his participation in the learning process. In addition to grafting extra education onto the regular school experience, proponents of compensation have attempted to nip deficiencies in the bud through preschool programs like Project Headstart.

For the most part, however, compensatory education is a prescription that deals with *symptoms,* with strengthened doses that have been ineffective before—more trips, more remedial reading, etc.—without real differences in kind. It is essentially an additive, or "band aid" approach that works by augmenting and strengthening existing programs. It builds layers onto the standard educational process in order to bring the strays into the fold and to fit them into the existing school mold. The assumption is that the schools need to do somewhat more for disadvantaged pupils, but it does not presume that the school itself is in need of wholesale re-examination.

Enormous effort, ingenuity, and funds have been invested in compensatory education, but the evidence gathered from even the best efforts indicates that they are having little significant impact on the problem of low achievement among disadvantaged children. The proponents of continued compensatory intervention argue either that not enough effort and resources have yet been applied or that greater attacks must be made on factors external to the schools (typically, family stability, housing, and income), or both.

But the compensatory approach is viewed with increasing distrust by the parents of academic failures both because the techniques are not achieving their goals, and because these parents are rejecting the premise that the fault lies in their children. Doubts are also beginning to arise among educational strategists disappointed by the failure of incremental inputs to the existing system to make a substantial difference.

Desegregation

Since the 1954 Supreme Court decision, a principal motivating factor in efforts toward integration has been the assumption that Negro pupils' achievement improves in an integrated school environment. The Coleman Report tends to support this view, and the U.S. Commission on Civil Rights is unequivocal in stating: "Negro children suffer serious harm when their education takes place in public schools which are racially segregated, whatever the source of such segregation may be. Negro children who attend predominantly Negro schools do not achieve as well as other children, Negro and white."[1]

In most urban settings, integration has proved elusive, if not impossible. The

---

[1] U.S. Commission on Civil Rights, *Racial Isolation in the Public Schools* (Washington: U.S. Government Printing Office, 1967), I.

failure to achieve integration to any significant extent was due first to massive white resistance. Now it is even less likely to occur in our lifetime because of the growing concentration in the inner city of Negro and other nonwhite minorities. The only possible plan for achieving integration in many large cities, metropolitan integration across present school district boundaries, seems politically unfeasible.

Moreover, minority group members themselves show a growing shift away from integration at the option of the white majority. The new focus of Negro and other racial-minority parents is on power and control over the schools their children attend. The changing mood springs not only from the poor record of integration efforts, but also from a revolt against the condescension perceived by minority group members in the school desegregation efforts of the post-1954 decade. First, many of them resent the fact that integration is, under current power arrangements, an option of the white community. Second, they believe that the dependent status of the Negro in American society is perpetuated by the notion that the only way to help the black child is to seat him alongside white children. Beneath this mood is a quest for stronger racial identity and pride, and a desire to gain more control of their own destiny. The initial desire for integration was based, say many Negro spokesmen, on the belief that parents in predominantly white schools exercised enough power to insure that the school offered quality education, in which Negro pupils should share. The converse is powerlessness, further destruction of identity, and increasing disconnection from the larger society.

The implication for public education is greater participation by Negroes in control over predominantly Negro schools. This is rather different from the "separate but equal" doctrine, since some "black power" philosophers reason that when Negroes achieve quality education under their own aegis, they will then be prepared to connect (integrate) with the white society on a groundwork of parity instead of deficiency. A good school then would be defined not by the kind of children who attend it, but by the quality of the education offered by the school. In short, they seek connection as equals.

The goals of integration, therefore, must be broadened to restore a quality that has been sidetracked in the emphasis on the educational-achievement goal of desegregation. That is, we must reaffirm our commitment to connect with one another as human beings. We must recognize that viewing diversity and differences as assets rather than unfortunate barriers to homogeneity has as positive an effect on human growth and development as the teaching of academic skills. All of which is to suggest that militant Negro demands for participation in control of public education is actually a means of greater *connection* to society, precisely opposite from the connotations of separatism usually associated with "black power."

Model Subsystems

In an effort to explore new and improved learning strategies and techniques, experimental units are being created in which educators hope to develop improved training, retraining, curriculum, and methodology patterns—and, lately, greater community participation—that may be demonstrated and disseminated throughout entire school systems. Within a school system, a subunit may consist of one or a cluster of schools. Projects under Titles III and IV of the Elementary and Secondary Education Act are seeking to create subsystems on a regional basis, through consortia of institutions.

Although some colleges and universities have for many years maintained experimental undergraduate subsystems (honors colleges, for example), the trend toward this mode of intervention in public schools may have started with a progress report (by a panel headed by Jerrold Zacharias) to the U. S. Commissioner of Education in March, 1964. The report led to the creation of a model subdivision in the Washington, D.C. Public Schools. At about the same time, the Syracuse, N.Y. Public Schools (in the Madison Area Project), and later the Boston Public Schools, created subsystems in a deliberate attempt to provide the total system with a development and training conduit for successful innovative practices. The most recent, and most visible, instances of model subsystems in a large urban establishment are three experimental school clusters in Manhattan and Brooklyn, including the Intermediate School 201 complex. These differ from earlier subsystems in that they are governed by community-based boards, although they must still seek ultimate approval on any number of basic decisions from the central Board of Education.

Many see the subsystem as a means for involving new institutions and persons outside the educational establishment with the urban schools. In New York City, for example, New York University, Teachers College, and Yeshiva University have "adopted" single schools or clusters of schools. Antioch College has assisted an experimental subsystem school in Washington, the Adams-Morgan School, and is seeking to adopt schools in Philadelphia and Dayton, Ohio. In addition to colleges and universities, community agencies, research and development centers, the Peace Corps and Vista veterans, private industry, and the professions are seen as possible sources of new talent and ideas introduced through model subsystems.

Intervention through model subsystems represents substantial progress toward a realization that "more-of-the-same" approaches have limited utility. It represents a refreshing intellectual concession that the educational process and system may share responsibility with the learner for his failure to achieve. It also borrows a leaf from scientific, technological, and industrial enterprises in its commitment to research and development.

The vogue for subsystems is developing rapidly despite scant experience with them and even scantier evidence of success. There are intrinsic constraints in the organizational framework within which dependent subsystems seek to explore the avenues of change. First, experience suggests that the model subsystem may lack the autonomy and freedom it needs to follow findings through to their ultimate conclusion. More likely than not, explorations into new school patterns call for breaking the rules, and the mother system is frequently unwilling to give her precocious, adventurous children much latitude. Furthermore, subunits too often depend for their new energies and resources on imported consultants who do not become integral members of the existing structure. And, as a practical matter, the educators selected to head subunits are often irreversibly captive to bureaucratic rigidity; their underlying identification is likely to be with the large system that sanctioned the experiment (that is, with the status quo) rather than with the new territory the experimental subunit seeks to explore. The experimental systems also are under pressure to produce results quickly. The mother system, which itself may be in disarray due to years or decades of decline, nonetheless is impatient to evaluate the subsystem, and perhaps vested interests are only too ready to label it a failure if it does not turn out a shining record of extraordinary achievement in a year or two. Whether the subsystem is dependent or largely autonomous, it is not likely to affect an entire system that is governed by an adept and hierarchy-hardened bureaucracy and conditioned by fixed patterns of behavior. Moreover, the educational substance of subsystems has, up to this point, been fragmented. The experiments tend to concentrate on one or another piece of improved instructional practice—team teaching, new careers for the poor, role playing, teacher training, or reading, for example—but seldom with the form and structure of the total system.

Parallel Systems

One set of approaches to quality education does not take the form of intervention in public education; rather, it calls for opportunities for students to escape into a parallel system. Such approaches assume that if the poor (or others) cannot reform public education, they should be afforded options to it.

Mario D. Fantini

A few privately managed schools have been established in urban ghettoes, and several others are in the planning stage. Precedents for such schools exist in southern Freedom Schools (notably Neil Sullivan's school for Negro pupils deprived of educational opportunity when the Prince Edward County, Virginia, public schools closed to avoid integration). Some northern counterparts include Harlem's Academies of Transition and the New School for Children in Boston's Roxbury section. The Urban League-sponsored street academies are sending more than 75 per cent of their students—hard-core rejects from the public school system —to college.

Of considerable potential significance to urban education is an act approved by the Massachusetts Legislature late in 1967 which enables the State Department of Education to assist and sponsor experimental school systems operated by private nonprofit corporations. Assuming a greater role in education and urban problems, states could establish yardsticks, "educational TVA's," by which to measure the effectiveness of different forms of educational innovation.

Project Headstart schools are also "private" in the sense that they exist apart from the public school system and are not subject to its rules and regulations governing personnel, curriculum, and other matters. Some of these schools are financed under Federal tuition grants and foundation funds, and efforts are being made to obtain support for others from business and industry. A special hybrid, a publicly-financed but totally independent school system (an enclave apart from the regular New York City system) with a per-capita budget received directly from the state, was proposed in 1967 by the Harlem chapter of CORE, though it failed in the New York State Legislature.

Nonpublic schools have advantages; they do not have to deal with distant and entrenched bureaucracies, with school boards unfamiliar with their particular needs, or with teachers' unions. They are free to hire teachers from a variety of personnel pools and to sidestep rigid credential-granting procedures. They may even abandon such practices as tenure and retain, promote, or discharge teachers purely on the grounds of merit and performance. If the schools are governed by boards with a substantial representation from the pupils' parents, they are likely to be more responsive to the children's needs and thereby encourage better rapport and partnership between the home and the school. In the most general sense, they afford the poor the choice that is open to many middle-class parents: to educate their children elsewhere if they are dissatisfied with the performance of the public schools. And if enough private schools are available, the pattern ushers in an entrepreneurial system in which parents can choose, cafeteria-style, from a range of styles of education—Montessori, prep school, Summerhill, and others.

Carried to its logical conclusion, however, the parallel-school approach would reduce the scope of public education, if not dispense with it altogether. The establishment of private schools sufficient to handle significant numbers of poor children would require public support and, in effect, establish a private system of publicly-supported schools. Middle-income parents would demand similar privileges. For financial reasons alone, the parallel-school approach is hardly likely to become widespread in the foreseeable future; moreover, the scheme would founder on political, if not constitutional grounds. Finally, since private schools are not subject to public control, there would be no guarantee against the organization of programs by special interest groups for ends inimical to a free and open society. Support of such enterprises at public expense would be intolerable.

These arguments are, of course, no reason to discourage programs that enable more low-income pupils to attend private schools. Private schools could serve a valuable yardstick function if they were run under conditions that simulated the resources and inputs of public education—particularly comparable per-capita expenditures, and admission policies that would embrace a range of low-income pupils, including the "disruptive." But that is the limit of their usefulness as an alternative to improved public education, for they could never serve the majority of the children of the poor.

Total System Reform

Since the compensatory approach has apparently failed, since desegregation is not a realistic short-range prospect, since model subsystems do not give much evidence yet of realizing their promise, and since parallel systems are basically an avoidance of the challenge to reform the schools where most children will continue to be educated, the latest—and, in my view, most promising—approach to intervention is reform of total school systems, structurally and otherwise. There are several approaches to total system intervention.

One approach is to provide new leadership for the system as a whole, while leaving the system's form and structure basically intact. This approach is exemplified by trends in Philadelphia, where a reform-minded central school board, including former Mayor Richardson Dilworth and a new superintendent of schools with a record of innovation are attempting to strengthen the effectiveness of the old system with the infusion of new staff and new styles. Pittsburgh, too, is improving the efficiency of the existing system, within the operational definition of quality education as achievement according to norms.

Another approach consists of reorganization of the system into quasi-autonomous districts—i.e., decentralization. Washington, D.C. has begun moving in this direction, beginning with single model schools. The Passow Report on the District's schools recommends a total system reform by decentralizing the system into eight subsystems of approximately equal size.[2]

Still another form is the proposed merger of the school systems of two entire political jurisdictions—the city of Louisville and Jefferson County. The Louisville-Jefferson County merger differs markedly from the piecemeal metropolitan experiments noted earlier. In this case, the new metropolitan system is to consist of a number of subdistricts, each with considerable autonomy yet federated into a single system to preserve the best of the worlds of bigness and smallness.

In the subsystems, models of excellence must swim against the tide of the status quo system. The total approach has no such constraint; there is no boring from within, for everyone starts at the reform gate at the same time. In a federation of autonomous subsystems, each with an equitable share of resources, instructional practices would operate in an open, competitive market. The most successful models would be on display as a challenge to other school systems to adopt their approaches or surpass them in performance.

New Energy Sources

The intervention proposed in November, 1967 by the Mayor's Advisory Panel on Decentralization of the New York City Schools—the Bundy Report—adds a crucial new energy source to the total system pattern.[3] Administrative decentralization of large school systems had been in the wind. (New York City itself had for the last six years begun loosening the reins of a highly centralized system.) But the Bundy Report's proposals go well beyond administrative arrangements into a form of public engagement in the process of education that is without precedent in large urban systems; and, in a sense, without much real precedent even in many suburbs and small cities.

The Bundy Report was significantly titled *Reconnection for Learning*. The

[2] A. H. Passow, *Summary of a Report on the Washington, D.C. Public Schools* (New York: Teachers College, Columbia University, 1967). (Mimeographed.)

[3] *Reconnection for Learning: A Community School System for New York City* (New York: The Mayor's Advisory Panel on Decentralization, 1967).

plan calls for more than a redistribution of power; it also provides new means of energizing school reform. Reform requires fuel. Sustained school reform needs not only ideas, but human resources and dynamic support from the public and the profession. All too often, the energy for educational reform consists only of a few professionals, practitioners or veterans who have shifted their struggle from the front lines to universities or the author's desk. The Bundy plan expands the base of energy to include the most numerous, and possibly the most powerful, energy source: parents and the community-at-large.

It offers the professional who is working for improvement within the system a powerful ally who is also highly motivated to reform the system. Ghetto parents especially have come to the same verdict as the most astute students and practitioners of education: that urban education is failing and desperately in need of reform.

But professional recognition of this energy concept is slow to come, for it assumes an altogether different professional-lay relationship from what now prevails. In the last several decades, education—in self-defense and for other reasons —has rapidly become professionalized. There has been an inverse correlation between professionalization and parents' involvement. Two other forces have tended to keep parents from participating in the education process. One, earlier in the cycle, though persisting in the urban ghetto, was the low level of the parents' own education relative to the teachers'. The immigrant, regardless of his desire for education for his children, was hardly likely to challenge the assigned authority represented by a native-speaking, better-educated teacher. The other factor, of course, is the growing size and impersonality of public school systems in large cities.

Even well-educated, middle-class parents who seek to engage in *meaningful* school decisions are deterred short of effectiveness by the inertial mass of the system or by the aura of professional exclusivity. Even the atmosphere in school buildings discourages parental presence (parent visiting days two or three times a year are prime evidence) and most parents visit school only in response to trouble. Thus, we have carefully-drawn boundaries for how far parents, singly or in parent-teacher associations, may go, even in asking questions of professionals. A sophisticated PTA member may nag at a school board that does not offer French in elementary school, but she will rarely ask for research results (or for research to be initiated) on the effectiveness of the school's language instruction. Still less is she apt to ask for such information as the school system's criteria for teacher selection or for evidence of its aggressiveness and imagination in recruiting teachers. Even when probing questions are asked, information is often safeguarded as being in the professional domain alone. Only now are some school systems beginning to accumulate and release performance data on a school-by-school basis.

But perhaps the role of the parent should go far beyond asking pointed questions. Should parents have a voice—preferential if not determinative—regarding school curriculum? Should parents have a say in the kind of teacher they feel is best suited to the needs of their children? These are questions to which most professionals—and, indeed, many parents—would offer a reflex negative. Yet, within the framework of basic standards and goals, there are many options. Mathematics may be taught in any number of ways, and there are a variety of approaches to foreign languages. If the school is dedicated to instilling learning *skills,* content is as much a means as an end, and one choice will often serve as well as another. Why then should not the choice represent what is most meaningful to a particular community? Very often the professional choice is only one of several objectively reasonable choices; his word is final because he has a monopoly on the authority. If community involvement is to be real, if parent-teacher parnership is to have any meaning beyond lip-service, the proper role for the professional would be to outline the educationally-sound alternatives, and to afford the parents and the community a choice among them. Parallels may also be found in such other aspects as selection of materials, personnel policies, and allocation of resources.

Although, as suggested, the parent has never been a true partner in the education process, at least the concept of lay and local control of public education has a long historical tradition. But the tradition has been diluted and is largely impotent against the force of a professional monopoly.

Professional educators have not ignored parents or the community. Elaborate structures and devices have been fashioned—parent-teacher associations, visiting days, American Education Week, parent education programs, dissemination of information—ostensibly to "inform" the parent. The administrator who seeks a "happy" school (or "tight ship," as the case may be) will see that his parents are paid some attention or even a degree of deference. He will be patient in explaining homework policies. Schools of education include community relations in their curricula; and in many systems, advancement through the administrative ranks requires a certain number of credits in community relations.

The chief motivation of most professionals in community relations is to make *their* system work more smoothly. One defect of this goal is that it is one-sided, for if a prevailing system is dysfunctional, anything that maintains it is a deterrent to reform. Perhaps a more serious defect is the assumption that parent participation is so special that it requires special attention and designated periods—similar to the well-intentioned but fundamentally insensitive Brotherhood Weeks. In short, the existing concept of parent and community participation in education is basically misdirected toward supporting the schools' status quo.

The analogue of this interpretation with respect to pupils is adjustment to the culture and environment of the school, even if the school environment has no relation to the pupils' needs or interests. Pupils are judged on how well they fit in —whether the mode of the school be folded hands, quiet in the halls, short haircuts, or an irrelevant curriculum with teaching methods that fail to diagnose the learning style of individual pupils.

Such school systems are essentially one-way avenues. The school and its staff lay out their wares and the "consumer" either accepts them or goes hungry. The schools are acting *upon* raw material; if the material resists shaping and molding, it is discarded and labeled defective. In such a system, conscious or unconscious consumer preferences do not count. There is no feedback loop from parents or pupils; and lacking feedback, the system is not likely to respond to changing conditions and needs. It is to such inflexible, tuned-out systems, as well as to the environment or psyche of the learner, that one must look for the causes of pupil failure, dropout, or tuneout.

The Goals of Effective Participation

What would be the purpose of real parent and community participation? We begin from the position that when people have a part in their institutions, they share responsibility for them and are more likely to pay close attention to the stated mission and actual performance of the institution.

Thus participation has a positive effect on the participants as well as the system. For example, as parents in East Harlem became more engaged in the education process, "quality education" replaced "black power" as the slogan. Responsibility comes with the power of an effective voice. In the train of responsibility, judgment, stability, and dedication to constructive purpose are likely to follow. The pattern of the revolutionary is that upon assumption of power, he shifts from destroying institutions to building order and new institutions (of his own kind, to be sure).

Participatory democracy in education should also give parents and community a tangible respect for the intricacy and complexity of the professional problems in urban education. It is not likely that parents who have gained admission as true partners in the process will oversimplify and lay the blame for educational failures solely on the professional. As things stand now, low-income communities *outside* the system understandably lay the blame squarely on the assigned professionals: "You are paid to teach, to deliver a certain product. When overwhelming numbers of our children fail to learn, you are not delivering. You are not meeting your professional obligation." The syllogism is simplistic: it ignores the fact that professional talent can be thwarted by a system, and it does not take into account extra-school factors in teaching and learning. But it is an altogether natural response from parents to whom the system provides no access and offers but two alternatives: total resignation and apathy; or anger, protest, and, sooner or later, some form of retaliation.

Skeptics who concede the right of parents to participate in the education process nevertheless question their technical qualifications to engage in educational decisions; the question is raised particularly (though not exclusively) in relation to low income, poorly educated parents. But the question should be not what parents know now, but what they can come to know about the technicalities of education. That they want to know is suggested by the few instances in which they have become more or less equal partners in the process. Their concerns soon broaden; they begin to ask, for example, who are the most talented reading specialists in the country, because we want them to help us. In qualifying for school board membership, too, they seek training for themselves—something rare among would-be school board members even in wealthier communities.

Admitting the public to the education process, therefore, should result in the addition of many new hands and minds to the tasks. These would be true partners, who participate in the enterprise and know it from their own experience, who do not simply take the established goals and procedures of the enterprise as virtues because its professional managers say so.

The school, after all, is only one site of the total curriculum to which children are exposed. Considerable learning takes place at home and in all manner of community institutions including the street corner, the church, the press and other mass media, and neighborhood organizations. As parents are admitted to participation in the schools' education process, they will become better equipped "teachers" of that part of the "curriculum" in which they are the prime agents —rearing in the home. Studies under Basil Bernstein of the University of London's Sociological Research Unit have illuminated discontinuities of socializa-

248

tion among the home, the child's peer group, and the schools.[4] Continuity could be restored if parents participated in the formal education process.

Greater public engagement in the public education process should also add political strength to pressures for increased financial support for education; a "parents' lobby" with unprecedented motivation and commitment might arise. Nor should the possible effects on parents in their own right be overlooked. Few people can engage in a social cause and not themselves be transformed. Relevant education in an institutional setting that is willing to experiment in the art—and yes, the mysteries—of learning and teaching is such a cause. It could bring into the lives of men and women working at tedious jobs, or leading lives of boredom (factors by no means peculiar to low-income groups), a new *spirit* in an activity with immediate relevance to their own families. This is to say nothing of the possible chain-reaction that meaningful engagement in the education process could have in stimulating parents to enlarge their own education.

Thus the realignment of the participants in public education could produce rich yields for all the main participants:

—for the parents, a tangible grasp on the destiny of their children and opening to richer meaning for their own lives.

—for professionals, surcease from an increasingly negative community climate and, more positively, new allies in their task.

—for the children, a school system responsive to their needs, resonant with their personal style, and affirmative in its expectations of them.

And finally there is the goal of participation for its own sake, an intrinsic concomitant—and test—of democracy. Education could no doubt be conducted efficiently if it were contracted out as a technical service, without the furniture of lay boards, community relations, and so on, especially if quality is defined strictly in terms of grade-level achievement. But in an open society, the process of participation itself is a social and educational value, despite the inefficiencies it may entail.

This is more than an alternative approach to halting the spiral of public education's failure. It is a design for social reconstruction.

---

[4] See, for example, Basil Bernstein, "A Socio-linguistic Approach to Social Learning" in J. Gould (ed.), *Social Science Survey* (New York: Pelican, 1965).

Appendix

Notes on Contributors

Index

A Brief Summary of the Coleman Report*

JAMES S. COLEMAN

Johns Hopkins University

The *Equality of Educational Opportunity* Report contains seven sections dealing with different aspects of educational opportunity (sections 2-8), a summary of the Report (section 1), and technical appendices (section 9) which are separately bound.

Of the seven sections dealing with equal educational opportunity, sections 2 and 3 have been seen as the most relevant to questions of school policy, and it is almost exclusively the conclusions represented in these sections that have been the subject of the discussion and controversy surrounding the Report. These sections describe the results of a national survey which covered approximately 4000 elementary and secondary schools. This large survey study was designed to identify the extent and sources of inequality of educational opportunity among six racial and ethnic groups (Negroes, Puerto Ricans, American Indians, Mexican Americans, Oriental Americans, and whites).

In this summary, I will first review briefly the range of topics that were investigated in the less well-known sections of the report and then summarize the major findings of sections 2 and 3 which have been the focus of controversy.

* To this summary, prepared especially for the present book, is appended the table of contents of the Coleman Report itself.

Section 4 describes the results of a survey of colleges and universities in which Negro and white teachers are trained. Since nearly all white students are taught by white teachers, and most Negro students (nearly all in the South, fewer than half in the North) are taught by Negro teachers, the results of this survey show the level of skill to which the teachers of the next generation of Negro and white students have been brought, giving some indication of the degree to which inequalities of opportunity may be self-perpetuating through racial matching of teachers and students.

Section 5 shows the distribution of Negroes and other non-whites in colleges with various characteristics. The basic data on characteristics of colleges were taken from existing records, principally those from the regular surveys of the Higher Education Branch of the U.S. Office of Education. No new data were collected for section 5. However, since the Office of Education did not begin collecting data on the racial composition of student bodies before 1965, this section contains the first tabulation of the distribution of Negroes and of other nonwhites in colleges with various characteristics. The characteristics include a number ordinarily used to assess the quality of a college: student-faculty ratio, percentage of the faculty with doctoral degrees, average faculty salary, expenditure per student, the presence of Phi Beta Kappa and AAUP chapters, and library resources.

Section 6 addresses an aspect of educational opportunity that could not be studied in the main survey of public schools: nonenrollment, or school dropout. Since the main survey was based on a sample of schools, the rate of nonenrollment at given age levels could not be determined. Consequently, data on nonenrollment for whites are reported from two sources: the 1960 decennial census, and a special addition to the October 1965 Current Population Survey of the Census Bureau. These tabulations show nonenrollment for whites and nonwhites aged 16 and 17 years old grouped by various other social characteristics: region, sex, metropolitan-nonmetropolitan, religion, and white-collar vs. non-white-collar father's occupation.

Section 7 consists of excerpts from a number of qualitative community studies carried out as part of the over-all study. These community studies examined the social and political forces involved in achievement of, or resistance to, racial integration in the schools. The studies were carried out in metropolitan areas and smaller communities, in the North and the South, and thus examined attempts to overcome both *de facto* segregation and *de jure* segregation.

Section 8 reports on four special analyses that were carried out from the data of the large national survey. One is an analysis of the performance of children who had participated in Project Headstart. The second is an examination of the effect of a foreign language spoken in the home upon verbal skills. The third and fourth are analyses of differences in the availability to Negro and white students of guidance counselors and vocational education. These last two analyses are extensions of the analysis of section 2, carried out for these two school resources.

This elaboration of the outline shows the variety and range of topics covered in the report. I will make no attempt here to summarize the results from all these sections. Although these sections give comprehensiveness and in some cases can provide statistics for reference purposes, there are only two sections of relevance to the central policy questions that have arisen from the report, sections 2 and 3. It is only the results from these sections that I will discuss.

Section 2 constitutes an examination of the inequality of educational opportunity through a comparison of objective characteristics, most of which can be regarded as "resources" of the school or measures of its quality, in schools attended by each of the groups under study. These groups were American Indians, Puerto Ricans (living in the United States proper), Mexican Americans, Oriental Americans, other whites, and Negroes. The latter two groups were compared both nationally and in eight kinds of locations: the metropolitan Northeast, Midwest, South, Southwest, and West, and the nonmetropolitan North, West, South, and Southwest. Therefore, it is a straightforward statistical description of the input resources of the schools in the survey, which were obtained from the superintendent's questionnaire, the principal's questionnaire, the teacher's questionnaire, and data from the students themselves.

The aim of section 2 is to give some indicators of inequality of opportunity by measuring qualities of inputs to schools, the most traditional conception of what constitutes school quality. It used the characteristics of schools that principals, superintendents, and school boards traditionally employ in comparing the "quality of education" their schools provide. These are items such as teachers' salary, the number of books in the library (and books per student), the age of buildings and of textbooks, the degrees of teachers and principals, specialized facilities and curricula, free kindergarten, and nearly all the objective measures of schools that exist in principals' records or that can be obtained from averaging responses of teachers to questionnaires. In addition, some less traditional measures of schools were used in comparing schools attended by each of the groups in question: the attitudes of the principals and teachers about their school, about their students, about the kinds of students they would most prefer to teach, and attitudes about school policy related to integration (for example, busing). In addition, teachers took a short vocabulary test. Finally, the chapter contains measures of another input to schools that obviously affects the opportunity of each student in the school: the characteristics of other students in the school. Their socioeconomic background and characteristics of their home environment, their race, their attitudes, and their aspirations were included in these tabulations.

The results of all these statistical comparisons can be summarized in only the most superficial way. They show differences between schools attended by each of the minorities and whites, and in particular between schools attended by Negroes and whites in the same geographic region.[1] In general, the differences show whites attending schools with greater resources, although this is not uniformly true, and perhaps the most striking point is the small size of the differences. The differences between locales (in particular, North-South differences, and to a lesser extent, metropolitan-nonmetropolitan differences) are for most resources strikingly greater than within-locale or national differences between schools attended by minority students and those attended by whites.

This finding has been one of the conclusions in the Report most subject to attacks by its critics, who argue that differences in the resources of schools attended by Negroes and whites are masked in one way or another. It is true that the reported differences do not show everything—for example, the fact that it probably costs more to run a school at the same level in the ghetto than in a suburb. To compete successfully for the same teachers, urban systems must pay higher salaries; among other things, depreciation on textbooks and buildings is greater, and the tabulation of numbers of books in the library does not show the quality of the books. Nevertheless, the criticism probably stems largely from the preconceptions that influence perception: many persons, white and Negro, when they see a school attended largely by black students, unconsciously depreciate it, seeing it as inferior, and then search for physical reasons to justify this perception.

---

[1] An additional analysis compares the schools attended by the average minority group student and average white within the same county or metropolitan area.

The differences that do show up strongly in the mass of statistics in section 2 are largely differences in the student bodies. The fact that school boards do not control this input into the schools does not make it less important to a child who enters. Thus, although these differences emanate from the aggregate of students in the school, they are no less real for each student there.

The most striking of these differences is the racial difference in student bodies of schools attended by the average Negro and the average white. This segregation is greatest in the South and greatest in elementary grades, so that the segregation is greatest at elementary grades in the South, next in secondary grades in the South, next in elementary grades in the North, and least in secondary grades in the North.

Stemming fundamentally from this racial segregation, and from the lower economic and educational backgrounds of Negro students, the social and academic characteristics of the student environment experienced by the average Negro and the average white are very great—greater in fact than differences in any other characteristics of their respective schools.

Next to differences in student environment are the differences among teacher characteristics for Negro and white students, differences that are least in length of training, salary, and other external characteristics, and greatest in attitudes and scores on the vocabulary test. These differences too stem largely from the racial matching of students and teachers, a matching that is greatest in the South, but existent in the North as well. Thus one might summarize these differences in school characteristics by saying that the major differences stem from the racial segregation of student bodies, and the racial matching of teachers and students. There are some differences in other inputs to schools, but these are not as large as had been generally believed.

Section 3 focuses on the outputs of schools, using achievement of various sorts as measures of output. The aim of the report was to use achievement output as the criterion by which various input differences might be evaluated: by assessing what inputs to the schools were most important for achievement, the relative importance of the input differences found in section 2 could be determined, and in fact, by applying weights to these differences in terms of their relevance to achievement, a measure of the over-all inequality of opportunity for achievement could be constructed. The report was only partially successful in this, never reaching the final stage of providing such a measure. Nevertheless, the success was sufficient to be relevant to broad policy questions (in contrast to specific policy questions, such as the relative importance of providing bigger libraries or newer textbooks, or integrating schools by busing or by creating larger school district boundaries).

In the measurement of achievement itself, in section 3.1, a number of results were evident. In all areas of achievement tested (verbal skills, mathematical skills, and in higher grades, tests in practical knowledge, natural sciences, social sciences, and humanities), results were similar. The whites and oriental Americans achieved at comparable levels in all grades tested (1, 3, 8, 9, and 12), and the other minorities achieved at a level sharply lower, with Negroes and Puerto Ricans achieving lowest of all. Over the span of grades from 1 to 12, the relative achievement of low-achieving groups declined. For Negroes, this decline occurred in all areas except the metropolitan North. The decline was greatest in the South, and greatest of all in the nonmetropolitan South. Thus in the nonmetropolitan South, Negro students at grade 12 were about one and a half times as far below whites in that region as at grade 1 (about 1.5 standard deviations compared to about 1.0 at grade 1).

When the relative importance of school factors for achievement was assessed, achievement for each racial group separately was regressed upon various school factors, after family background characteristics were controlled. This control was carried out so that those school factors most highly correlated with family background would not spuriously show a high relation to achievement. In carrying out this control, however, the analysis showed what had already been well-known: the powerful relation of the child's own family background characteristics to his achievement, a relation stronger than that of any school factors.

In assessing the importance of various school factors for achievement, the school factors were grouped into three large clusters, and the additional variance in achievement accounted for by each cluster—after controlling on the student's own family background, and in some analyses, after controlling on other school factors as well—was examined. The clusters were teachers' characteristics, all school-facility and curriculum characteristics excluding teachers, and characteristics of the student environment, obtained by aggregating student characteristics in his grade in school.

The general result was that the factors that, under all conditions, accounted for more variance than any others were the characteristics of the student's peers; those that accounted for the next highest amount of variance were teachers' characteristics; and finally, other school characteristics, including per pupil expenditure on instruction in the system, accounted for very little variance at all. The total variance accounted for by these three sets of school factors was not large—in fact, an analysis of variance showed that only about 10 percent of the variance in achievement lay between schools (for each racial group separately), most of it residing within schools.

Another result was that the variance in achievement accounted for by school characteristics was least for whites, and most for southern Negroes outside metropolitan areas. The inference was drawn that it is in general for the students from poorest family backgrounds that school characteristics were most important for achievement, but the analysis did not directly test this.

These results of the analysis of the relation of school characteristics to achievement have produced the largest portion of controversy surrounding the Report—a result which is to be expected, since they constituted the major causal inferences in the Report, and causal inferences from statistical analysis are always subject to debate, whether the issue be smoking and lung cancer or school factors and achievement.

The results clearly suggest that school integration across socioeconomic lines (and hence across racial lines) will increase Negro achievement, and they throw serious doubt upon the effectiveness of policies designed to increase non-personal resources in the school. A simple general statement of the major result is that the closest portions of the child's social environment—his family and his fellow-students—affect his achievement most, the more distant portion of his social environment—his teachers—affect it next most, and the non-social aspects of his school environment affect it very little. This of course is an oversimplification because of the interactions of some of these factors; but the results remain, with clear implications for school policies designed to increase the achievement of minority groups and lower-class white students.

James S. Coleman

Contents of the Coleman Report

Notes on Contributors

BILL AYERS is Director of The Children's Community School, Ann Arbor, Michigan. He was previously a community organizer and a teacher in an experimental school in Cleveland. He is co-author of an article to appear in a forthcoming collection, *Beyond Dissent: Papers from the New Left.*

SAMUEL BOWLES is Assistant Professor of Economics at Harvard University and Research Associate at the Center for International Affairs and at the Center for Studies in Education and Development, both at Harvard. Professor Bowles has published in the *Journal of Human Resources* and *Quarterly Journal of Economics.* His new book, *Planning Educational Systems for Economic Growth,* will be published by the Harvard University Press in 1969.

KENNETH B. CLARK is President of the Metropolitan Applied Research Center, a member of the New York State Board of Regents, and Professor of Psychology at City College, City University of New York. Professor Clark has been particularly interested in the areas of education and social psychology. His recent publications include *Desegregation, an Appraisal of the Evidence* (1953), *Prejudice and Your Child* (1955), and *Dark Ghetto* (1965).

DAVID K. COHEN is a lecturer in the Harvard Graduate School of Education and Senior Research Associate in the Graduate School's Center for Educational Policy Research. During 1966-1967 he was Director of the Race and Education Project, U.S. Commission on Civil Rights, and in 1967-1968 he was Visiting Associate at the Joint Center for Urban Studies of the Massachusetts Institute of Technology and Harvard University. He is the principal author of *Racial Isolation in the Public Schools* (1967).

JAMES S. COLEMAN, Professor of Sociology at Johns Hopkins University, is the senior author of the Coleman Report and had major responsibility for the design, administration, and analysis of the survey on which the Report is based. He has worked primarily in the sociology of education. Other recent publications include *Community Conflict* (1957), *The Adolescent Society* (1961), and *Adolescents and the Schools* (1965).

NOEL A. DAY is Senior Member at The Organization for Social and Technical Innovation in Cambridge. He has served as Executive Director of St. Mark Social Center in Boston and Director of the Seminar on Disadvantagedness, an NDEA Summer Institute at Dartmouth. Interested especially in urban sociology, he is the author of several articles concerning the Negro in Boston.

HENRY S. DYER is Vice President of Educational Testing Service and has served as Associate Director of the College Entrance Examination Board. He has contributed articles to the *Journal of Negro Education* and *The Educational Record*. His interest in measurement of the performance of educational systems is reflected in his leadership in the preparation of the three-volume *Plan for Evaluating the Quality of Educational Programs in Pennsylvania* (1965).

MARIO D. FANTINI is Program Officer for the Ford Foundation and Executive Secretary, Mayor's Advisory Panel on Decentralization of the New York City Schools. He has directed several pilot programs in Syracuse, N.Y., centering upon developing more effective ways of educating disadvantaged and inner-city children. The author of many articles, he has recently published a book with Gerald Weinstein entitled *The Disadvantaged: Challenge to Education* (1968).

CHARLES V. HAMILTON's current interests include political modernization and black politics in America. Dr. Hamilton taught at Lincoln University in Pennsylvania, Rutgers University, and Tuskegee Institute before becoming Professor of Political Science and Director of the Graduate Program in Urban Studies at Roosevelt University in Chicago. His publications include co-authorship (with Stokely Carmichael) of *Black Power: The Politics of Liberation in America* (1967) and several articles on the Negro and American politics.

IRWIN KATZ is Professor of Psychology at the University of Michigan and, until 1966, was Professor of Psychology and Director of the Research Center for Human Relations at New York University. Dr. Katz has edited, with Martin Deutsch and Arthur Jensen, *Race, Class, and Psychological Development* (1968) and has written on the intellectual performance of minority group children in the *American Psychologist* and the *Nebraska Symposium on Motivation*.

DAVID L. KIRP is Instructor and Assistant to the Dean at the Harvard Graduate School of Education. A recent graduate of Harvard Law School, he has taught writing at Harvard College for several years. He recently prepared a writing seminar offered as part of a pre-law summer program for Negro juniors and seniors. Mr. Kirp is currently interested in urban political and social problems.

HERBERT KOHL is Director of the Teachers and Writers Collaborative, Teachers College, Columbia. He previously taught in the New York City public schools. His most recent book is *36 Children* (1967).

GERALD LESSER is Professor of Education and Developmental Psychology and Director of the Laboratory of Human Development at Harvard University. He is particularly interested in cultural influences upon learning, personality, and motivation. In addition to numerous articles in educational and psychological journals, he has collaborated in the writing of several books, including *Emotional Disturbance and School Learning* with D. H. Clark (1965), *Contemporary Issues in Thematic Apperceptive Methods* with J. Kagan (1961), and *Personality and Persuasibility* with C. I. Hovland, and others (1959).

DANIEL P. MOYNIHAN is currently Director, Joint Center for Urban Studies of the Massachusetts Institute of Technology and Harvard University; Professor of Education and Urban Politics at the Harvard Graduate School of Education; and member of the Institute of Politics of the Kennedy School of Government, Harvard. He is the author of numerous books and articles. Recent publications include *The Assault on Poverty* (1965) with Margaret S. Gordon and others.

THOMAS F. PETTIGREW is Associate Professor of Social Psychology at Harvard University. His major interest in American race relations is reflected in his authorship of *A Profile of the Negro American* (1964) and his work as consultant to the U.S. Commission on Civil Rights and the U.S. Office of Education.

SUSAN S. STODOLSKY, formerly Research Director of the Preschool Project at Harvard University, is Assistant Professor in the Department of Education at the University of Chicago. She is interested in the early cognitive and social development of children, especially the disadvantaged, and in observational procedures in educational research.

NEIL V. SULLIVAN was appointed Massachusetts Commissioner of Education in September 1968. Formerly Superintendent of Schools, Berkeley Unified School District, he is a co-author, with Thomas Maynard and Carol Yellin, of *Bound for Freedom* (1965) and is currently writing a book reflecting his confidence in the promise of school integration.

ALAN B. WILSON is Associate Professor of Education and Lecturer in Sociology at the University of California. He has taught in elementary schools and in recent years has been a member of the staff of the Survey Research Center, University of California. In addition to journal articles, he is the author or co-author of *Education of Disadvantaged Children in California* (1966); and *Educational Consequences of Segregation in a California Community* (1966).

Index